KT-375-532

WITHDRAWN

N 0065768 9

Desertification

For Lucy

Desertification:
Exploding the Myth

David S.G. Thomas
and
Nicholas J. Middleton

JOHN WILEY & SONS
Chichester · New York · Brisbane · Toronto · Singapore

Copyright © 1994 David Thomas and Nicholas Middleton

Published 1994 by John Wiley & Sons Ltd,
  Baffins Lane, Chichester,
  West Sussex PO19 1UD, England
  Telephone National Chichester (0243) 779777
  International +44 243 779777

Reprinted June 1995, August 1996

Other Wiley Editorial Offices

John Wiley & Sons, Inc., 605 Third Avenue,
New York, NY 10158-0012, USA

Jacaranda Wiley Ltd, 33 Park Road, Milton,
Queensland 4064, Australia

John Wiley & Sons (Canada) Ltd, 22 Worcester Road,
Rexdale, Ontario M9W 1L1, Canada

John Wiley & Sons (SEA) Pte Ltd, 37 Jalan Pemimpin #05-04,
Block B, Union Industrial Building, Singapore 2057

British Library Cataloguing in Publication Data

A catalogue record for this book is available from the British Library

ISBN 0-471-94815-2

Typeset in 10/12pt Palatino by Florencetype Ltd, Kewstoke, Avon
Printed and bound in Great Britain by Biddles Ltd, Guildford and King's Lynn

Contents

Preface

Being geographers with research and other interests in drylands, we have long been aware of the significance attached to desertification as a major environmental issue. We were also aware of the pitfalls, limitations and controversies attached to certain aspects of the phenomenon, especially regarding its definition, delimitation and relationship to natural events such as drought.

In 1991 we were approached to write the text for the United Nations Environment Programme's *World Atlas of Desertification*. This principally involved describing and explaining the outcome of a recent attempt to quantify and define the scale and nature of desertification. In part the writing process involved visits to UNEP's Nairobi offices to find out more about the new assessment project (GLASOD) and to collect information for the text of the atlas. The Nairobi visits opened our eyes to many issues concerning desertification, especially its politicisation, and the many doubts and concerns that surround its representation in the literature and the media.

One evening in Nairobi we decided that there was a strong case to be made for producing a short book that attempted to analyse together the range of scientific, social and political issues surrounding desertification. There have of course been several books published on the subject. These range from the tightly-written volumes that address the occurrence of desertification such as Alan Grainger's *The Threatening Desert*, those that try and view the issue from a more social perspective such as Spooner and Mann's *Desertification and Development* published over a decade ago, to books that are poorly defined and poorly focused, and add little to the clarity or understanding of the problem. By attempting to address social, environmental and political aspects of desertification, we hope to provide an integrated perspective. It is our belief that it is difficult to assess the significance of desertification without exploring how it grew to be treated as a major environmental issue, and how it links to certain aspects of development and aid, as well as to specific aspects of society and environment. The title of the book was chosen because desertification has received a rough ride in media and scientific quarters in recent years, with its very existence being questioned.

Several people have helped us in the course of thinking about and writing this book. We had both fruitful and awareness-raising discussions with various people in Nairobi, while in the UK practical assistance has come from Paul Cole of the Cartographic Unit, University of Sheffield Geography Department, who drew all the figures. In virtually all cases where these have originated from existing sources they have been amended, reworked, added to or edited for their use in this book, with the initial sources identified in the figure captions themselves. We are very grateful to publishers and authors who have given us permission to use their diagrams. Every effort has been made to trace the copyright holders of diagrams. If, however there are inadvertent omissions these can be rectified in any future editions. Acknowledgements are due to Earthscan Publications (Figures 3.4 and 4.1), Allen and Unwin (Figure 5.1), Cambridge University Press (Figures 5.3 and 7.9), Ian Scoones (Figure 5.4), Oxford University Press (Figure 2.2), Routledge (Figures 5.5 and 7.1), John Wiley and Sons (Figures 6.3, 8.2 and 8.8), Professor Anders Rapp (Figures 4.3 and 8.1), UNEP (Figures 7.3, 7.4, 7.5, 7.6 and 7.9). All the photographs are our own with the exception of Figure 5.7, which is a NASA space shuttle photograph, and Figure 8.3 which was kindly supplied by Jeremy Perkins.

List of abbreviations

AVHRR	advanced very high resolution radiometer
CRU	Climatic Research Unit
DC/PAC	Desertification Control Programme Activity Centre
DECARP	Desert Encroachment and Rehabilitation Programme
DESCON	Consultancy Group for Desertification Control
DTCD	Department of Technical Cooperation for Development
EC	European Community
ECA	Economic Commission for Africa
ESCAP	Economic and Social Commission for the Asia–Pacific Region
ESCWA	Economic and Social Commission for Western Asia
FAO	Food and Agriculture Organization of the United Nations
GAP	General Assessment of Progress
GEMS	Global Environment Monitoring System
GIS	Geographic Information System
GLASOD	Global Assessment of Soil Degradation
GRID	Global Resource Information Database
GVI	global vegetation index
GWP	global warming potentials
HUI	herbivore use intensity
IADIZA	Instituto Argentino de Investigaciones de las Zonas Aridas
IAEA	International Atomic Energy Agency
IAWGD	Inter-Agency Working Group on Desertification
ICASALS	International Centre for Arid and Semi-Arid Land Studies
IGADD	Intergovernmental Authority on Drought and Development
IGN	Institut géographique National
IIED	International Institute for Environment and Development

IPAL	Integrated Project in Arid Lands
IPCC	Intergovernmental Panel on Climatic Change
ISRIC	International Soil Reference and Information Centre
ISSS	International Society of Soil Science
IUCN	International Union for Conservation of Nature and Natural Resources
LSU	livestock unit
MSS	multispectral scanner
NASA	National Aeronautics and Space Administration
NDVI	normalised difference vegetation index
NGO	non-governmental organisation
NOAA	National Oceanographic and Atmospheric Administration
PACD	Plan of Action to Combat Desertification
PCC	potential carrying capacity
SADCC	Southern African Development Coordination Conference
SLEMSA	soil loss estimation model for southern Africa
TM	Thematic Mapper
UN	United Nations
UNCED	United Nations Conference on Environment and Development
UNCOD	United Nations Conference on Desertification
UNDP	United Nations Development Programme
UNEP	United Nations Environment Programme
UNESCO	United Nations Educational, Scientific and Cultural Organization
UNHCR	United Nations High Commissioner for Refugees
UNIDO	United Nations Industrial Development Organization
UNOSTD	United Nations Centre for Science and Technology
UNPACD	United Nations Plan of Action to Combat Desertification
UNSO	United Nations Sudano–Sahelian Office
USA	United States of America
USAID	United States Agency for International Development
USSR	Union of Soviet Socialist Republics
UNICEF	United Nations Children's Fund
WFP	World Food Programme
WHO	World Health Organization
WMO	World Meteorological Organization
WRI	World Resource Institute

Prologue

Desertification has been described as one of the world's most pressing environmental issues. It has also been described as a myth. This book attempts to present and evaluate the scientific, political and social information needed to gain a clear understanding of desertification.

The myth of desertification

There are four main parts to the apparent desertification myth:

1. According to United Nations data, desertification affects one third of the world's land area. It is a voracious process which rapidly degrades productive land, especially in drylands.

2. Drylands are fragile ecosystems that are highly susceptible to degradation and desertification.

3. Desertification is a, if not the, primary cause of human suffering and misery in drylands.

4. The United Nations is central to attempts to understand and solve the desertification problem.

To evaluate each of these parts, to see if there is indeed a myth, it is necessary to examine the desertification issue using the evidence that is available to us. This is the purpose of the nine chapters that follow.

1 Introduction

Desertification is a real problem, but there is something awry in the way it is understood, analysed and presented. (Spooner, 1989:112)

What are we talking about?

Desertification is widely viewed as a major environmental issue in scientific, political and even popular circles. What it exactly is, and the environmental processes that it entails are, however, often far from clear. The literature on the topic is fraught with confusions and contradictions, generalisations based on a lack of data and uncertainties stated as facts. In recent years it has even been questioned whether desertification actually exists (Binns, 1990; Hellden, 1991).

The purpose of this book is to attempt to unravel the major confusions and doubts related to desertification, including those with political, social and scientific slants to them. In doing so we hope to present a clearer picture of how desertification gained its status as a key environmental and social issue and of what are and are not justifiable aspects of the topic. To do this we will take a broad look at desertification, from its origins as an environmental issue to the actions proposed and taken for its attempted solution.

In 1977 the United Nations Conference on Desertification (UNCOD) was held in Nairobi and attended by official representatives of 95 countries, 50 UN offices and a myriad of NGOs (UN, 1977a). UNCOD can perhaps be seen as the birth of the modern age for desertification; it was certainly seen as generating more post-conference discussion than any previous UN conferences (Tolba, 1987). If it was not the beginning of clarity regarding what desertification is, what causes it and where it occurs then UNCOD was certainly the start of a period when the word entered popular, political and scientific vocabularies as a term for a major environmental problem or group of environmental issues.

Desertification is perhaps unique as an environmental problem as for over a decade its lifeblood as a focus of investigation and concern has come from a semi-autonomous office within the UN called the Desertification Control Programme Activity Centre (DC/PAC), which has described desertification as 'a geological leprosy' (UNEP DC/PAC, 1987). DC/PAC was set up in 1985 by Dr Mustafa Tolba, then Executive Director of the United Nations Environment Programme (UNEP) as a means of dealing directly with the Plan of Action to Combat Desertification (PACD), which was an outcome of UNCOD in 1977 (UNEP–UNCOD, 1978).

This is not to say that desertification, or the perception of it as a problem, was new in 1977. The late 1960s and 1970s saw a series of environmental and human crises, associated with severe drought and population pressures in the countries on the southern fringe of the Sahara. These crises were a source of scientific, political and humanitarian concern (e.g. Le Houerou, 1968; Rapp, 1974; Rapp *et al.*, 1976). A desertification study group was established by the International Geographical Congress in 1972 (Grove, 1977) and a world bibliography of the problem was published in 1976 (Paylore, 1976).

The United Nations' interest in drylands dates from two decades earlier, with the establishment of the UNESCO arid zone programme in 1952, which ran for ten years. The Sahel problems led more specifically to the establishment of the United Nations Sahelian (later Sudano-Sahelian) Office (UNSO) in 1973. This office was charged with coordinating recovery and rehabilitation efforts in the drought affected region, but rapidly led to recognition that drought relief measures alone would be insufficient for tackling the social and environmental problems at stake (Verstraete, 1986). Consequently in 1974 the UN General Assembly adopted resolutions that led directly to UNCOD.

Desertification is certainly not new and may have been occurring for millenia (Grainger, 1990); according to Spooner (1989) it can be traced back to the mediaeval period, the ancient world and probably the neolithic. In the twentieth century, the general issue at stake and trigger of UNCOD – detrimental changes in the environment on the Saharan fringe – had been the subject of reports nearly half a century earlier (Bovill, 1921; Stebbing, 1938; Jacks and Whyte, 1939) while developments in desert-like conditions were also recognised elsewhere (e.g. Lowdermilk, 1935), not least in the USA (Brown, 1948), South Africa (Schwarz, 1919) and Australia (Walls, 1980). The word desertification itself dates from 1949 (Aubreville, 1949). What was new in the 1970s was the conceptualisation of desertification as a serious problem, of global rather than local significance, and as something important for the political agenda.

Since the 1977 watershed, desertification has become big business, politically sensitive and a major North–South aid issue. For example, President Kountche of Niger used the need to fight desertification as an excuse to halt his country's democratisation process (Warren and

Agnew, 1987). Desertification has certainly turned out to be regarded as one of the biggest environmental issues of the last two decades (Goudie, 1990; Hellden, 1991) and is in the World Bank's 'top ten' of major global environmental problems. During the period from the mid 1970s to the early 1980s billions of dollars of aid went into the Sahel region, at a time when the environmental and human consequences of the major drought figured highly in the political and popular thinking of socially conscious groups in the developed world. Desertification was rarely far behind in these thoughts for as Spooner (1989:118) has noted, 'there has been a tendency to take for granted that desertification, famine, drought and poverty should be found together'. Yet perhaps as little as 1.5 per cent of foreign aid entering the Sahel countries during this period was spent on ecological and conservation projects that would improve the environment in the long term (Timberlake, 1985).

Desertification has also burgeoned as a theme of investigation in the scientific and academic world. Notwithstanding what was produced prior to the 1970s, since UNCOD, desertification has been the basis of scientific reputations and the theme of hundreds if not thousands of published articles, books and 'grey literature' documents. In the awareness sense, it was perhaps the first 'big' environmental issue, preceding others such as global warming, the ozone hole and acid rain in its adoption by the popular and pseudo-scientific press and its appeal to the growing public environmental concern expressed by the increasing 'green' awareness that proliferated in the developed world in the 1980s.

This introduction is a selection of some of the central issues concerning the significance of desertification. It is an environmental issue that has major social, economic and political angles. It is an issue, though not new to the late twentieth century, that has certainly caught the imagination as a problem that needs urgent action. Its effects are not limited to the developing world, or just to the poorest people, but it was problems involving these, especially in Africa, that centred concern on it and led to action being taken by the UN. We will return to the themes raised above later in the book, but now we must consider a central issue: what is desertification?

What is desertification?

So far we have avoided direct discussion of what desertification actually is. Some clues about this and its environmental and social significance come from the literature. UNEP, the overseer of international efforts to tackle the phenomenon, refers to it as the 'sands of change' (UNEP, 1987)

UNITED NATIONS
ENVIRONMENT PROGRAMME

UNEP Environment Brief No 2

sands
of change:

why land becomes desert and what can be done about it

Poor land management and environmental pressures are degrading many of the world's dryland areas. Despite international efforts to halt desertification, the problem is worsening: one-third of the Earth's land area, and as many as 850 million of the world's poorest people, are potentially at risk.

Key facts

The problem ...

- about 3500 million hectares of land – an area the size of North and South America combined – are affected by desertification;

- every year about 6 million hectares of land are irretrievably lost to desertification, and a further 21 million hectares are so degraded that crop production becomes uneconomic;

- the rural population affected by serious desertification rose from 57 million people in 1977 to 135 million in 1984;

- the situation is likely to become extremely critical in the rainfed croplands by the year 2000, and to be little better elsewhere;

- desertification is caused largely by human action – or lack of it ... it follows that it can also be arrested by human action;

... and its solution

- desertification causes annual losses of about US $26,000 million compared to the US $4500 million a year needed to control it – about three-quarters of what is needed is being spent but the remaining quarter is critical;

- although more money is needed, the most successful attempts to control desertification have been cheap, local, small in scale, and run by those personally affected;

- the technical solutions, such as reforestation, improved farming techniques and better land use, are well known and have been successfully applied in many areas;

- in spite of this, the battle is being lost ... a massive new effort to control desertification is required if declining productivity, erosion, famine and political chaos are to be avoided.

Figure 1.1 'Sands of change'. The cover of a UNEP publicity document, 1987

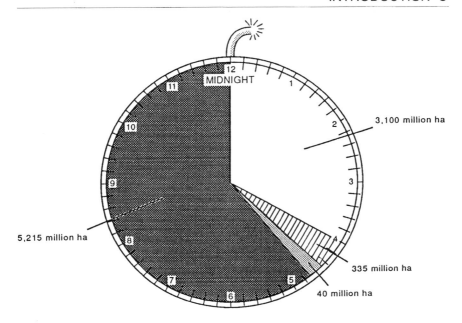

LAND MODERATELY OR SEVERELY AFFECTED BY DESERTIFICATION
(40% of the world's productive land)

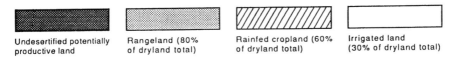

| Undesertified potentially productive land | Rangeland (80% of dryland total) | Rainfed cropland (60% of dryland total) | Irrigated land (30% of dryland total) |

At the rate of 27 million hectares lost a year to the desert or to zero economic productivity, in a little less than 200 years at the current rate of desertification there will not be a single, fully productive hectare of land on earth.

Figure 1.2 'The timebomb of desertification' (after UNEP, 1987)

(Figure 1.1), while expressions such as 'the spreading desert', 'deserts on the move' and 'desert creep' have frequently appeared, building on the idea espoused in an African context by Bovill (1921) of 'the encroaching Sahara'. Good examples of the recent treatment of this issue in this manner are from Smith (1986) who suggested that 'the Sahara continues to creep forward, claiming an area the size of New York State every decade' and Vinogradov (1988, in Rozanov, 1990) who noted that the area of shifting sands in Kalmykia, central Asia, had grown by 300,000 hectares between 1983 and 1989 due to 'anthropogenic desertification'. Globally, UNEP has used a similar concept to warn that desertification amounts to a time bomb that will ultimately destroy all productive land on earth (Figure 1.2).

Although there are undoubtedly cases where the expansion of aeolian processes and development of desert sand dunes has occurred due to human activities, the simple concept that desertification is the physical advance of deserts misrepresents a complicated situation and the range of issues and processes that are actually under consideration. Though widely used to emphasise what desertification might be and embodied within sections of political, pseudo-scientific and popular thought, the 'marching desert' theme has been the subject of increasing contempt and criticism, though it is a perception that is difficult to shake off (Dregne and Tucker, 1988). As Mabbutt (1985:1) so correctly noted, 'the symbol of the palm tree disappearing under the advancing sand dune is locally warranted, but as a general view of desertification it could lead to mistaken combative strategies'.

More recently scathing scientific monographs have appeared on this topic (Warren and Agnew, 1987) together with papers bearing titles such as 'Is desertification a myth?' (Binns, 1990) and 'Desertification – time for an assessment' (Hellden, 1991). Rejection of the emotive image has even filtered through to the public press, with articles such as 'Few grains of truth in the shifting sands' (Pearce, 1992). The concept of deserts progressively and clearly moving over productive land, usually in the form of a readily measurable front of mobile sand dunes, may be appealing in its simplicity, visualisation and potential for raising political and public awareness, but it is not the form that desertification commonly takes. Put simply, desertification is more like a sporadic rash than an advancing tide (Goudie, 1990).

While it is easy to say what desertification generally is not, it is another matter to determine what it actually is. The issue of what we are dealing with will arise many times in the course of this book, and to some extent it is central to many of the complex debates and criticisms that have arisen amongst those attempting to understand and tackle the problem. It is therefore useful at this stage to examine some of the key themes that arise in the desertification definition debate.

What's in a definition?

The term desertification has been used to refer both to processes of change and states of the environment. In a review of the concept Glantz and Orlovsky (1983) identified over one hundred definitions that had appeared in the literature. As a UNEP DC/PAC representative has recently noted, the term has been used indiscriminately and consequently much confusion has arisen (Mendoza, 1990).

This is not too surprising. In an interesting article Dregne (1987) has suggested that the use of desertification in the title of the 1977 UN conference (UN, 1977a) was a stroke of political genius. The conference appears to have been planned initially as a means of addressing the socio-economic problems caused by drought in the Sahel countries (Mabbutt, 1987a). It is unclear how the 'd' word entered the title, for its use prior to that had been restricted, not appearing in an English language publication until the early 1970s, but as Dregne (1987:8) notes:

> Desertification carried the connotation of disaster and required no explanation. Practically everyone knew intuitively that desertification was bad, irrespective of what it referred to. And if it was bad, something should be done to stop it. Few persons ever asked what 'it' was. As I recall, the UNCOD consultants spent at least a year discussing desertification before we got round to asking what the term meant.

Arguing about what the correct definition is can be a futile activity, but it is also of significance if the problem is as extensive as has been suggested and if solutions are to be sought. When desertification is big business, correct definition and delimitation of the issue is necessary. UNEP–UNCOD (1978) estimated that the economic loss caused by desertification was US$42,000 million per year with a 20-year control programme requiring US$4,500 million each year, of which US$2,400 million p.a. would need to go to developing countries. The ratio of economic losses caused by desertification to the cost of remedying the problem was estimated at about 10:1 (Gigengack *et al.*, 1990). In 1991 the cost of tackling the issue was further revised for presentation to the 1992 United Nations Conference on Environment and Development (UNCED) at Rio de Janeiro to up to US$292,000 million over 20 years to stop desertification or US$107,000 million for a medium programme of basic corrective measures (US$5,300 p.a.) for 81 developing countries (UNEP, 1991).

Since UNCOD, the production of its Plan of Action to Combat Desertification (UNPACD) (UN, 1977; UNEP–UNCOD, 1978), and the coordination of big desertification control budgets, the problem seems to have become worse (Rozanov, 1990). UNPACD aimed to have solved the problem, which meant to have halted and reversed desertification, by the year 2000. Yet according to Rozanov (1990) it is likely that by then the problem will have deteriorated beyond its level at UNPACD's inception. Two general reasons might be suggested for this. First, although the total funding of aid projects related to desertification from 1978 to 1983 was at about the level estimated as necessary, only about ten per cent was actually spent on direct control projects (Gigengack *et al.*, 1990). Second, Odingo (1990a) has suggested that the unrealistic 20-year target was a consequence of too much faith being placed in finding a technological solution to desertification. Inappropriate conceptualisation of the problem was accompanied by a lack of understanding of its nature and a lack of serious attempts to define it, particularly for the benefit of those attempting to implement solutions and make decisions.

How can solutions be achieved if definitions are uncertain and the subject of controversy? UNEP does have definitions that it uses, but these have been criticised, by Warren and Agnew (1987) among others, for fudging the key issues, confusing processes, and not even understanding what the causes are. A common source of confusion or difference of opinion, for example, is the relationship between meteorological drought and desertification, with the two variously being seen as basically the same issue, cause and effect (see Agnew and Anderson, 1992), the former as one of many potential catalysts for the latter (Dregne, 1983a), or drought as an extreme natural event that can act with human causes to create desertification (Sabadell *et al.*, 1982). Dregne (1987) has observed that in pre-UNCOD consultant discussions the initial focus was on drought as the cause, but a gradual shift away from this stance took place. Some components of desertification may even contribute to drought (Charney *et al.* 1975; Hulme, 1989).

It is certainly true to say that different experts, used by UNEP to calculate the scale and extent of desertification, have considered different issues or defined the problem in different ways and that UNEP has changed and refined its definition over time. This in itself may be a valuable aspect of the scientific development and coming-of-age of the problem, and an indication of just how little was known of the processes involved when the severity of desertification was first estimated. But it can also be used to suggest incompetence, especially when large budgets are involved and when solutions are attempted prior to the nature of the problem being understood. While arguments over a precise definition and disputes over terminology might be futile, knowing what is actually going on is not.

Definitions

Desertification is frequently regarded as a process (e.g. Glantz and Orlovsky, 1983; Rozanov, 1990), but it is also used to describe an end state of a process or processes, for example in Aubreville's original usage (1949) where he referred to the creation of desert conditions in humid parts of West Africa. In a recent book it is argued that desertification is best reserved for the ultimate step of land degradation, the point when land becomes irreversibly sterile in human terms and with respect to reasonable economic limitations (Mainguet, 1991).

Process and state are often blurred or not distinguished, as in the case of the definition of the United Nations Desertification Secretariat (UN,

1977a) where both were included. Usage can often be unclear and very generalised and the types of environment or climatic regime in which it occurs may or may not be specified. If desertification is treated as a process, this can result in a glossing over of what actually takes place, for usage in this sense is simply a blanket term for a whole range of specific biological, chemical and physical changes in the environment. As such, desertification is a shorthand term, rather than a specific process with a specific cure.

Although the issues at stake will arise throughout the book, we can briefly examine some of the main aspects of the definition issue. The UNCOD definition of desertification (UN, 1977a), of which only the first sentence is usually quoted was:

> the diminution or destruction of the biological potential of the land that can lead ultimately to desert-like conditions. It is an aspect of the widespread deterioration of ecosystems and has diminished or destroyed the biological potential, i.e. the plant and animal production, for multiple use purposes at a time when increased productivity is needed to support growing populations in quest of development.

This specifies both the general process and what it leads to and as such appears simple, straightforward and unambiguous to the extent that Dregne (1987), for example, wondered why it was not widely adopted. One reason may well be that its breadth rendered its actual use impractical, for example in terms of attempts to quantify desertification (Dregne et al., 1991). Another is that it is not confined to any specific biome, and therefore becomes a blanket term for any form of degeneration that reduces productivity. The picture was further complicated by a later attempt by FAO/UNEP (1984) which defined the problem from a more human perspective, including the general contributory factors, the areas affected and the general environmental outcome. Desertification was stated as being:

> A comprehensive expression of economic and social processes as well as those natural and induced ones which destroy the equilibrium of soil, vegetation, air and water, in the areas subject to edaphic and/or climatic aridity. Continued deterioration leads to a decrease in, or destruction of the biological potential of the land, deterioration of living conditions and an increase of desert landscape.

Assessments by Odingo (1990a) and Rozanov (1990), direct responses to requests to clarify the position that UNEP should adopt, contributed to the most recent UN official definition of desertification, now called 'desertification/land degradation' as:

land degradation in arid, semiarid and dry subhumid areas resulting mainly from adverse human impact.

This was adopted by UNEP in February 1990 (Mendoza, 1990) and used for example in the assessments of the scale of the problem in the UNEP *World Atlas of Desertification* (Middleton and Thomas, 1992). Unlike the earlier UNCOD definition, this UNEP definition specifies the environments in which land degradation is termed desertification, reflecting both common (but not exclusive) usage and the types of environment that were the trigger for UNCOD in 1977. It also reflects and extends the shift in focus from drought as the cause, in the pre-UNCOD discussions, through equal prominence being attached to humans and climate (during and subsequent to UNCOD), to the dominant view today of people as the main cause of desertification.

It is interesting that the 1990 UNEP definition has avoided both the process and the effect included in the earlier UNCOD and FAO/UNEP explanations. As footnotes to the definition, UNEP also notes that land in land degradation includes soil and local water resources, the land surface and vegetation, with degradation implying a reduction in the resource potential caused by one or a series of processes acting on the land (e.g. Mendoza, 1990; Dregne *et al.*, 1991; Middleton and Thomas, 1992).

Although this definition still embodies a vagueness that might receive criticism, it does at least partly answer the charge often levelled at UNEP of oversimplifying the issue (e.g. Warren and Agnew, 1987; Nelson, 1988). It also firmly returns the emphasis to desert margin areas, it embodies the notion of the land's utility to humans as a key factor in making desertification the issue that it is often perceived to be and it suggests that the loss of potential for sustainable use, one of the key points raised by Warren and Agnew (1987), is of significance. The definition does not however specifically address the degree of change or the permanency of degradation. This is significant, as Nelson's (1988) definition for the World Bank included the premise that desertification reduces the productive potential to an extent which can neither be readily reversed by removing the cause nor easily reclaimed without substantial investment.

In this vein, Warren and Agnew (1987) hint that a component of Aubreville's (1949) 'commonsense' meaning, the creation of desert conditions, is useful in that it indicates a loss of productivity, with the lack of potential for productivity being a major characteristic of natural deserts.

What about the people? Social aspects

So far this introductory discussion has made little reference to people, of which some 650–850 million may be affected (Rozanov, 1990), other than as a cause of desertification and indirectly as victims, yet degradation ought to perhaps be seen principally as a social problem (Blaikie and Brookfield, 1987). In many respects this reflects the way in which people are often included in desertification studies. This may in turn be a reflection of the way that communities have been treated by major aid projects: as inanimate recipients. Yet there are wider human issues relating to why people cause desertification, to why the problem seems to get worse despite, or even because of, organisations such as UNEP, and to the conceptualisation of desertification by all interested parties.

Notwithstanding the previous discussion on changing or evolving definitions of desertification and its environmental attributes, the lack of a real social component in many considerations of desertification may be important, perhaps even in explaining why the problem may have been accelerating in the post-UNCOD period. There are also major potential conflicts between the environmental and social components of and solutions to desertification. At one extreme this boils down to the survival of the physical system, the ecological viewpoint, and the survival of individual people, the social component (e.g. Spooner, 1982).

Another way of viewing desertification is as a total social phenomenon (Spooner, 1989), total in its potential direct and indirect effects on everyone and total in that people are involved in all its stages, not just as cause and victim. Attempts to add or properly reinstate the social dimension into desertification studies (e.g. Spooner and Mann, 1982; Spooner, 1987 and 1989), are as essential as understanding its environmental characteristics if programmes of desertification control or management are to have any success (Figure 1.3).

It is clear that since UNCOD it is the natural scientists rather than the social scientists who have gained most positions of importance in official desertification circles. UNEP DC/PAC is dominated by soil scientists and others in related disciplines, for example ecologists and physical geographers. Definition problems apart, they are able to describe and quantify the problem from the perspective of the affected environment, which is exactly what the most recent GLASOD assessment of desertification does, with increased precision (see Chapter 7). They are even able to promote the best soil management strategies and make more refined ecological pronouncements on, for example, range management, sustainability and resilience in drylands. Further, they are able to be quite clear that desertification is not just a scientific problem but a human

Figure 1.3 Maize cultivation on sandy soils in the Cuenca de Oriental in central Mexico. Many approaches to the desertification issue have tended to concentrate on the physical problems of overusing resources in drylands. Reinstating the social dimensions of the debate leads to the more frequent posing of the question: 'why are such marginal lands being used for cultivation?'

one too. Yet Spooner (1989) notes that scientists do not go to social scientists for explanations or considerations of the human components, perhaps because they do not visualise difficulties in understanding the human role. Instead, they go to the policy makers and politicians, making recommendations on combative solutions or with requests for funding for projects.

One of the problems with understanding the human component of desertification that Spooner (1989) has highlighted is that scientists seem to assume that the motives of people who cause desertification are all the same. But just as the links and relationships between desertification, drought and famine are complex (e.g. Glantz, 1989), so are those between desertification, people, poverty and resource issues. Desertification is not solely associated with specific types of social and cultural groups. It was once widely held, for example, that nomadic pastoralism, which is both a land use type and a socio-political grouping, was a major factor in desert margin degradation (e.g. Lamprey, 1983). Now it is widely perceived by researchers as a sound strategy for environmental utilisation in drylands (e.g. Sandford, 1983; Hogg, 1987; Moore, 1987), not just because it is more attuned to the dynamics and nature of these environments but because it makes better use of grazing resources that are available on a seasonal basis than fixed point ranching, for example (Livingstone, 1991).

Linked to this, the argument has been extended to infer that desertification in developing countries is frequently a consequence of abuse of common property rights (Picardi and Siefert, 1976); the often quoted concept of the tragedy of the commons (Hardin, 1968). This concept has been applied to the use of communal rangeland, to the activities of subsistence farmers and to the collection of firewood, all of which have been proposed as key causes of desertification processes (e.g. Grainger, 1990). The solution to these problems has sometimes been seen in the implementation of greater regulatory schemes (Perrier, 1986) or changes in land use to more westernised systems, such as ranching (Cousins, 1987). But these solutions totally ignore the complexity of many indigenous systems and the wide range of strategies that are embraced within, for example, pastoral nomadism, which in drylands may range from highly opportunistic approaches to those that make very conservative use of available resources (Sandford, 1982).

From the social perspective the very idea of the tragedy of the commons has been severely criticised (e.g. Livingstone, 1977 and 1991; McCabe, 1990), not least because the use of many common access systems is in fact regulated by various social mechanisms (Blaikie and Brookfield, 1987; Jodha, 1987; Peters, 1987). The concept of abuse of a common system, for example through the accruing of large personal livestock herds, ignores many issues that require careful assessment at the human–physical interface. These will be considered in later chapters but include the aforementioned dynamics of dryland vegetation communities in response to both climatic variability and grazing pressures, the thorny issue of the carrying capacity concept and the dynamics of livestock numbers (e.g. Sandford, 1983; Abel and Blaikie, 1989) which can fluctuate just as significantly as vegetation cover, and the social component of stocking levels, which can mean that what may appear as high from a simple environmental standpoint may not be from a social perspective (Abel *et al.*, 1987; Livingstone, 1991).

It is not usually sufficient for an anti-desertification policy or plan of action simply to have environmental goals, however laudable they may be. This can be illustrated with respect to pastoralist issues. If stocking levels are reduced on, possibly misguided, environmental grounds, it can also reduce the capacity of the environment to support people (Abel and Blaikie, 1989). If nomadic pastoralism were replaced by ranching in the Sahel, Jahnke (1982) has estimated that the number of people that could be supported would be just one-fiftieth of present levels, while changes to commercial agriculture in Niger had significant effects on both traditional cultivators and pastoralists who had previously adopted a system of mutual benefit on common lands (Franke and Chasin, 1981).

We are aware that desertification does not just occur in developing countries. The most recent UNEP survey suggests, for example, that 79 million hectares of susceptible drylands in North America have been degraded to varying degrees by desertification processes (Middleton and Thomas, 1992). Poverty is sometimes seen as a significant issue in its occurrence, so that even in developed countries desertification affects or is caused by poorer social groups. However, this view does not withstand scrutiny either. Poverty may often be present, but it is certainly not exclusively so. It may be more appropriate to suggest (Spooner, 1989) that the common denominator amongst those who supposedly cause desertification is that they do so while pursuing what seem to them reasonable objectives. This is not necessarily just seeking food as part of a subsistence livelihood, but can be the pursuit of profit in conjunction with highly mechanised or technologically advanced agriculture. Consequently there is affluence desertification and poverty desertification, and their effective control will require different types of political, economic and educational intervention.

Aid and desertification

Another aspect of desertification to consider relates to overseas development assistance or aid. UNCOD implied that desertification as a problem could be solved, setting a 20-year agenda to do so (UNEP–UNCOD, 1978). We have already alluded to some of the problems with the implementation of PACD, including its overt reliance on technological solutions (Odingo, 1990a). Further problems perceived by UNEP are that large-scale funding for desertification-specific projects has not been forthcoming and that their plan of action may have been too environmental in its focus (Kassas *et al.*, 1991). Others might suggest that such an interventionist programme, with its emphasis on aid from donor nations or organisations, has its own attendant problems. From one point of view aid agendas have tended to be set by the donor countries, which may have contributed to the small amounts being spent directly on control mechanisms or on essential research (Dregne, 1985), which do not yield 'glossy' rapid results (Kassas *et al.*, 1991). Some aid projects may even have exacerbated desertification by encouraging the spread of inappropriate agricultural methods, by supporting irrigation schemes that then suffer from salinisation, and by improving infrastructures and access to previously remote areas.

Aid and desertification can be considered from a broader social perspective too, in which it is not necessarily beneficial for recipients (e.g. Bauer, 1988). Regardless of the complex links and entwinements between desertification, famine and poverty, many of the social groups directly affected by desertification in developing countries are, like the land affected, marginalised (Spooner, 1989). Trying to tackle desertification through the normal types of government-to-government aid intervention may only serve to increase this situation. Aid programmes involving centrally rather than locally made decisions can separate the people affected from the decisions taken concerning their destiny, reducing the effectiveness of traditional decision-making processes and undermining social structures that have not necessarily been causing desertification but rather have been under stress. Consequently groups can be separated from the environment upon which they depend for survival, their potential contributions and local knowledge can be ignored (Blaikie, 1989), and local issues in specific degradation problems can be overlooked as a general model is applied without adaptation to a specific situation (Thompson, 1988).

This book

In the preceding pages we have given a brief indication of some of the key dilemmas and problems concerning desertification, its evolution into a major world issue, its relationship to environment and society and its treatment as an institutional, scientific and social issue. In the following chapters we will expand and develop these themes in an attempt to provide not only a reasoned account of its status and development as a major environmental issue but also as an indication of the way it has developed in a political context. We feel that it is essential to do this because so often desertification is considered as an environmental issue without much thought being given, in particular, to the role that the UN has played in its popularisation and its presentation. Desertification also needs to be viewed in the context of the changing scientific awareness of its relation to a range of environmental factors and with respect to the social and human aspects that give its understanding great urgency.

Chapter 2 considers the development of ideas about changing deserts and the role of anthropogenic activities as contributions to desert expansion, in the period preceding UNCOD. Chapter 3 concentrates on the institutionalisation of desertification, centred upon UNCOD and UNEP. This is followed by an evaluation of the central tenets used to support its position as a key environmental issue. Chapters 5 and 6 examine the causes of desertification and why they occur, while in Chapters 7 and 8 the central scientific issues and recent developments in the understanding of dryland environments are explored. Chapter 9 looks to the future of desertification, of the institutions that investigate it, of scientific inputs and of those people affected by it.

2 The history of desertification

The people are living on the edge, not of a volcano, but of a desert whose power is incalculable and whose silent and almost invisible approach must be difficult to estimate. (Stebbing, 1935:510)

The history of human occupation of drylands appears to be punctuated with numerous examples of productive land being lost to the desert, either through mismanagement and overuse of the environment or through natural changes in the environment itself, or a combination of the two. This chapter looks at the the long history of ideas concerning desert marginal degradation up to the calling of the United Nations Conference on Desertification in Nairobi in 1977.

The ancient world

Evidence of mismanagement and calamity comes from some of the earliest dryland civilisations. Ancient records and archaeological excavations combine to show that salinisation and siltation began to plague Lower Mesopotamian irrigation schemes from about 2400 BC (Jacobsen and Adams, 1958), playing a significant role in the eventual collapse of the Sumerian civilization. Temple surveyor reports, which described fields as free from salt in 2400 BC, recorded sporadic salinity in the same areas 300 years later. Increasing salinity is also suggested by the changes in crop types grown, as indicated by counts of grain impressions in excavated pottery from sites in southern Iraq. In 3500 BC, the proportions of wheat and barley were roughly equal, but by 2500 BC the more salt-tolerant barley accounted for more than 80 per cent of the crop, and barley's share had risen to 98 per cent by 2100 BC. Similarly, yields of irrigated crops fell over the same period, attributable to rising concentrations of salt and the build-up of silt in irrigation and drainage channels.

Overuse of water for irrigation and subsequent salinisation appear to be a common cause of decline in agricultural settlements through history. It was an important reason behind the collapse of agriculture and abandonment of the Khorezm oasis settlements of Uzbekistan, for example, dating from the first century AD, although successive invasions also played their part (Mainguet, 1991). Increasing salinity is also the probable key to explaining the many ancient oases that have been buried beneath the shifting dunes of the Taklamakan Desert in China's north-western Tarim Basin (Zhao Songqiao, 1986). The oases of Kuga, Xinhe and Xayar, to the north of the basin, developed during the Han (206BC–AD220) and Tang (AD618–907) dynasties on the alluvial fans of the Tienshan Mountains, but were abandoned after poorly-managed irrigation systems allowed salinisation and waterlogging to degrade the cultivated land.

In other areas, however, the loss of productive land on desert margins has been attributable to largely natural environmental changes. The abandonment of Sueyang, a flourishing oasis during the Tang dynasty in the Hexi Corridor running east–west along the northern foot of the Qilian Mountains in north-east China, provides a rather different story of agriculture and settlement losing out to the desert. About 33,000 hectares of irrigated land were cultivated around the town using water from an alluvial fan of the River Changma, but when the river's course changed about AD700–800 the town had to be abandoned. Today the ruins of Sueyang are partially submerged beneath a sand sheet of small dunes and sparse shrubs (Zhu Zhenda and Liu Shu, 1983).

Explanations of past desertification events are continually subject to re-evaluation as new evidence becomes available however. The identification of natural environmental changes in the Negev Desert, involving a gradual desiccation of the climate from about AD300, has put a question-mark over conventional explanations of deserted Byzantine towns in present-day southern Israel (Issar and Tsoar, 1987). The decline and abandonment of six towns founded by the Nabateans in the first century BC, which developed sophisticated water harvesting on surrounding terraces, has long been put down to conquest by Moslem-Arab nomads (Evenari et al., 1971). However, geological and geographical evidence suggests that the Negev enjoyed a more humid climate from about 100BC to about AD300, after which it became more arid, reaching a critical threshold at around AD500 when the decline of these settlements began.

The invasion and settlement of areas by outsiders is a widely-cited reason for the onset of environmental degradation in historical times. In Latin America, the conquests by the Spanish, bringing technologies and methods of resource use from their more temperate climes, are often blamed for desertification and land degradation. For example, IADIZA (1992), traces the origins of desertification in Argentina to the Spanish conquest and subsequent colonisation, noting that the process has been accelerated in the last 150 years by a new phase of European immigration into the country.

In a similar vein, the arrival of the Spanish in the Coquimbo region of central Chile saw the start of over-intensive use of local resources. Wheat cultivation and the grazing of livestock on increasingly marginal lands have closely tracked copper mining activities in the region. The resultant establishment of invasive vegetation communities and the persistence of some native species, both being less productive than species lost (Figure 2.1), have reduced the region to a 'zone of extreme poverty' as designated by the Chilean government (Chile, 1980).

However, a note of caution has been sounded recently over the ease with which invading Iberians are blamed for upsetting traditional, supposedly harmonious systems of resource use. Analysis of lake sediment cores in central Mexico indicates that pre-Hispanic indigenous land uses in the Lake Patzcuaro basin were not conservationist in practice. Several periods of accelerated soil erosion prior to the arrival of the Spanish, and of the same magnitude as during Spanish colonial times, suggest that the introduction of the plough had no more severe impact on soil loss as traditional agricultural methods (O'Hara et al., 1993).

Progressive desiccation

It was in Central Asia, during the early years of this century, that ideas of a post-glacial gradual drying-up of the environment were developed by authors such as Kropotkin (1904), Huntington (1907), Coching (1926) and Stein (1938). The concept of post-glacial 'progressive desiccation' was based on the twin tenets that wet conditions characterised the glacial phases of the Pleistocene and that aridity had increased since the warming of the Pleistocene ice sheets in the Holocene. Travellers in Central Asia pointed to dry water courses and lakes and abandoned settlements as evidence of this desiccation and suggested that deteriorating environmental conditions had spurred successive nomadic invasions of their more civilised neighbours during periods of increased aridity. Not all investigators of the time agreed with these views, however. Sven Hedin, the Swedish explorer, for example, thought that much of the apparent desiccation could be explained by rivers shifting their courses (Hedin, 1940).

Similar ideas were put forward in southern Africa in the nineteenth and early twentieth centuries. Desiccation was suggested by explorers such as David Livingstone (1857), and the concept was further propounded in both hydrological studies (e.g. Brown, 1875) and popular literature (e.g. Macdonald, 1914). Grandiose schemes to divert rivers and flood depressions were proposed to reverse the threat of ever-worsening droughts (Schwarz, 1923), although a government commission sent to the Kalahari to investigate in 1925 cast doubt on the validity of the ideas and the evidence used to back them up.

The progressive desiccation theme was also expounded in West Africa

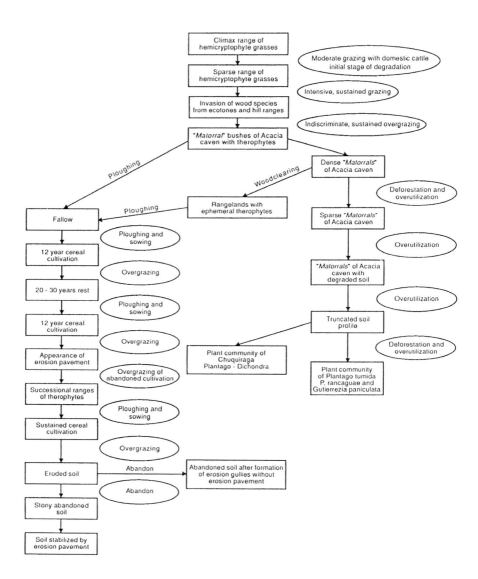

Figure 2.1 Stages in the retrogression of ecosystems in the interior plain of the Coquimbo region, Chile (after Chile, 1980)

in the early decades of this century. The Sahara was said to be encroaching southward onto the Sudan zone along its entire southern front, from the Red Sea coast to the Atlantic. Wells were drying up, lake levels were falling, rainfall was declining, pastures being depleted and trees were dying (Hubert, 1920; Renner, 1926; Bovill, 1929; Stebbing, 1935, 1938). 'The threat to the West African colonies', as Stebbing (1935:506) put it, rang alarm bells in the colonial offices of London and Paris and an Anglo-French Forestry Commission was sent to conduct field investigations into the problem in the late 1930s. But the Commission's findings did not support the desiccation hypothesis (Jones, 1938), suggesting instead that human actions were leading to sand dune reactivation and the lowering of water tables.

The Dust Bowl

The 1930s Dust Bowl of the American Great Plains is one of the best known dryland environmental disasters in history. While the Great Plains have long been typified by recurrent drought and accompanying windstorms, the scale of the events in the 1930s was unprecedented. The widespread dust storms, most severe from 1933 to 1938, affected most parts of the Great Plains, but the core of degradation comprised the western third of Kansas, southeast Colorado, the Oklahoma Panhandle, the northern two-thirds of the Texas Panhandle and northeast New Mexico.

The blame for the tragedy of the 'Dirty Thirties' has largely been lain at the feet of the pioneering farmers who ploughed up the grassy plains for wheat cultivation. Cultivation started in the Great Plains in the late 1870s, with subsequent waves of new settlers arriving from the east during years of high rainfall. A surge of new homesteads sprang up between 1914 and 1930. Farmers ploughed ever greater areas of grassland, spurred on by high wheat prices which also allowed the increasing use of mechanised agricultural techniques brought from the temperate latitudes of western Europe. Worster (1979) has emphasised the drive of social and economic forces in the mismanagement of the Plains, the product of a culture set on dominating and exploiting the land and its natural resources. But when drought hit the Great Plains in 1931, the lack of regard for the climatic and pedological suitability of the region for wheat farming was dramatically exposed (Lockeretz, 1978). Unprecedented large-scale wind erosion was the result. By 1937 the US Soil Conservation Service estimated that 43 per cent of a 6.5 million hectare area in the heart of the Dust Bowl had been seriously damaged by wind erosion.

Coming as it did at the same time as the Great Depression, the Dust Bowl resulted in permanent changes to the lives of hundreds of thousands of Americans. The 'Okies' and 'Exodusters', as the outmigrants from the Great Plains were known, contributed to one of the largest migrations in American history as farmers and their families who had lost everything in the burning winds upped sticks and moved out. An estimated 3.5 million people left their farms during the decade, moving into nearby towns, or further afield to the west coast, to look for alternative work (Worster, 1979).

The ecological catastrophe on the Great Plains in the 1930s traumatised the USA and had a long-lasting effect on a generation of western scientific thinking. It is probably no exaggeration to say that the events of the 'Dirty Thirties' had as significant an effect on science as concerns over the ozone hole and greenhouse warming have had in the late 1980s and early 1990s. One far-reaching effect was to put human-induced soil erosion to the forefront of the perceptions of mid-latitude farmers and administrators operating in drylands in other parts of the world. Images of the US Dust Bowl 'caused Agricultural Officers all over British Africa to examine their own localities for signs of this menace' (Anderson, 1984:327).

But the Dust Bowl also inspired major advances in wind erosion research and soil conservation techniques, most notably the work of Chepil and his colleagues at the US Department of Agriculture. Two decades of field research produced predictive equations (Chepil et al., 1963; Woodruff and Siddoway, 1965) and a seminal work on the physics of wind erosion and its control (Chepil and Woodruff, 1963).

Despite the fruits of this research into the wind erosion system and soil conservation techniques, the annual reports of the US Soil Conservation Service on land damage in the Great Plains leave little doubt that the factors responsible for wind erosion are still not being adequately controlled (Fryrear, 1981). Thirty to forty consecutive years of data for the Texas Panhandle show yields of sorghum declining by 67 per cent and kafir by 59 per cent. Although soil losses by water erosion, the effects of cropping practices and insect and disease may have combined with wind erosion to cause these yield declines, it is clear that improvements in cultivation practices and crop varieties have not kept pace with the factors responsible for decreased crop production.

Drought in the area in the 1950s again resulted in massive wind erosion from agricultural land (e.g. Laprade, 1957), this time damaging more land than in the 1930s, and soil loss in the 1970s dust storms was on a scale comparable to that in the 1930s (Lockeretz, 1978). The events of the 1970s bore sad witness to the fact that political and economic considerations had outweighed the need for prudent land management. Large tracts of marginal land had been put into dryland wheat cultivation during the mid-1970s driven by high levels of exports, particularly to the USSR. A Federal Wheat Disaster Assistance Program was introduced to compensate farmers for losses due to wind erosion, thus removing the disincentive to plough up marginal areas. New centre-pivot irrigation technology was also adopted to water the new cropland, necessitating the removal of linear wind breaks planted since the Dust Bowl era to help prevent wind erosion (McCauley *et al.*, 1981). Perhaps the worst single dust storm event occurred after two years of drought, in the Portales Valley area of eastern New Mexico in late February 1977. The dust palls were tracked on satellite imagery, obscuring 400,000 km² of ground surface of south central USA, and out over the Atlantic Ocean (Purvis, 1977).

The Sahel

While numerous examples can be cited of desertification throughout history in many of the world's drylands, it was events in the African Sahel in the 1970s that thrust the issue to the forefront of the global environmental agenda. A number of events coincided in the 1970s to elevate the desertification issue in the minds of the world community. First, the countries of the Sahel entered a phase of severe drought in the late 1960s after a period of good rainfall years in the 1950s. This in itself was not an unprecedented situation for the peoples of the Sahel, who had experienced droughts before. But in every Sahelian country except Ethiopia this drought came after a long period of colonial rule, with all the effects on traditional societies and economies which that entails: 'The transformation of a relatively self-sufficient pre-colonial economy was far from complete when the droughts of the seventies and eighties struck. Market penetration was proceeding, population was multiplying, but the tenurial links between the people and their land remained substantially undisturbed' (Mortimore, 1989:192). In most cases the countries of the Sahel had experienced a steadily declining rainfall during the first few years after independence in 1960, to be faced with a severe drought before their tenth birthdays (the exceptions are Sudan, independent in 1956, and Ethiopia which has been self-ruling for most of this century).

The effect of the drought was human suffering on a huge scale, primarily because these countries had much larger populations than in the past, but also because in many cases traditional food production had been sidelined by colonial authorities in favour of crops grown for western markets. The other clinching factor in the equation was the state of the global communications media, which meant that for the first time in history pictures of starving fellow human beings could be beamed straight into the living rooms of the western developed world. The sorry pictures were caused not simply by drought, the concerned audiences in the west were told, but also by an insidious environmental plague known as desertification.

History of desertification in the western Sahel

The impact on the world community of the 1970s disasters in the Sahel belie the fact that the region has a long history of human environmental impact. The US National Research Council suggest that

> Evidence of human occupation in the Sahel dates from approximately 600,000 BP. Since that time, selective hunting and gathering, bush fires, agriculture, herding, charcoal production, the destructive exploitation of forest products, and other activities have contributed greatly to the modification of Sahelian ecosystems. No areas, however remote from human settlement, have been left undisturbed. (National Research Council, 1983:24).

Bush fires have been used as a management tool by hunters in the Sahel since the earliest recorded writings, dating from Roman times. Modern herders use the same rationale as ancient hunters in using fire to encourage tender green pasture for animals in areas cleared of coarse, inedible vegetation left from the previous season. Many researchers believe that centuries of burning have altered the Sahel's vegetational character (e.g. Harden, 1963). Regular burning favours perennial grasses with underground stems that regenerate rapidly to produce new green shoots and the invasion of fire-resistant trees and shrubs.

Traders, who have been plying the trans-Saharan routes carrying salt, cloth, precious stones, gold dust and slaves for 2500 years (Figure 2.2), have also had an impact on the desert-marginal environment. Widespread destruction of *Acacia tortilis* to produce charcoal is suggested as perhaps the principal impact by the National Research Council (1983). Riley (1817) quotes a Moroccan active in the trans-Saharan trade in the late eighteenth century who describes caravan traders clearing large tracts of acacia to make charcoal which was used for trade and emergency rations for the camels (numbered in their thousands) as well as fuel during the journeys.

Another acacia species, the *Acacia senegal*, has suffered widespread destruction in the Mauritanian Sahel dating from the fifteenth century when the Dutch first established a coastal trading centre at Arguin for the export of gum arabic to be used for the textile printing industry. Production of gum arabic, a storage product of the *Acacia senegal*, has gradually shifted southward through the centuries and it seems likely that tapping methods which stress the tree and leave it less resistant to drought and disease are at least in part responsible for the *Acacia senegal*'s depletion (National Research Council, 1981). In the twentieth century the destruction has continued around Boutilimit, Togba and elsewhere in Mauritania with far-reaching implications for local economies. The trees also provide browsing, support honey production and wood and fibres used in rural manufacturing, while their extensive root systems help to maintain soil structure and stability.

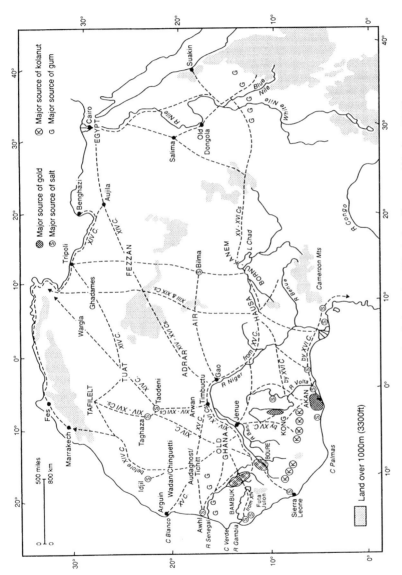

Figure 2.2 Ancient trade routes across the Sahara (modified after Fage and Verity, 1978)

Several other environmental impacts can be traced from the increasing European influence in Sahelian latitudes. The introduction of advanced firearms, which dates from the European involvement in the slave trade, has had a number of knock-on effects for wildlife and consequently vegetation. Many authors have commented on the abundance of wildlife in the Sahel in historical times (see, e.g. Blake, 1914–1942) and the National Research Council (1983) quote a variety of sources testifying to Sahelian people's partiality for bush meat.

The spread of firearms has had a predictable effect. Travellers' reports indicate that wildlife populations have steadily declined throughout the Sahel since the sixteenth century. The loss of birds and browsing herbivores has had an impact on vegetation through their former roles in the growth-stimulation response and seed dispersal of trees and shrubs (e.g. McNaughton, 1976). Modified habitats have, in turn, meant the loss of other wildlife species once important in seed dispersal.

The other significant aspect of more widespread firearms has been to remove the disincentive for herders to allow their animals into forests and thickets. Formerly these areas were homes to predatory wild carnivores, and thus to be avoided. But as wild carnivores have been eliminated so herds have entered the woodlands, resulting in widespread removal of protective understorey and seedlings. The consequence has been a serious disruption of the ecology, with wildlife habitats destroyed and a reduction of precipitation interception and groundwater recharge. Many of the wild animals and plants lost or severely depleted were formerly used by rural populations as famine foods during periods of shortage.

While trans-Saharan trade has long had an environmental impact (see above), the development of modern transport methods and networks has brought its own forms of damage. The introduction of wood-burning steamships on the region's rivers, which dates from the 1830s on the Niger, heralded a significant new pulse of deforestation on riverbanks. Rail transportation, which began with the inauguration of the Dakar–Saint Louis line in 1885, had similar effects, both to fuel the steam engines and to clear the way for tracks and build bridges. In more recent times, building new roads has produced similar results. The development of new transport networks has also been associated with the growth of new settlements, the spread of farmers and the increase in exploitation and transport of natural products, particularly trees, all having a discernible impact on local environments.

The Sahel in the 1960s and 1970s

Hence the events in the Sahel during the late 1960s and early 1970s, which sparked an unprecedented new interest in and concern for desertification both in the Sahel and elsewhere, should be seen in the light of a long history of human impact on the desert marginal environment.

In 1968 the rains in the western Sahel came early and were heavy, but stopped at the beginning of May. By the time these had returned in June seedlings had shrivelled and died in the fields. Animals were dying of hunger by the end of the 1969 dry season, and when rains failed again in 1970 the situation worsened. The small harvest was soon exhausted and an estimated three million people were in need of emergency food aid in the six countries of the western Sahel – Senegal, Mauritania, Mali, Burkina Faso, Niger and Chad. Rains in 1971, 1972 and 1973 were also below average. Estimates of the number of people who perished during this first phase of the prolonged Sahelian drought range from 50,000 to 250,000, while animals died in their millions. Less hardy sheep and cattle suffered most; the UN Food and Agriculture Organisation (FAO) estimated that 3.5 million head of cattle died in the Sahel in 1972–73 alone.

Although it was clear that drought played a major part in this catalogue of disaster, the conveners of UNCOD threw their net wider. The key problem was identified as a chronic process of land degradation in which people were playing a pivotal role. Although there was much debate as to the relative importance of human action and a lack of rainfall, drought was seen primarily as a catalyst which exposed the deleterious effects of long-term degradation by people. Four prime causes of desertification in the Sahel were identified: overcultivation, overgrazing, deforestation and mismanagement of irrigated cropland. These were the offending actions that needed to be understood and controlled.

But this was not all. Although the disaster in the Sahel in the early 1970s undoubtedly prompted the convening of UNCOD, the desertification problem which lay behind the suffering was by no means confined to tropical Africa. Desertification was seen as a global threat, affecting both rich and poor nations alike. While the immediate outcome was obviously more critical in sub-Saharan Africa, similar problems were also sapping the economies of developed countries like the USA and the USSR. It was becoming a problem of global significance, a problem that some authorities and politicians felt only the UN, with a remit for global agendas, could properly face. In 1977 hundreds of international experts attended the UN Conference on Desertification in the Nairobi headquarters of the UN Environment Programme: their mission was to agree on a Plan of Action (UNPACD) to combat desertification and to bring it under control by the year 2000.

3 Institutional developments

The word desertification, created four decades ago, became a trap which ambushed scientists, planners, donor countries, governments of the affected countries, and the mass media! (Mainguet, 1991:16)

In this chapter we will examine the role of the United Nations in shaping desertification into a major world issue. This will inevitably focus on the role of the UN Conference on Desertification (UNCOD) as a catalyst for both the designation and delimitation of the problem and its control. However, the aim is to go further in order to explore the part that institutions, particularly the UN Environment Programme (UNEP), have played in directing the means and mechanisms employed in attempts to tackle desertification. Rather than looking principally at the specific physical-control methods the organisational aspects will be considered, the scales at which they have operated, their successes and pit-falls. In doing so we will look again at some of the major arguments over definitions hinted at in Chapter 1, and we will look at the way in which the extent of desertification at the global scale was established, as this has been used as important ammunition in designating desertification as a high priority problem.

Background and aims of UNCOD

UNCOD was primarily a response to a regionally-specific event, the so-called Sahelian 'Great Drought' of 1968 to 1973 (UN, 1977a). This drought and its associated famine, human suffering and the environmental degradation discussed in Chapter 2 raised western consciences, leading to a major programme of international aid, mainly in the form of food, which in 1974 was worth approximately $200 million (UN, 1977a). This aid was predominantly directed at alleviating a specific situation, famine, rather than tackling longer-term consequences of the drought, such as restoring food production to degraded arable lands and the recovery of pastures. The United Nations Sudano-Sahelian Office (UNSO), established in 1973, was charged with handling rehabilitation of the drought-affected areas, based on the assumption that the drought was the major problem and that 1973 was its last year.

It was soon apparent that the consequences of the drought, or at least related events, were highly significant, not least that environmental recovery was perceived as a long process and that some irreversible damage may have occurred in part through the imprint of human actions upon the climatically-stressed environment, leading to desertification. In December 1974 the UN General Assembly passed resolution 3337 (XXIX) which called for an international conference on desertification to be organised for 1977. This resolution was introduced by the delegates from Upper Volta (now Burkina Faso), which had been particularly badly affected by the consequences of the drought.

Although UNESCO had recognised the significance of arid land degradation through its Arid Zone Programme, this resolution effectively put the issue on the world stage: desertification was 'officially' born as a global issue. Though the focus, especially in the western public eye, has often been on desertification as principally a developing world issue, inextricably linked to famine, poverty, under-development and population growth, it must not be forgotten that it also has expressions, sometimes serious, in the developed world, notably in North America and Australia but also in parts of southern Europe (e.g Vokou et al., 1986; Aru, 1986).

UNCOD had three central aims (Verstraete, 1986):

1. to increase global awareness of desertification;
2. to collect together all the available scientific and technical knowledge on the problem and its possible solutions;
3. to instigate and commence a programme to combat desertification.

This very broad remit was ambitious, given the actual state of understanding of desertification in the late 1970s. It has previously been noted (Chapter 1) how one of the consultant experts used by the UN to prepare for the conference on desertification considered that the issue evolved in its pre-UNCOD stages without ever being properly defined (Dregne, 1987). Indeed, the confusion over definitions and areas affected by desertification has persisted, a consequence of the complexity and range of ecological and environmental processes involved as well as of disparate scientific, social and political interests in the problem. The importance of definitions can be overstressed but an appropriate definition was vital if UNCOD's aims, particularly the third, were to be met.

UNCOD's first two aims were partly accomplished by the preparation of documentation provided for the representatives of the 95 governments attending the conference in Nairobi from 29 August to 9 September 1977. This documentation consisted of four main parts. The first was a World Map of Desertification, prepared at a scale of 1:25,000,000 by FAO, UNESCO and WMO (UN, 1977c). The map attracted much attention (Verstraete, 1986) but depicted desertification hazard rather than occurrence, though at the conference and since it has often been treated as showing actual desertification (Dregne, 1987; Mabbutt, 1989).

The second part of the documentation was an overview and a series of reviews of key themes necessary for understanding desertification, subsequently available to a wider audience in modified versions as a book (UN, 1977a). The reviews covered climate and desertification (Hare, 1977), ecological change (Warren and Maizels, 1977), population and society (Kates et al., 1977) and technology (Garduno, 1977).

For the third part of the documentation the UN commissioned and organised six detailed case studies of desertification, in Chile, Tunisia, India, Niger, the Indus Valley and the Tigris Euphrates Valley. The first two case studies covered summer rainfall areas, the second two winter rainfall areas and the last two areas were affected by salinisation and waterlogging due to poor irrigation practices. The UN studies were supplemented by a further six case histories provided by the governments of Australia, China, Iran, Israel, the USSR and the USA (Mabbutt and Floret, 1983). By including only one Sahel country, these studies effectively illustrated the world-wide extent of desertification, but specifically confined it to a dryland context.

The final documentation consisted of feasibility studies for means of combating desertification, with a specifically cooperative transnational focus. They consisted of ecological monitoring programmes in southwest Asia and South America, greenbelt projects in North Africa and the Sahel, implying the concept of creating a cordon to stop the advancing desert, a livestock and range management project in the Sahel and a groundwater project in northeast Africa and Arabia (Spooner, 1989).

It has been suggested that the representatives of specific countries, notably those from the Sahel, had a more poignant and pressing agenda at UNCOD (Dregne, 1987; Spooner, 1989), namely to secure aid for their immediate problems. However, on paper at least the main outcome of UNCOD was the production of the Plan of Action to Combat Desertification (UN, 1977b; UNEP–UNCOD, 1978), subsequently referred to as UNPACD or the Plan of Action, and the designation of UNEP as its executor.

The Plan of 'Action'

UNCOD's Plan of Action to Combat Desertification was divided into four parts. Its main points are well summarised in Grainger (1990). UNPACD contains some very significant points and embodies a wider recognition of the scope and nature of factors contributing to desertification than it is often credited with. Overall though and befitting a document produced by committees, it is replete with platitudes and good intentions, not untypical of the type of material that stems from major international and intergovernmental conferences. Looking at the Plan of Action 15 years after UNCOD, it comes across as a recipe for inaction and discussion rather than action. On its own, it contains no specific focal points or strategies; rather it is a statement of good intent and generalised issues.

The 28 recommendations are divided into priorities requiring national and international action. Overall they embrace three central objectives (Mabbutt, 1987a): stopping and reversing desertification processes; establishing sustainable land-use practices, and the social and economic development of population groups directly affected by desertification.

National and regional action

Section A of the Plan of Action contained seven areas of recommendations for national and regional action. The first six of these covered desertification evaluation and land management; a statement on the role of urbanisation and industrialisation in ecological change; anti-desertification measures; socio-economic aspects; drought insurance and strengthening national science and technology.

Under these headings countries were advised to assess the magnitude of desertification, its causes and effects, 'by monitoring dryland dynamics, including the human condition' (UNEP–UNCOD, 1978, recommendation 1). It was also recommended (recommendation 12) that the social, economic and political factors with a bearing on desertification should be analysed. Several recommendations refer to using ecologically sound or 'better' practices, presumably a reference to sustainability, with regard to land-use planning, range management and arable agriculture practices. It was also noted that special account should be taken of the needs, wisdom and aspirations of people. Reference is additionally made to a broader remit of social, health and educational aspects of societies affected not only by desertification but by drought.

The section ends with a final, seventh area as recommendation 22. This states that programmes to combat desertification ought to be formulated along the lines of national development plans. To some extent this reflected and attempted to capitalise on awareness of the often perceived link between desertification and underdevelopment in many countries. If general national planning was required for development, it ought to include consideration of desertification (Spooner, 1989). Although this recognises some of the macroscale issues in desertification, in a political sense it also opened the door to the belief that national plans could cure the problem without detailed local understanding. Planning in a manner that takes variations in conditions and circumstances, both social and environmental, into account would clearly require considerable local study, and to be effective and useful national anti-desertification plans would have to do so. The subsequent emphasis on the national plan of action has been considerable. Such plans were frequently coordinated or aided in some form by UNEP, and examples of the weighty documented outcomes of such national assessments abound in the library of UNEP DC/PAC (e.g. Tunisia, 1985; Mali, 1987; Mauritania, 1987). Their actual value and contribution to desertification control, beyond being a further bureaucratic layer in the desertification business, has been questioned (Dregne, 1987; Odingo, 1990b) and is considered further below.

The international response

Section B of PACD focused primarily on the role of the UN, its various agencies and other international bodies such as the World Bank in tackling desertification, as well as recognising the need for cooperation by neighbouring states to deal with a problem that does not respect national frontiers. As well as charging the UN with establishing a viable approach for the monitoring and forecasting of desertification, three of the components of recommendation 23 make particularly interesting reading. Of note are the promotion of effective dryland range-management, the provision of financial assistance for the sedentarisation of nomads, and support for research into dryland energy sources.

The first of these stresses the importance attached at UNCOD to rangeland degradation, an issue which in the desertification context has more recently become fraught with debate over the relationships between natural patterns of climatically-induced vegetation change and dryland dynamics (e.g. Mace, 1991; Tucker et al., 1991). It is further complicated by considerations of ecological resilience and recovery (e.g. Warren and Maizels, 1977; Warren and Agnew, 1987; see Chapter 8) and relationships between vegetation change and soil degradation (Middleton and Thomas, 1992).

The detrimental role of pastoral nomads, a popular scapegoat for desertification in the eyes of both scientists (e.g. Lamprey, 1983) and African governments, is also clearly but somewhat surprisingly conceptualised in PACD by the support given to sedentarisation programmes. In fact prior to UNCOD, UNESCO and UNEP had commenced an Integrated Project in Arid Lands (IPAL) in northern Kenya in 1976 that had included settlement as a programme of land-use development in a traditional area for pastoral nomads. This was despite earlier studies under the auspices of the UNESCO Arid Zone Programme recognising that nomadism in drylands occurred in the very environments essentially unsuited to permanent settled pastoralism (Bremaud and Pagot, 1968). The inclusion of the settlement aspect in recommendation 23 may well have reflected part of the broader political agenda of some participant countries at UNCOD, well noted in a wider context by Horowitz (1979).

Action and implementation

The final two sections of the Plan of Action addressed recommendations for implementing desertification control programmes and other action to be taken. In part they cover bureaucratic aspects of organisation, planning and assessment at national levels and within the UN. In particular, responsibility for the follow-up of UNCOD and implementation of UNPACD was given to UNEP (recommendation 27). Recommendation 28 outlined possible funding opportunities for desertification control projects, including the setting up of the subsequently very unsuccessful 'Special Account'. It also included six specific desertification control projects which extended directly from the transnational monitoring projects that formed part of the preliminary conference documentation.

Definitions and assessments

UNCOD was very successful in placing desertification squarely on the agenda of environmental issues but it was less than clear on stating what the issue and its extent actually were. In Chapter 1 it was observed that UNCOD's working definition was the 'diminution or destruction of the biological potential of the land' (UN, 1977a), though others were also present in the conference documentation. The World Map of Desertification (UN, 1977c) worded it as:

> the intensification or extension of desert conditions ... leading to reduced biological productivity, with consequent reduction in plant biomass, in the land's carrying capacity for livestock, in crop yields and human wellbeing.

A further more graphic example given by Warren and Maizels (1977) was:

> the development of desert-like landscapes in areas which were once green. Its practical meaning. . . is a sustained decline in the yield of useful crops from a dry area accompanying certain kinds of environmental change, both natural and induced.

In the same document, Garduno (1977) differed from Warren and Maizels (1977) in being narrower in respect to causation:

> Desertification is the impoverishment of arid, semi-arid and some subhumid ecosystems by the impact of man's activities.

Notwithstanding the differences in these definitions, a central principle exists: the reduction of the biological potential of the land.

Subsequent assessments of desertification (e.g. Mabbutt, 1989; Odingo,

1990a) have indicated various limitations in UNCOD's definition (see also Chapter 1). One of these is that the focus on ecological aspects and indicators of desertification has essentially ruled out the use of social indicators in determining the scale of the issue (Mabbutt, 1989), yet people are both causes and victims of desertification. A further, equally fundamental but ecological problem is that a reduction in biomass is not necessarily a consequence of a long- (or even short-) term reduction in biological potential. This confusion persists in many quarters and is closely linked to scientific vagaries about desertification. As has been previously noted and will subsequently be developed (Chapter 6), biological indicators of desertification, employed in often-cited studies of desertification's extent (e.g. Lamprey, 1975; Dregne, 1983a) have their own limitations when they are not properly considered in the context of dryland ecosystem dynamics.

In 1977 there were no clear assessments of the scale of the desertification problem. The assessment given at the conference was in terms of the area that potentially could be affected, as derived from the desertification hazard map and related documentation (FAO *et al.*, 1977; UN, 1977c). The often quoted figure of 3800 million hectares was a derivative of this (see Chapter 4). This figure was legitimately used by UNEP for awareness- and fund-raising purposes, but subsequently entered the folklore of desertification and virtually achieved the status of a fact. Elsewhere in the UNCOD documentation it is clear that the conference secretariat saw desertification as a dryland issue, indicated in some of the definitions above and emphasised in UN (1977b). For example:

> Desertification arises from the interaction between a difficult, unreliable and sensitive dryland environment and man's occupation and use of it. (paragraph 52:17)

However, it was also recognised that physical impacts could extend beyond the immediately affected areas (UN, 1977b, paragraph 25), for example through the effects of dust storms and enhanced runoff.

The participants at the conference did not always see desertification in a dryland context. The UNCOD Secretariat had invited representatives of all UN member states to the conference. It has already been noted that some nations saw the conference as an arena for political bargaining and the airing of national interests, a charge also levelled at the 1992 Rio de Janeiro UN Conference on Environment and Development (UNCED). The focus of the 1977 conference, on desertification and drylands, directly excluded about a quarter of Africa and a range of other developing countries from consideration. This meant that they were effectively barred from the potential economic and other benefits of subsequent aid directed at desertification.

At UNCOD scientists argued, for example, against the inclusion of post-deforestation degradation in humid areas as part of the desertification issue, while politicians from developing countries wished the general development issue to be central to the desertification debate (Spooner, 1989).

After UNCOD

The approval of the Plan of Action by the UN General Assembly late in 1977 allowed UNEP to establish mechanisms to fulfil its role in UNPACD's implementation. UNEP desertification activities operate through a tripartite system consisting of DC/PAC, the Consultancy Group for Desertification Control (DESCON) and the Inter-Agency Working Group on Desertification (IAWGD) (UNEP, 1982a). UNEP's Desertification Branch, subsequently renamed as the Desertification Control Programme Activity Centre (DC/PAC) was established at UNEP's Nairobi headquarters where it remains today as the overseer of the day-to-day operation of desertification control activities. DC/PAC states its role as principally one of a catalyst, not only of monitoring programmes and of the progress of UNPACD but generally to promote awareness of the issue of desertification and to assist and advise in the preparation of projects for desertification control. It also coordinates the activities of various other UN agencies (Figure 3.1), but it does not implement action.

DC/PAC acts as the secretariat to two further groups established in 1977–78. DESCON consists of representatives of relevant UN agencies and organisations, such as UNDP, UNEP, UNESCO, FAO and WMO as well as various government representatives, inter-governmental organisations and the World Bank. It considers projects for desertification control submitted from various sources and effectively has acted as a forum for project vetting and evaluation and proposing financial sources for worthy projects.

The Inter-Agency Working Group on Desertification (IAWGD) is the third part of UNEP's approach to implementing UNPACD, and had met 16 times by 1989. Many UN agencies such as UNDP, UNESCO and FAO had considerable expertise in activities relevant to desertification prior to UNCOD (Verstraete, 1986) so that IAWGD's role was essentially seen as one of facilitating cooperation and coordination between groups, and seeing to the implementation of projects relevant to UNPACD.

The bureaucracy of desertification

One political scientist has considered that giving the remit for overseeing UNPACD to UNEP actually damaged its viability (Schulz, 1982). Within

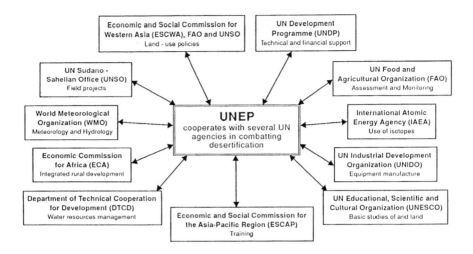

Figure 3.1 UNEP's links with other UN agencies engaged in anti-desertification activities

the UN, UNEP had and still has relatively little political clout compared with longer established bodies such as UNDP and FAO, which also had a global presence. In the 1970s the FAO was not always perceived as the most appropriate organisation to deal interactively with developing nations because of its background in the colonial era and outmoded methods (Weiss and Jordan, 1976).

Conversely UNDP was seen as more progressive and at UNCOD there was a significant lobby to give it joint jurisdiction, with UNEP and one other body, over UNPACD (Schulz, 1982). The sole award to UNEP, with its comparatively low resourcing, relatively small staff, limited global representation and absence of executing authority (meaning it can only recommend projects rather than directly implement them), may have unwittingly contributed to the problems that arose in keeping desertification high on the political agenda and in getting activities established.

In 1984 a report was produced (UNEP DC/PAC, 1984) that outlined the efforts of UNEP in the implementation of the Plan of Action. It clearly indicates DC/PAC's role as a catalyst rather than as a direct contributor to the specific control of desertification. This might cynically be seen as adding to the bureaucratic obstacle of getting actual control measures implemented. A more sympathetic view, appropriate to UNEP's overall role in the desertification issue, might be that a central coordinating body could be the best way to galvanise the action, information and expertise from disparate sources that would be necessary to tackle such a major world issue. The subsequent discussion may help to evaluate an opinion with respect to these views.

Twenty-five UNEP anti-desertification projects are listed in UNEP DC/PAC (1984). Five of these projects actually predated UNCOD. Of the remaining twenty, three were training programmes, two in China and one in the USSR, that included practical field skills in aspects of soil reclamation and dune stabilisation, one was a training programme for government officials, and three were related to the transnational projects that had been presented at UNCOD. Of the remainder, all bar one involved support for various seminars, conferences and institutional support within the UN. The one other project, number FP/1700-80-01, involving UNEP, FAO, UNESCO, WMO and ISSS, the International Society of Soil Science, and with a total budget of nearly $700,000 over three years, concerned the development of a rigorous methodology for the assessment and mapping of desertification.

In an internal report on the activities of the UN (Bertrand, 1985), it is noted that many UN projects tend to be training courses for a small number of individuals and reports on problems and issues rather than actual practical projects. Large sums are spent on fees and expenses for external consultants (Hancock, 1989). UNEP did at least support some projects dealing with actual anti-desertification measures. DC/PAC prepared, assisted in or advised on the preparation of 16 projects that were presented to DESCON for evaluation and approval (UNEP DC/PAC, 1984). These projects were concerned with the practical task of combating desertification, though with a broad remit. For example, DC/PAC and DESCON approved a five-year, $3.5 million project for strengthening the Tunisian seed bank, a $16.7 million sand-dune-fixation project funded by the Libyan government, and a two-year agricultural development project in Yemen to which UNEP contributed nearly one third of the $1.4 million cost.

DESCON also reviewed projects from sources beyond UNEP. At its second meeting, in 1980, for example, it considered seven projects submitted through UNEP and twenty from UNSO. All but one of these were supported to various degrees and by 1982 eight were fully funded, ten partially and four withdrawn due to lack of financial backing. By 1987, however, when DESCON met for the sixth time, it was questioning its own existence due to diminishing financial and participatory support. In the seven years since its second meeting 74 projects had been considered but only 28 had sufficient support for their implementation, with less than half of the necessary funding being secured.

Financial aspects

UNCOD, UNPACD and the publicity that they received, together with the establishment of an infrastructure within the UN organisation directed to facilitate institutional activities in the field of desertification control, implies that a mechanism had been established to keep desertification high on the political and environmental agenda, thereby securing the interest needed for its effective control and eradication by the UNPACD target year 2000.

However, only a few years after UNCOD obstructions to the Plan of Action's implementation were being highlighted (UNEP, 1981). UNEP (1981) noted that while most of the technical and scientific knowledge required for the control of desertification existed (a point that may itself be inaccurate: Odingo, 1990a) major financial problems affected project implementation. Not only were the developing nations suffering from desertification confronted by competing demands for scarce financial resources, but the UN's own efforts were severely hindered by financial shortfalls.

With the implementation of UNPACD, a Special Account had been established to receive funds for desertification projects. In his report to the 36th UN General Assembly, Mostafa Tolba, Secretary General of UNEP and a major force behind UNCOD, proposed a range of sources appropriate to giving the Special Account a predictable source of income (UNEP, 1982b). These included an international tax on trade flows at 0.1 per cent, funds from sea-bed mining, a trust fund from the sale of gold and communications satellite 'parking fees'. These were in addition to the anticipated government contributions, interest-free loans and support from organisations such as the World Bank (Verstraete, 1986). Even if estimates of the total cost of desertification control are not considered in detail because funding could also come from routes outside the UN, by 1988 only $45.5 million had entered the Special Account, which compares with the projects supported by DESCON requiring $122.4 million (UNEP, 1988). It is also interesting that the first seven countries to make contributions were from the developing world: Bangladesh, Brazil, Chile, Mexico, Panama, Sierra Leone and Sudan. The response, financially or otherwise, to the Special Account from the developed world was nonexistent.

UNEP also has its own budget within the UN and it is interesting to examine the component used in a desertification context. From UNCOD until 1983, total UNEP expenditure on desertification was $16,690,026 (UNEP DC/PAC, 1984). Almost 20 per cent of this was spent on what are called Programme and Programme Support Costs, essentially the administrative costs of running DC/PAC, including salaries, consultancies and from 1980 an annual contribution to the administrative costs of UNSO. The remainder, $13,309,576, was directed at actual projects. Overall, UNEP's contribution to anti-desertification activities during this period represented less than ten per cent of its total budget (UNEP DC/PAC, 1984).

National plans: rhetoric or action?

Within UNEP a lot of stress was placed on the production of National Plans of Action to Combat Desertification, for two main reasons that were compatible with the overall Plan of Action. First, they put desertification on the political agenda of, usually, developing countries and second, they gave the opportunity for the incorporation of anti-desertification measures within the overall framework of development.

National plans were, and remain, one of the central catalytic activities of UNEP. Examples of national plans for which preparation commenced soon after UNCOD were Jordan and Mexico along with some of the 18 countries whose efforts were further assisted by UNSO, including Djibouti, the Gambia, Niger and Senegal by 1982. Some plans, such as Syria's, were completed relatively quickly while others, such as that for Jordan, took five years or more. The variable pace of producing national plans was reported in an early assessment for UNEP on the activities of DC/PAC (Richardson, 1984). This pointed out that only meagre results had been achieved, in the form of two plans and a further nine in draft form. This was seen as hardly a heady start for the UN's official anti-desertification activities.

UNEP has also contributed to the preparation of regional plans. Their value is that they may permit anti-desertification programmes to be formulated with greater recourse to environmental conditions rather than to national political issues and boundaries, though on the whole the latter have a considerable bearing on what can realistically be achieved. An example of a recent regional plan is that produced for the Kalahari–Namib region (SADCC, 1990) under the auspices of the Southern African Development Coordination Conference (SADCC). This is at once both an example of a plan where environmental conditions and boundaries are allowed to override political boundaries for planning purposes, and one where political conditions, namely the exclusion of South Africa, limit the way in which the plan can be seen really to address the region's desertification issues (Figure 3.2).

The national Plans of Action to Combat Desertification tend to be a mixture of background data, on land use, general population statistics, relevant political information and in some but not all cases assessments of the nature and extent of desertification, and aims and objectives for desertification control including specific projects. The balance of individual documents tended to reflect the pre-existing level of perceived understanding of the desertification problem.

The plan for Mali (Mali, 1987) is dominated by eight priority projects, reflecting a country where desertification, drought and degradation had been central issues on the political agenda for several decades. Interestingly, even in 1987 when the plan was finally published, one of

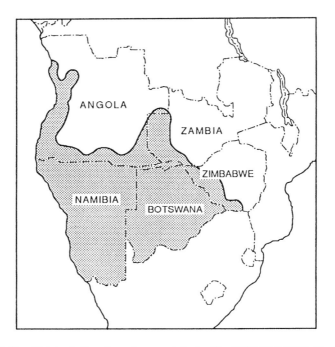

Figure 3.2 The Kalahari–Namib region, as delimited by SADCC (1990). Environmentally compatible areas in South Africa are excluded for political reasons

the projects is 'a green belt to prevent desert encroachment'. It is hard to believe that the experts contributing to the plan still conceived the desertification problem in this manner, and indeed this project is rather more than one involving the creation of a desert cordon. Perhaps such terminology was seen as making the project more saleable to potential donors. It is also interesting that the cost of most of the projects had not been evaluated, severely limiting their chances of being implemented.

By contrast the slim plan for Mauritania (1986) contains little actual detail of proposed projects but is primarily an outline of general strategies. The Jordan (1987) plan is a mix of statistics, a retrospective look at the failure of previous national plans and an outline of the environmental content of the 1986–90 national development plan. In Syria's (1987) Plan of Action, a number of anti-desertification demonstration projects are included.

If UNEP regarded national Plans of Action to Combat Desertification as a central component of its anti-desertification efforts, it is difficult to see how they have fulfilled this role in a useful manner. In a sense, they are a good reflection of the difficulties that a central coordinating and facilitating body such as UNEP can face. The plans in themselves do little in the realm of desertification control, while their variable nature and content even limit their value as a consistent data source. They do fulfil the role of establishing desertification as an issue to be dealt with by the internal administrative structure of the countries concerned. But in many cases even here the burden of dealing with desertification often appears to be shared by several ministries or departments (Mabbutt, 1987a), diluting the potential for effective action and increasing the bureaucratic burden. Without integration or coordination with other national planning activities, for example those relating to food production, it is also difficult to visualise how anti-desertification measures included in a separate plan could be viable goals. In short, their political, as distinct from environmental, viability might even be questionable (Dregne, 1983b).

The national plans could have provided an opportunity for countries to present their case to potential donor agencies for project funding. To some extent Mali's plan, for example, does meet this objective as it clearly spells out what are perceived to be major anti-desertification projects, though without costings it is difficult to see how donors can respond to them.

GAP

The ratification of the Plan of Action by the UN General Assembly included the requirement of regular assessments of progress towards meeting its goals. The first of these was due to be eight years after UNCOD but was brought forward a year to 1984, not least because of the efforts of UNEP's executive director and because the recurrence of drought and related problems in the Sahel region increased the need for urgency in assessing the activities of UNEP.

The UNEP Secretariat began preparations for the General Assessment of Progress, or GAP, in 1982 citing four main aims (Stiles and Sangweni, 1984):

1. an assessment of the current status and trend of desertification;
2. an evaluation of the effectiveness of anti-desertification efforts;
3. identification of factors limiting the implementation of UNPACD;
4. recommending future action.

The aims were to be achieved through various means, including an update of some of the UNCOD documentation, the circulation of a questionnaire on environmental and population matters to 91 countries experiencing desertification problems, the commissioning of reports from bodies such as UNSO and, possibly most important since it indicated a realisation of the inadequacy of existing data, the development of a systematic methodology for desertification monitoring (FAO/UNEP, 1984). Some of the information was assimilated by a consultant group and has subsequently been used in other reports (e.g. Mabbutt, 1989).

The GAP assessment (UNEP, 1984b), presented to UNEP's twelfth Governing Council session, included reiteration of some of the points made previously, not least involving concern about funding and the status of the Special Account (Walls, 1984; Stiles and Sangweni, 1984). Significantly, it also involved official realisation that the target of the year 2000 for solving the desertification problem was unrealistic (UNEP DC/PAC, 1987) and recognition that previous methods of assessment were inadequate and had been given insufficient prior attention (FAO/UNEP, 1984; Stiles and Sangweni, 1984).

The major message that came from GAP to the outside world was that by 1984 desertification had become a greater problem than it was in 1977, extending to 3500 million hectares. There is some confusion as to what areas were considered in the 1977 and 1984 assessments. Mabbutt, one of UNEP's expert consultants, suggests that the 1977 assessment considered arid and semi-arid regions alone (Mabbutt, 1989). The 1991 report of UNEP's executive director (UNEP, 1991) suggests that subhumid regions were also included in the 1977 assessment. Subhumid areas are seen as important because their highly seasonal and variable rainfall regimes, together with experiences of population pressure, made them particularly subject to human-induced degradation pressures.

GAP included the production of data on regional trends and extents of desertification (UNEP, 1984b). The detail in the data suggests considerable rigour in its collection and its presentation supposes a reliability and usefulness that belies the severe limitations present in the methods by which the information was collected. The 1984 assessment was in fact the first real attempt systematically to collect data on desertification's extent. However, the data from the assessment highlighted more about the inadequacy of the ability to collect reliable and systematic information on the problem than actually on desertification itself, which was clearly realised by some of UNEP's principal consultants (Mabbutt, 1987a, 1987b, 1989; Rosanov, 1990). Mabbutt (1987a:13) noted that:

> The GAP revealed, and was hampered by, a sad lack of information at the national level concerning the extent and nature of desertification...which reflected general shortcomings in its assessment and monitoring.

Mabbutt's use of the word 'shortcomings' is diplomatic, for few if any countries had actually been conducting monitoring exercises. The problem not only rested on the practical aspects of data collection, which were themselves significant because so much of the GAP status review was based on qualitative assessments, but with methodological issues.

These related to the standardisation of data collection procedures (Mabbutt, 1987a) and the more overriding issue of what was actually to be assessed – in other words, what desertification actually consisted of. The detailed data on desertification presented as part of GAP, so easily mistaken for a reliable knowledge of the extent of the problem, was not matched in the visual presentation of information. FAO and UNESCO were assigned the job of producing a world desertification map, which turned out to be a further presentation of desertification hazard (FAO/UNEP, 1984) rather than actual desertification. In the course of the map's production, it was recognised that data limitations precluded the production of anything more sophisticated (Stiles and Sangweni, 1984). A more detailed assessment of the degradation hazard was prepared for Africa as part of the same project, based on FAO/UNEP's (1984) provisional methodology for desertification assessment. The map extended beyond drylands and related to general soil conditions (Figure 3.3). Although the methodology behind such attempts indicates a striving for consistency of analysis, the outcome still fell short of indicating the actual occurrence of desertification. One of the GAP consultants was particularly concerned at the lack of hazard/status distinction and expressed disappointment at the official UN efforts (Dregne, 1987). A year before GAP, he had published his own global map (Dregne, 1983a; Figure 3.4), prepared in 1981. Although 'based on little data and a lot of opinions' (Dregne, 1987:9), this map has been widely used since despite its own lack of scientific foundation.

Post-GAP: rigour and publicity

The 1984 general assessment offered the opportunity of a turning point in UNEP's anti-desertification activities. If UNCOD was seen as a success in putting desertification high on the environmental awareness agenda then the seven years following it could hardly be seen as more than a failure, both scientifically and politically.

The assessments of desertification carried out for GAP or produced independently of it (Dregne, 1983a) can be noted for their lack of scientific foundation. As a means of providing baseline data for social and environmental action they were marked by their lack of rigour, lack of consistency and lack of a clear definition or methodological foundation. It is fair to say that UNEP was well aware of this (UNEP DC/PAC, 1987) and that in conjunction with the FAO and other agencies was attempting to resolve the lack of rigour (e.g. FAO/UNEP, 1984). At the same time, faced with the desire to keep the momentum of UNCOD rolling, UNEP was not afraid of using the poorly-defined statistics to show

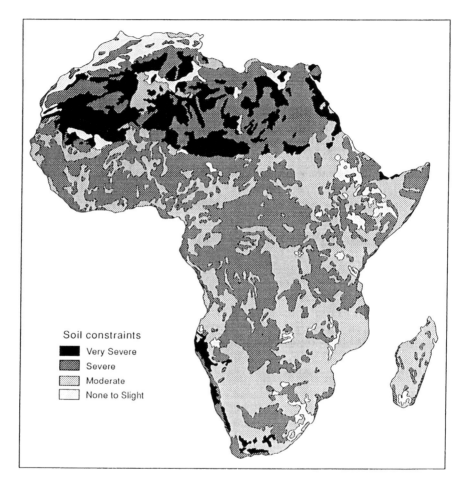

Figure 3.3 Soil constraints on African agriculture (based on a map in Stiles and Sangweni, 1984)

just how severe desertification was and to keep the political pot boiling.

The significance of this can be viewed from several angles. UNEP appears to have been keen to view desertification as a scientific and environmental issue with social consequences. Solutions, however, required political as well as scientific actions, not least in terms of funding anti-desertification projects and in terms of transnational cooperation. While recognising, and implementing, the need to spend time on valid data collection, methodological developments and understanding the environmental aspects of desertification, UNEP also needed to increase its

Figure 3.4 Dregne's (1983) map of the world status of desertification (redrawn from Grainger, 1990)

political effectiveness, both with respect to potential donors for anti-desertification projects and in terms of assisting poorly-resourced developing countries. In 1983, UNEP therefore embarked on the first phase of a Desertification Information Project (UNEP, 1984a), aimed at politicians and the general public in western nations.

At the same time, UNEP also focused and extended its methodological and assessment efforts, not just to give a better understanding of desertification but to enhance scientific credibility. Phase two of the FAO/UNEP mapping project began in 1983 and has increasingly utilised outside agencies to assist with fundamental issues such as defining and understanding the nature of dryland climates as well as drawing on internal UN expertise including UNEP's Global Environmental Monitoring System (GEMS). Even by 1990, 13 years after UNCOD, IAWGD was still recommending desertification assessment as the principal joint activity of UN agencies in the anti-desertification field (UNEP, 1990a). This highlights the complexity of the issue, but perhaps also just how much had previously been taken for granted about knowing what the problem actually was.

In its facilitating role, UNEP revised its efforts in the light of GAP noting that desertification appeared to be accelerating in occurrence and that the problem was likely to be worse in the year 2000 than at the time of UNCOD, despite UNEP's efforts (Mabbutt, 1987b). From 1984, the focus of practical actions was to fall into seven categories (Walls, 1984):

• improving dryland land-use planning;
• concentrating efforts onto the most productive land under threat;
• improving water management;
• emphasising the importance of training and applied studies;
• concentrating on community level projects;
• overcoming the constraints on regional cooperation;
• launching a meaningful international effort.

The apparent breadth of these aims indicates that UNEP saw successful management of desertification as something that could be tackled at a range of scales. It is particularly notable that in the light of GAP, community-scale projects were specifically mentioned, giving recognition to the importance of taking local social and by implication environmental considerations into account at the grassroots level of applying control activities.

Ten years after UNCOD

The UN used the tenth anniversary of UNCOD to assess the institutional response to desertification. It was noted by Mabbutt (1987b) that the first decade since UNCOD was really a period of setting the agenda and of information exchange, reaffirming and recognising the limitations of progress identified by GAP. As we have noted above, most of the problems identified as a consequence of the general assessment related to definition aspects and retaining political awareness, not least because of the financial implications of not doing so. It is therefore interesting to consider the views of the United Nations Centre for Science and Technology (UNOSTD) on the success of UNPACD in addressing and tackling the desertification issue.

UNOSTD (1987) noted that the implementation of the Plan of Action had not been successful, but some of the reasons given for this appear at the same time to vindicate the route UNEP had been taking in its efforts while also highlighting limitations and contributory external factors. Socially, population growth in developing dryland countries was noted to be both a major draw on fragile ecosystem resources and a diversion for economic resources that might otherwise contribute to desertification control. At the national level the means by which desertification control was attempted were also criticised. In particular, the lack of incorporation of anti-desertification projects within overall national plans was noted, as was the disjointed nature of many projects which failed to assess the overriding key issues and consequences. Extending this to a broader scale, the lack of regional planning was seen as an obstacle to solutions to a problem that transcended national boundaries. The ambivalent attitude of the international donor community was also noted.

Whereas the GAP had in effect seen the problem of the ineffectiveness of UNPACD as due to a lack of understanding of the nature of the issue (scientific assessment and definition concerns) and to desertification's low position on the agenda of global concerns (publicity and ensuing financial problems), UNOSTD effectively identified structural limitations at the national level and population growth as the key causes of failure. UNOSTD (1987) suggested that the Plan of Action needed considerable revision if it was to contribute to desertification control.

The role of other agencies and institutions

The institutional aspects of desertification cannot be considered solely in terms of UNEP, though we believe that its role since 1977 has justified focusing on it and examining the ways it has attempted to publicise desertification as an issue and set the anti-desertification agenda.

Many other UN agencies, some of which have been mentioned, have played a role in the desertification issue before UNCOD, though since 1977 their activities have been increasingly linked through UNEP and DC/PAC's role of coordination through DESCON and IAWGD (see above). Desertification has not usually been seen as the central issue of bodies such as the World Bank, yet the finances available to such organisations place them in a better position actually to implement desertification-control projects. For example, between 1978 and 1983 the World Bank and other major donors such as specific western government agencies contributed to desertification-related aid projects in affected areas that in value came close to UNEP's estimate of the actual expenditure needed for desertification control. However only ten per cent of the $100 million concerned was spent on actual field control projects (Gigengack *et al.*, 1990).

The nature of some development assistance and aid, often linked to economic development, as in the case of the World Bank, may in fact contribute to desertification. Some aid-funded projects, established from development assistance loans, may have fostered inappropriate land uses and the expansion of activities into marginal environments. One observer has even described some projects as having near-apocalyptic impacts on the environment (Hancock, 1989). The struggle for economic growth has been the top priority, with little explicit concern given to detrimental environmental impacts (Goldsmith and Hildyard, 1988). Thus the 1973 drought rehabilitation programme in Somalia, funded by the World Bank, involved the settlement of nomads and the establishment of agricultural settlements that were soon affected by salinisation problems (UNEP, 1982a).

Conclusion

In Chapter 2 we saw that desertification was not a new environmental issue in the 1970s; similar environmental problems had been confronted by dryland populations earlier in the twentieth century and in previous centuries and millennia. The North American Dust Bowl was widely documented and publicised in the newspapers of the day but it was events during the 1970s, especially in the Sahel, that placed the plight of dryland peoples and environments squarely on the world stage. The distinctive aspect of the Sahelian situation was the role played by the media and politicians who were operating in a global framework. Global communications brought the suffering and plight of dryland peoples in Africa into the living rooms of the West and the UN politicians found a world-wide issue to be concerned about. Developing dryland nations, not long freed from the colonial powers, faced difficulties that appeared, at least to politicians, to be insoluble without financial aid and help from rich countries. The need to take action was therefore pressed home in both popular and official circles, without a clear environmental and social understanding of what the problems being faced really were. Sahelian problems were presented in an environmental context rather than blamed on the incompetence or actions of affected parties: the developing world could therefore legitimately go to the developed world and ask for assistance.

The UN was the obvious forum for such approaches, leading to the 1977 conference in Nairobi. Whether the UN was best equipped to deal with desertification and related problems in terms of being able to react to short-term disasters and longer-term scientific issues is debatable. Whether desertification as a problem is best tackled or coordinated through the UN, especially through one of its lesser bodies, UNEP, is also questionable.

In this chapter we have highlighted the central issues that have arisen from institutional, particularly UNEP, involvement in desertification, which suggest that the activities following on from the Nairobi conference were neither successful in their short-term impact nor in their ability to set a clear agenda for future research and anti-desertification activities. UNCOD was not the scientific or policy springboard that it was hoped it would be. With hindsight it seems to have triggered many problems, of understanding and of action, that manifested themselves in the ways in which desertification was conceptualised, represented and approached as an environmental, social and political issue in the decade that followed. UNCOD's one success appears to have been to bureaucratise the issue and create an apparent but hollow framework for its understanding and solution. How this took effect is considered in the next chapter.

4 The institutional myth

Desertification has become an 'institutional fact' . . . one that an institution wanted to believe, one that served its purposes. (Warren and Agnew, 1988:7–8)

The global extent

Part of UNEP's original remit from the UN General Assembly was to provide regular assessments of the global extent of desertification, and this mission has formed a central part of UNEP's efforts against the problem, both in preparation for UNCOD and since. The ways in which these assessments have been made and how the resulting data have been subsequently used provides a valuable insight into both the workings of the international body itself and the emergence of the desertification issue on the world's environmental agenda.

UNEP have made three separate assessments of the global extent of desertification. The first in 1976–77 for UNCOD in 1977, the second in 1983–84 as part of the General Assessment of Progress (GAP) in 1984, and the third (GAP II) was in time for the UN Conference on Environment and Development (UNCED) in 1992.

1977 UNCOD

Timberlake (1985) has suggested that UNCOD was 'one of the best UN conferences ever in terms of scientific data and explication of an issue'. Part of the documentation presented at the conference was a number of world maps showing desertification and an estimate of the global areas affected. Estimate is the key word here. Delegates realised that hard data on the actual occurrence of desertification were lacking for most areas of the globe and hence estimation was the best that could be done. The map and associated estimates which have proved to be most durable were prepared by FAO, UNESCO and WMO and were in fact an estimation of desertification hazard rather than actual occurrence (UN, 1977c; see Figure 4.1). Desertification hazard was assessed as moderate, high or very high through a subjective evaluation of climatic conditions, the

Figure 4.1 The 1977 UNCOD desertification hazard map

inherent vulnerability of the land and the pressure put upon it by human or animal action. There is some confusion, however, as to which climatic zones were included in this assessment (see Chapter 3, p42; Mabbutt, 1989; UNEP, 1991). The assessment was made by a limited number of consultants with experience in drylands world-wide. The global figure for the area at risk from at least moderate desertification was put at 3970 million hectares.

To quote UNEP DC/PAC, these data presented at UNCOD revealed that:

> at least 35 per cent of the earth's land surface is now threatened by desertification, an area that represents places inhabited by 20 per cent of the world population. Each year 21 million hectares of once-productive soil are reduced by desertification to a level of zero or negative economic productivity, and six million hectares become total wasteland, beyond economic recoverability. (UNEP DC/PAC, 1987:1)

UNEP and associated agencies had done their best. In the absence of real data the best that could be done was an educated guess at the true extent of the problem and this was what was presented at UNCOD. Although in UNEP's own words: 'the map was based on existing geographical data which was [sic] not precise enough to assist future action in planning and guiding anti-desertification activities either at a national or international level' (UNEP, 1990b:25).

1984 GAP

When the time came to reassess the global extent of desertification, as part of the General Assessment of Progress (GAP) of the Plan of Action to Combat Desertification (PACD) which arose from UNCOD, an attempt was made to glean information from national sources in order to piece together a global picture of desertification. A questionnaire was circulated to the 91 countries with land areas inside the climatic limits of terrain susceptible to desertification. In the questionnaire, respondents were asked to give detailed data on the extent of desertification in their country.

The result was a failure. As Odingo (1990b:25) put it: 'Unfortunately the questionnaire did not contribute any significant data'. But the lack of reliable information coming from the GAP questionnaire was not surprising. Since there were (and indeed still are) precious few monitoring projects in operation, how could the information be anything but more estimates? And since the perception among some of those filling in the GAP forms was that the greater the desertification problem in their country the more likely it was that some aid money might come in to help them do something about it, the temptation was to find desertification to be as widespread as possible. This was when the questionnaires were filled out and returned. Most were not. In fact the initial response was so apathetic that UNEP had to hire consultants to help governments fill out the forms. Even so, most respondents found it 'difficult, if not impossible to complete it correctly' (Odingo 1990b:25).

Hence UNEP was forced to fall back on their consultants again to come up with some more of their own estimates on the global extent of the problem. Studies from two main sources were used, one from Mabbutt (1984), the other from Dregne (1983b).

Mabbutt's study, originally supposed to use the data from the UNEP questionnaire, was based largely upon several specially commissioned regional studies. He classified desertification status as moderate, severe or very severe according to a range of criteria which applied to different land uses.

For rainfed and irrigated cropland, desertification was deemed moderate if there was widespread erosion or salinisation and waterlogging with losses of up to 25 per cent of crop production. The desertification status was severe if crop production losses were between 25 per cent and 50 per cent, and very severe if they exceeded 50 per cent.

Moderate desertification on rangelands was identified in areas where there was a significant reduction in vegetation cover and deterioration in species composition, a significant level of erosion and a 25 per cent decline in carrying capacity. Loss of carrying capacity between 25 per cent and 50 per cent meant severe desertification, while a reduction of more than 50 per cent, making the rangelands economically unreclaimable, indicated very severe desertification.

Using these criteria, Mabbutt derived a new set of global estimates for the extent of desertification. His total figure for the area affected by desertification was 2001 million hectares, just over half the estimate presented at UNCOD seven years before.

Mabbutt's number was also significantly lower than that derived by Dregne (1983b). Dregne's criteria for classifying desertification were slightly different to Mabbutt's (see Table 4.1) and the number he came up with was 3271 million hectares.

This significant difference between Mabbutt's and Dregne's figures is not difficult to understand. First, it should be remembered that both numbers are estimates, based on a lot of educated guesswork and very few hard data. Hence such a difference is not surprising. The key divergence in the two authors' estimates is in the rangeland area estimated to be affected, proportionally by far the largest land-use type where desertification was thought to occur (the other two being rainfed and irrigated cropland). Dregne's figure for the extent of desertified rangelands was 3072 million hectares, while Mabbutt's estimate was 1615 million hectares (Figure 4.2). Dregne excluded about 600 million hectares of slightly

Table 4.1 Criteria for estimating degree of desertification (after Dregne, 1983b)

Desertification class	Plant cover	Erosion	Salinisation or water-logging (irrigated land) ECc* x 10³ (mmhos)	Crop yields
Slight	Excellent to good range conditions class	None to slight	<4	Crop yields reduced by less than 10 per cent
Moderate	Fair range conditions class	Moderate sheet erosion, shallow gullies, few hummocks	4–8	Crop yields reduced by 10–50 per cent
Severe	Poor range conditions class	Severe sheet erosion, gullies common, occasional blow-out area	8–15	Crop yields reduced by 50–90 per cent
Very severe	Land essentially denuded of vegetation	Severely gullied or numerous blow-out area	Thick salt on nearly impermeable soils	Crop yields reduced by more than 90 per cent

Note: * ECc – electrical conductivity, a measure of soil salinity

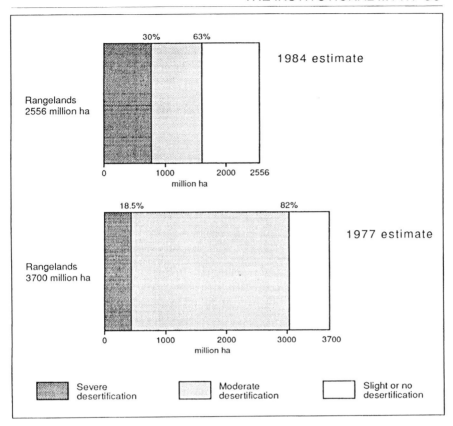

Figure 4.2 Estimates of rangeland areas affected by desertification. The 1984 estimate here is that produced by Mabbutt prior to UNEP's efforts to reconcile the differences between the estimate here and that produced by another consultant (see text). Interestingly enough, Mabbutt's original estimate of 1615 million hectares was still published by UNEP in its Desertification Control Bulletin. (Diagram from data in Mabbutt, 1985)

desertified rangeland in natural deserts such as the Sahara, the Taklamakan and Arabia, where natural biological productivity was too low to support grazing, hence human impact was minimal. But Mabbutt also excluded other large areas of what he considered to be remote, unwatered or otherwise difficult terrain, which although classified as rangeland was seldom if ever used as such.

Like both estimates as a whole, the difference is largely one of personal opinion, but after these estimates were initially considered by UNEP Mabbutt was asked to make a second estimate, including these 'unproductive' rangelands. The new global figure he came up with, having adjusted the rangeland estimate, was 3475 million hectares. Hence:

According to GAP, desertification threatens the wellbeing of 850 million people and embraces an area of some 3.5 billion hectares, of which 3.1 billion hectares are pasture lands, 335 million hectares are rainfed croplands, and 40 million hectares are irrigated agricultural lands. Desertification causes approximately 21 million hectares annually to loose their productivity, even to the point at which their use becomes totally unfeasible from an economic point of view. (Rozanov 1990:49)

In other words, GAP showed that the total desertified area on earth was then made up of 75 per cent of the productive area of the world's drylands and 40 per cent of the world's productive area. The number of people who inhabited lands undergoing desertification had increased by 35 per cent over the number presented to UNCOD in 1977. In the seven years since UNCOD, desertification had extended and intensified in all its forms and was affecting 67 per cent of the rural population of the world's susceptible drylands, including 80 per cent of the Sudano–Sahelian region. Accelerating desertification was shown in five regions, two of them in Africa, one in West Asia, one in South Asia and one in South America.

1992 GAP II

If UNEP had learned anything from the experiences of GAP, it was that there is no substitute for hard data, since detractors from the GAP estimates could legitimately observe that estimates can be massaged to show what is required, especially in the absence of a clearly defined methodology. Since one of the other significant developments at GAP was the presentation of a new provisional methodology for desertification assessment (FAO/UNEP, 1984), it seemed reasonable to assume that this would form the basis of future calculations on the global extent of desertification. However, this was not the case.

When the time came for the next reassessment, as part of GAP II, UNEP used a soil degradation data base, GLASOD (Oldeman, 1988), which had not been developed specifically for desertification studies but for human-induced soil degradation in all environments. The methodology used for GLASOD represents definite progress from those used in the previous assessments. Although GLASOD still incorporates a significant degree of subjectivity, it is based on a more rigorous and consistent set of guidelines than previous assessments and draws its estimates from a much larger pool of regional soil degradation experts, adopting the approach to which Dregne (1989) refers as 'structured informed opinion analysis'. GLASOD methodology, dealt with in detail in Chapter 7, has divided the global land area into 21 regions, and drawn together existing data and impressions from experienced local experts for each region, sub-divided in turn into mapping units based on physiographical realities. Assessments of the degree and extent of human-induced soil degradation for each mapping unit has been made using a detailed and consistent set of indicators for each of four main degradation processes: water erosion, wind erosion, physical deterioration and chemical deterioration.

The GLASOD data, stored in a Geographic Information System (GIS), was used to assess soil degradation in a newly-defined target area of susceptible drylands. There were two important components to the newly-defined susceptible drylands. First, the climatic zones deemed susceptible to desertification were further refined from previous assessments, to include arid and semi-arid drylands as before, but this time only including dry subhumid areas as opposed to all subhumid areas. The second important difference between this and previous delimitations of susceptible drylands was that for GAP II time-bound datasets were used, for the period 1951–80, to come up with a new assessment of just where the susceptible drylands were (UNEP, 1992). The important aspects of the new approach were that this represented a delimitation of drylands at the time of the GLASOD assessment and that the strict, replicable methodology allowed future delimitations to be made in the same way for future time periods. The significance of this issue is further developed in Chapter 6.

The GLASOD data for human-induced soil degradation indicated that 1016 to 1036 million hectares of land were experiencing desertification, less than one-third of the area estimated in both the 1977 UNCOD and the 1984 GAP assessments (Table 4.2). The precise figure varies according to which UNEP source is consulted (UNEP, 1991; 1992; Dregne et al., 1991).

The assessments using GLASOD data were published by UNEP in a document presented at UNCED (UNEP, 1992). However, as the Introduction to this book points out, UNEP regards soil degradation as just one aspect of desertification, albeit a very important one. Degradation of vegetation, which might not necessarily also involve degradation of soil, is regarded as another important aspect of desertification.

The study of vegetation degradation is an area which has seen some significant shifts in thinking by rangeland ecologists in the years since GAP, to the extent whereby the concept of carrying capacity, an essential tenet of the 'overgrazing' phenomenon, has been closely scrutinised and to some extent found to be inapplicable in the highly dynamic dryland ecosystem (see Chapter 8 for a detailed discussion). But nonetheless, a second assessment of vegetation degradation desertification was also commissioned by UNEP as part of the GAP II reassessment. This assessment, made by Dregne's institution, the International Centre for Arid and Semi-Arid Land Studies (ICASALS), used more or less the same approach as earlier assessments. The estimate for the extent of rangelands with vegetation degradation, but no soil degradation, was 2576 million hectares. Toulmin (1993) notes that included within this is forest that has been cleared for cultivation.

Hence, the conclusion of the GAP II assessment, which combined the GLASOD data with the ICASALS estimate, was close to the previous two assessments, at 3592 million hectares (Table 4.3).

Table 4.2 UNEP estimates of areas affected by desertification in the form of human-induced soil degradation (after UNEP, 1991)

	million ha	% of total drylands
Degraded irrigated lands	43	0.8
Degraded rainfed croplands	216	4.1
Degraded rangelands	757	14.6
Total	1016	19.5

Statistical castles in the sky

Having reviewed the methodologies used for estimating the global extent of desertification, it is interesting to go on to scrutinise the basis of statements of desertification rates which are so often referred to in the academic literature and in popular and political circles. A few examples from the 1980s illustrate the sorts of definitive statements commonly made, referring to areas that range in scale from individual countries to whole deserts and to the world itself. In a document outlining UNEP's work in combating desertification, UNEP (1984a) said that 'currently, 35 per cent of the world's land surface is at risk . . . each year, 21 million hectares are reduced to near or complete uselessness'. Warren and Agnew (1988:2) quote a statement made in March 1986 in which US Vice-president Bush was being urged to give aid to the Sudan because 'desertification was advancing at 9 km per annum'. The President of the World Bank is quoted by Forse (1989:31) as saying that 'We must stop the advance of the desert . . . in Mali the Sahara has been drawn 350 km south by desertification over the past 20 years'. Smith (1986) suggests that 'the Sahara Desert continues to creep forward, claiming an area the size of New York state every decade'. And Suliman (1988:27) cites a Sudanese government programme for desert encroachment control in saying that 'it has been esti-

Table 4.3 UNEP estimates of type of drylands deemed susceptible to desertification, proportion affected and actual extent

	1977 UNCOD	1984 GAP	1992 GAP II
Climatic zones susceptible to desertification	Arid, semi-arid & sub-humid	Arid, semi-arid & subhumid	Arid, semi-arid & dry subhumid
Total dryland area susceptible to desertification (million hectares)	5281	4409	5172
Percentage of susceptible drylands affected by desertification	75	79	70
Total area of susceptible drylands affected by desertification (million hectares)	3970	3475	3592

mated that 650,000 square km of the Sudan had been desertified over the last fifty years and that the front-line has been advancing at the rate of 90 to 100 km annually during the last 19 years'.

A number of problems arise when considering statements of this kind. First, we must bear in mind a point made elsewhere in this book: the fact that the advancing desert margin is a misleading image to conjur up, since rarely is this the pattern that actually occurs, an aspect which was acknowledged at UNCOD itself (UN, 1977a). With this point in mind, the reader may start to become suspicious of the sort of statements quoted above, in which case the obvious area to turn to for confirmation is the factual basis for such statements. Herein lies another problem, however, since rarely are such claims backed up by simultaneous presentation of, or indeed reference to, survey methods used, or primary data based on physical measurements. Consequently, it is often impossible for the reader to assess the validity of these descriptions or statements. Indeed, without the means for verification which are all too often conspicuous by their absence, the reader suspects, all too probably rightly, that these proclamations, used with the sort of confidence which should be based on good science, are in fact little more than hollow political statements used to drum up concern; they are guesstimates or, at best, estimates.

And yet the statements continue, and it seems that the more often they are made the more acceptable they become, reinforcing their very existence so that with time they are accepted without question. How can they possibly be wrong if wherever we turn we are faced with such announcements? It seems that if something is said enough times it becomes an accepted reality. In the words of Warren and Agnew (1988:7), who borrow a concept from Thompson et al. (1986), 'Desertification has become an "institutional fact"', defined as one which an institution wants to believe because it serves its purpose, in this case presumably to maintain the institutions themselves and/or the flow of aid to countries affected, particularly the Sahel. Irrespective of whether the claims for desertification's rampant progress can be substantiated, they must continue to be made, for without the claims and the awareness that they engender the work of the institutions and individuals making the claims becomes suspect.

It is sometimes difficult to assess what the UNEP figures are intended to mean. An estimated 3970 million hectares affected in 1977 was revised in the 1984 GAP report to 3475 million hectares (UNEP, 1984b). Sometimes the data are referred to as the area threatened by desertification, other times as the area embracing the problem (Rozanov, 1990) or the actual area affected by it (Dregne et al., 1991). Taking the supposed area affected and the proposed rate of desertification, dramatically increased from the UNCOD figure to one variously reported as 21 million hectares a year (Rozanov, 1990) or 27 million hectares a year (UNEP DC/PAC, 1987), UNEP has certainly used these figures to dramatic effect in its publicity (see Figure 1.2), noting that:

> At a rate of 27 million hectares lost a year to the desert or to zero economic productivity, in a little less than 200 years at the current rate there will not be a single, fully productive hectare of land on earth. (UNEP DC/PAC, 1987:17)

However, although undoubtably dramatic, this statement causes further confusion, since it implies that desertification can happen well beyond drylands and affect all climatic zones. It is only when someone starts to question seriously the basis of such 'facts' that their shaky foundation is exposed.

5.5 km a year

The notable exception to the lack of evidence to support statements as to the progress of desertification is a study carried out by Lamprey (1975) in a mission planned and executed by the Sudanese National Council for Research and Ministry of Agriculture, Food and Natural Resources, and supported financially by the UN and International Union for Conservation of Nature and Natural Resources (IUCN). The study was carried out in October and November 1975, in central western Sudan, in the regions of Northern Darfur and Northern Kordofan and in the Nile Valley north of Khartoum. Its purpose was to make an up-to-date assessment of the status of desert encroachment and ecological degradation as a preliminary step towards a fully integrated research and development project.

The vegetational edge of the desert was mapped by aerial reconnaissance and ground support vehicles. Although the boundary between true desert and grassland and sub-desert scrub was diffuse, the team was able to identify it to the nearest five kilometres (Lamprey, 1975). The approximate boundary which was mapped was then compared to the boundary drawn in 1958 after a survey of Sudan's vegetation (Harrison and Jackson, 1958). Comparing these two lines indicated that the desert's southern boundary had shifted by 90–100 km between the two dates (Figure 4.3). The average rate of advance was thus 5.5 km a year over 17 years.

Lamprey's survey also found other evidence of desertification in the area, in the form of a large expanse of active dunes in Northern Kordofan which had not been mapped in the 1958 study. In 1975 these dunes were apparently drifting southward, engulfing the scrub vegetation and threatening cultivated fields and villages in their path.

Bearing in mind the inherent variability of desert ecosystems, an immediate questionmark is raised over the validity of assessing an average rate of advance from just two 'snapshot' surveys 17 years apart. This suspicion of Lamprey's conclusions has been confirmed by more recent work done in Northern Kordofan by geographers from the University of Lund. Remote-sensing techniques have been combined with field observations, national statistics on crops, population and precipitation, and spatial modelling to examine desertification in Sudan.

Hellden (1984) was able to identify the vegetational desert boundary on false colour satellite imagery of Lamprey's area for 1972 and 1979 and found no change in its location between the two dates, both being in approximately the same position as that located by Lamprey's study. Hellden also established that the vegetation boundary drawn by Harrison and Jackson (1958) and used as a baseline by Lamprey was not actually surveyed but taken as the 75 mm isohyet. Hence, in a later précis of his 1984 paper, Hellden (1988) concluded: 'There does not seem to be any evidence for the Lamprey conclusion that the Sahara desert had advanced 90–100 km in the area during the period 1958-1975.'

The threat of the moving sand dune field was also questioned. The dunes, supposedly encroaching into the Kheiran region north of El Obeid, were reported as early as 1911 (MacMichael, 1911), and ground-based observations combined with aerial photographs for 1962, and satellite-image analysis for the years 1972, 1973 and 1979 did not confirm that the dune system was rolling southward (Hellden, 1984). Indeed, the inter-dune depressions between the transverse dune ridges at the

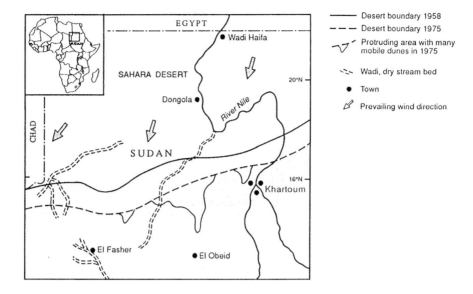

Figure 4.3 Lamprey's advancing Sahara (see text; diagram after Rapp *et al.*, 1976)

southernmost tip of the supposedly advancing sand dune complex have been cultivated at least since the beginning of the 19th century and are still cultivated today.

Other members of the Lund team have also investigated the findings of Lamprey and those of others working in Sudan, including the suggestion that desertification is occurring through the expansion of existing village and water-hole perimeters stripped of vegetation through overgrazing and fuelwood-cutting (Born, 1965; DECARP, 1976). Changes in vegetation and biomass in Kordofan were studied by Olsson (1985), comparing air photographs from the beginning of the 1960s with satellite data from 1972 and 1979, light aircraft surveys from 1975 and field surveys in the years 1982–84. Ahlcrona (1988) also used air photographs taken in the early 1960s to compare the situation in parts of Kordofan and White Nile regions with satellite images from 1972, 1975, 1978 and 1983, complemented with field surveys in 1984 and 1985. None of these studies verified the creation of long-lasting desert-like conditions in Sudan during the 1962–84 period on the scale proposed by other authors. No major shifts in the northern limit to cultivation were identified, no major changes in the position of sand dune fields, and no trend in the creation or growth of denuded patches surrounding 103 villages and water holes examined over the period 1961–83. No major changes in vegetation cover or crop productivity were identified which could not be explained by the variability of rainfall. A severe drought impact was discernible on crop yields in the 1965–74 period, but this was followed by a significant recovery with the return of the rains.

A concept out of hand

The severe questionmark put over Lamprey's work in the Sudan by the Swedish geographers, when combined with the knowledge of the estimates and guesswork involved in the global assessments of desertification, has put the desertification issue under the spotlight in recent years (e.g. Nelson, 1988; Binns, 1990). Criticism of the global statistics issued by UNEP have been countered by Mainguet, a former UNEP employee, who asks: 'what is best? To have approximate statistics which have a value for political decisions but not for scientists, or to have nothing? At least they provide a start which can be confirmed or disproved' (Mainguet, 1991:42). This is a fair point to make *vis à vis* the UNCOD estimates, but it does not justify the continued 'fudging' of the statistics which appear to characterise subsequent estimates. Further, the distinct lack of monitoring programmes instigated by UNEP in the post-UNCOD period rather begs the question: what have UNEP been doing since 1977?

Some authors have questioned whether a global assessment of such a diverse and poorly understood phenomenon is possible, realistic or even useful (Warren and Agnew, 1988) given that solutions with any chance of success ought to be locally oriented. But there is a case to be made for assessing such issues on the global scale, if only to put the issue into perspective, identify more specific problem areas and to generate the political and economic will to do something about it.

However, in their efforts to publicise and raise awareness about desertification, UNEP appear to have sacrificed good science on the altar of expediency. Indeed, in their enthusiasm to publicise the issue, UNEP have been guilty of blurring the distinction between desertification and other forms of land degradation outside the dryland realm. Some UNEP publicity-seeking documents infer that desertification is happening or is being controlled in such non-dryland countries and regions as South Korea, Haiti, Central America and the foothills of the Himalayas (UNEP, 1987). It seems that the whole concept has got out of hand.

But UNEP are by no means the only guilty party in this respect. In their enthusiasm to jump onto an environmental bandwagon many other agencies have pushed the credibility of desertification to the limits. The proceedings of a symposium in the EC Programme on Climatology, entitled Desertification in Europe (Fantechi and Margaris, 1986) is a good example of this phenomenon. The symposium included papers on desertification by acid rain in Central Europe and soil degradation in Denmark. Not all the participants were convinced about the true nature of the conference, however. A. T. Grove's paper, for example, began with the words: 'Desertification in Europe is more appropriately called environmental degradation' (Grove, 1986:9). In the preface to the book, one of the editors, Fantechi, admits: ' . . . when mentioning the subject of desertification in Europe the most usual reaction is well that embodied in the title of Professor Mensching's paper: "Desertification in Europe?"', and according to the various interlocutors the question mark may express any nuance from candid astonishment to perplexity and beyond' (Fantechi and Margaris, 1986:v), but the editor goes on to say that most of the problems are semantic.

It is not just in academic circles that the desertification concept has got out of hand. In the field of overseas development aid many a project has been established and financed in the name of desertification which in fact has relatively little to do with the problem. In the 1980s, desertification became a catchword which had to be included in all good project proposals for dryland development aid. While it was noted in Chapter 3 that the special fund set up for desertification projects after UNCOD was a disaster, innumerable other development schemes were established in the name of desertification. This was recognised in some of the documents released by UNEP as part of GAP. Dregne (1984) points out that an analysis of project spending by four multilateral agencies (the World Bank, FAO, UNESCO and UNEP) and one major national donor agency (the US Agency for International Development or USAID) over the period 1978–83 totalled $10,000 million on projects that were said to have a desertification component. This sum is impressive, and at an average of $1667 million a year, is well in excess of the $388 million estimated annual cost of necessary land reclamation measures put forward at UNCOD. However, only about 10 per cent of this money was spent on direct field control of desertification. The remainder was channelled into projects which are better described under the much wider heading of rural development, such as improving water supplies, building feeder roads, establishing seed multiplication facilities and controlling animal diseases. Some of these projects, such as those aimed at reducing animal losses and digging more wells, may even make the situation worse.

Small is beautiful

To some extent this is a chicken and egg situation. If desertification is to be seen in the wider social context, and thus begging of the question 'why do people indulge in land degrading practices?' (a question dealt with in more detail in Chapter 6), then wider rural development projects may, in the long run, help to combat the desertification problem. But in the immediate term desertification funding is arguably better spent on halting and reversing degradation, which in turn will lead to increased rural prosperity. In this sense, valuable lessons can be learned by the larger development agencies from the activities of some non-governmental organisations (NGOs). Analysis of a sample of NGO desertification projects worldwide as part of GAP indicated that more than half were directed towards field reduction of desertification, principally by reafforestation and soil conservation. A special emphasis was often put on community involvement and appropriate levels of information and education, and the costs of such NGO projects were often very much smaller than those spent by large donors (Dregne, 1984). In just one example, NGOs were praised for their successful approach to forestry projects in the Sahel with their strong emphasis on community orientation, relative to USAID projects (Weber, 1982). In UNEP's own words NGOs 'have been the most effective agencies to date in the battle against desertification . . . their actions have had an impact out of proportion to the money invested' (UNEP, 1987:7). To some extent this shift in emphasis towards smaller scale, flexible, locally appropriate and participatory projects has been taken on board by the larger multilateral and bilateral agencies (Warren and Khogali, 1992).

UNCED and its aftermath

The GAP II assessment of desertification and the GLASOD project were both presented as part of UNEP's contribution to the 1992 UNCED. GAP II was presented as the official interpretation of the status of desertification. Regardless of the philosophy of treating one or other as the 'correct' statistics, the scientific issues relating to which are explored in Chapter 5, UNEP's efforts in the desertification realm since 1977 were widely regarded as a failure, principally on political grounds (UN, 1992).

As we have noted, UNEP consultants had been hinting at the limitations of its efforts since the early 1980s (Mabbutt, 1987a). Financial, scientific, organisational and scale issues have all been levelled as contributary reasons for this (UNEP, 1981; Warren and Agnew, 1987; Rozanov et al., 1989). Attempting to apply technical solutions to a social problem and a poor scientific grasp of the issues concerned are also relevant points, which the subsequent chapters will explore.

The solution suggested at UNCED, in a resolution proposed by Malaysia, and subsequently adopted by the 47th UN General Assembly, was for the 'establishment of an intergovernmental negotiating committee for the elaboration of an international convention to combat desertification in those countries experiencing serious drought and/or desertification, particularly in Africa' (UN, 1992).

It remains to be seen whether this convention, with its June 1994 ratification date, will be any different from the 1977 Plan of Action in terms of its ability to tackle the issue or set policy alternatives for affected nations. The negotiations for the convention involve UN bodies, technical experts, politicians (the committee is chaired by Swedish Ambassador Bo Kjellen) and NGOs, who deal with hands-on, small-scale projects in affected areas. Pressures brought to bear on developing country governments by the international donor community for improved governance must be matched by a more equitable approach to power, decision-making and access ability to markets for third world exports (Toulmin, 1993). How much affected countries are genuinely interested in desertification *per se* or as a mechanism for attracting aid remains to be seen. However, the balance between these aspects will clearly contribute to how much scientific issues will set an agenda that undoubtedly requires political and social solutions.

Conclusion

UNEP's anti-desertification efforts have been dominated by attempts to present data on the shear magnitude of the phenomenon. The lack of scientific foundation of early quantification attempts, doubts surrounding the conceptualisation of desertification as the advancing desert front and the lack of clarity of the processes involved have not prevented politicians from using information based on these approaches to indicate the severity of the problem. Scientists have questioned the developing myths, but it is not until now that their voices have begun to be widely heard and increasingly accepted above the clamour created by the UNEP publicity machine.

Small scale anti-desertification activities are now being seen as appropriate measures to take. One of the documents for delegates at preliminary meetings for the new UN desertification convention even considers 'a strong role for . . . farmers, pastoralists, women and NGOs' in decision-making as a possible item for inclusion in the convention (UN, 1993:8). What this will mean in terms of actual activities supported by the UN, and the position these will take alongside all other actions, remains to be seen.

Despite its failings, the UN still claims a central role for anti-desertification activities: desertification is still being treated as a global problem requiring global coordination and actions, and may well be being used as a means to attract funds and actions to wider political issues affecting relevant developing nations. The dangers inherent in this approach should be obvious. At worst, key issues relevant to desertification are in danger of being lost in wider debates. However, it could be argued that this illustrates how unimportant desertification really is in terms of larger political and social ills.

5 Causes of desertification

\

It has come to be seen as describing a cause of poor agricultural development and declining yields. In fact desertification is more often a symptom of agricultural neglect and misuse. (Timberlake, 1985:60)

The actions people take that cause desertification are apparently well known and are certainly widely quoted. They are methods of land use which are inappropriate in the sense that they apparently lead to environmental degradation. Different authors have organised these causes in different ways (Warren and Agnew, 1988; Grainger, 1990; Mainguet, 1991) but generally they fall under the headings of overgrazing, overcultivation and deforestation. Salinisation on irrigated cropland, a clear-cut case of desertification resulting from human actions, is often viewed as a separate category from the aforementioned. A further category, termed bioindustrial activity in the soil degradation survey of Oldeman *et al.* (1990) is another apt addition.

The ways in which these inappropriate land uses result in degradation are also apparently well known, at least in theory. In practice, however, some of these classic desertification causes are by no means conclusive when subject to close scrutiny of the evidence, and areas deemed to be desertified due to a particular cause are all too often thought to be in such a state through the subjective, though in some cases experienced, eyes of a single expert or at best a group of experts. Just as widely cited figures of the global extent of desertification have been shown to be little more than estimates based on guesstimates, so many of the areas supposedly subject to desertification due to a particular cause are also largely based on subjective assessments as opposed to long-term environmental monitoring. This is a statement of the obvious, of course, since the global assessments are but an aggregate of local and regional assessments.

Overgrazing

Livestock-based livelihoods are an important component of both subsistence and commercial economic activities in drylands (Figure 5.1). Traditional pastoral–nomad systems have been important in northern Africa, some southern African areas, Arabia and central Asia for hundreds if not thousands of years. The drylands of the New World have

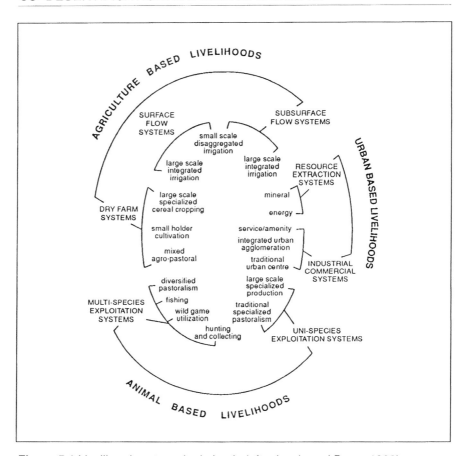

Figure 5.1 Livelihood systems in drylands (after Lewis and Berry, 1988)

been subject to extensive ranch-style pastoralism since the 1830s, the so-called Golden Age of ranching (Heathcote, 1983). In recent decades, ranching has also spread to areas formerly utilised on a nomadic basis. Figure 5.2 illustrates the extent to which livestock systems dominate land use in the Horn of Africa.

Pastoral nomadism, the village-based (or cattle-post) system and ranching, which in fact embrace a wide range of individual utilisation strategies, have all been suggested as contributing to desertification. Indeed, the emphasis placed on degraded rangelands in some of the assessments of the scale of desertification reported in Chapter 4 indicates the importance that has been attached to overgrazing as a cause of degradation. This description of degradation in Australia and the western USA summarises the general pattern that dryland range degradation has been perceived to take:

First came the removal of the edible species and thereby the encouragement of inedible species. Then, if pressures continued, the modification of soil and water conditions to the extent that all vegetation was removed and soil erosion became a major problem. Associated with this deterioration of the vegetation were rapid reductions in livestock carrying capacities, usually by massive deaths in droughts. (Heathcote, 1983:164)

Plant destruction is not solely achieved by eating, as trampling of plants, disturbance of root systems by scuffing and compaction of the surface reducing rainfall infiltration all contribute to damage. Traditional patterns of land use by dryland herders, especially nomadic ones, have sometimes been perceived as a poor use of the environment, yet at least one study has shown that in production terms these traditional systems are possibly up to ten times more efficient than ranching (Breman and de Wit, 1983). Degradation has especially been regarded as ensuing from situations when herd sizes are allowed to increase in an almost uncontrolled and seemingly irresponsible manner (Khogali, 1983; Cooke, 1983; Al-Sharif, 1990). However, beyond the rangelands of Africa and central Asia considerable problems have also been identified on ranches in the New World drylands of the American west (Harris, 1966; Heathcote, 1983) and Australia (Australian Government, 1978). By 1975 it was estimated that nearly one-third of the Australian arid grazing lands required soil conservation work to restore their potential with a further 22 per cent needing better management practices (Australian Government, 1978). A report given at UNCOD highlighted considerable degradation caused by over half a century of sheep grazing on ranches in the Gascoyne Basin of western Australia. The view was expressed that further grazing on 15 per cent of the area would lead to irreversible erosion (Williams *et al.*, 1977). Estimates for the rangelands in 11 USA dryland states (Hadley, 1977) show a complex picture of fluctuations in forage condition since 1930, with the stabilisation of conditions over time (see Table 5.1), perhaps due to reduced stocking or better management but also possibly indicating the problems of attempting to interpret trends for dryland conditions when only using data for 'windows' of time.

Table 5.1 Percentage rangeland forage conditions for 11 USA dryland states

Condition	1930-35	% 1955-59	1975
Improving	1	24	19
Unchanged	6	57	65
Declining	93	19	16

Source: Hadley (1977)

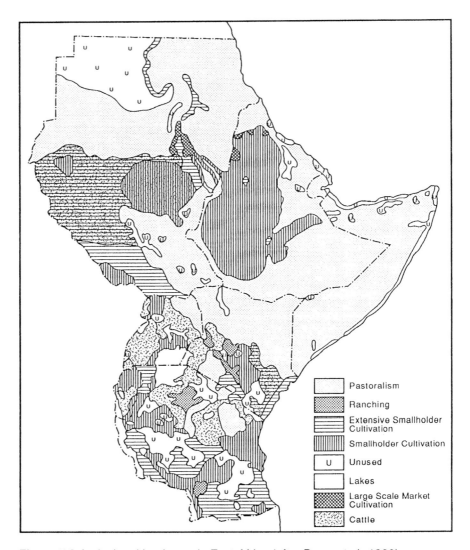

Figure 5.2 Agricultural land uses in East Africa (after Berry *et al.*, 1980)

The supplanting of traditional pastoral nomadism with organised ranching, as in the middle belt of Nigeria, or the spread of ranching into previously virgin potential pasturelands of, for example, the Kalahari, has faired little better in environmental terms according to some authors (Kokot, 1955; Cooke, 1985).

Rising livestock numbers in dryland grazing systems have particularly been seen to lead to desertification. Overstocking, expressed in terms of the concept of potential carrying capacity (PCC) has been widely used as an expression of the way in which herders mistreat the environment (World Bank, 1992). PCC is simply the number of livestock a unit of land in a given environment can support without detrimental impacts to the environmental system and without density-dependant mortalities in the livestock system (Scoones, 1989), and is therefore linked to the concept of sustainable production. Figure 5.3 shows potential carrying capacities for Botswana (Field, 1977), with data expressed as the land area needed to support one livestock unit (LSU) (see Table 5.2). PCC values can be calculated with respect to a simple parameter such as mean annual rainfall (e.g. Field, 1977) or in a more rigorous manner using a basket of environmental parameters.

Exceeding the potential carrying capacity has been seen as a common cause of overgrazing leading to general environmental degradation. As Grainger (1990) and others have recently noted, the overgrazing concept is not always as simple as it initially seems. In Chapter 8 we shall see how relationships between vegetation change and permanent degradation have not been adequately demonstrated in many cases. Other issues further complicate a simple interpretation of apparently high livestock numbers leading to degradation. The concept of carrying capacity and its utilisation in determining optimum stocking levels for a particular area is fraught with problems (Perkins, 1991). One considerable difficulty is that it is hard to reconcile carrying capacities with the natural temporal variability in dryland environmental conditions (discussed below). Stocking levels based on what an environment can support during drought years will leave considerable grazing resources unused in wet years.

The converse scenario might result in considerable stresses being exerted on environment and animals during droughts. However, drought may result in considerable declines in livestock numbers, as has occurred in both the Sahel and southern Africa, through mortality, low birth rates and, in some instances, sales (Perkins, 1990), which may

Table 5.2 Examples of livestock units used in the calculation of carrying capacities

1 LSU = 450 kg live weight			
Animal	Field (1978)	Meyer (1980)	Le Houerou and Grenot (1986)
Camel	-	1.0	1.16
Cow	0.7	0.8	0.81
Horse	0.6	1.0	0.80
Sheep	0.1	0.15	0.18
Goat	0.1	0.15	0.15
Donkey/mule	0.4	0.5	0.53

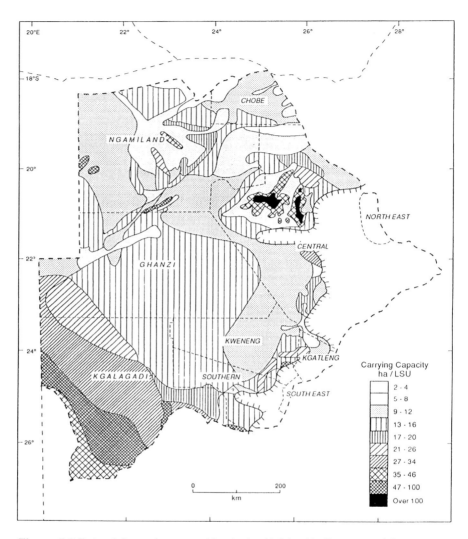

Figure 5.3 Potential carrying capacities in the Kalahari in Botswana (after Thomas and Shaw, 1991)

reduce the potential impacts of large livestock numbers on the environment towards the end of drought periods when it is most stressed. Such a strategy makes economic sense and is supported by McCabe's (1990) study of East African pastoralists. Taking a carrying capacity based on mean conditions satisfies neither the herder nor the environmentalist. Sandford (1982) notes that the two extremes on a continuum of possible stocking regimes are effectively conservationist and opportunist

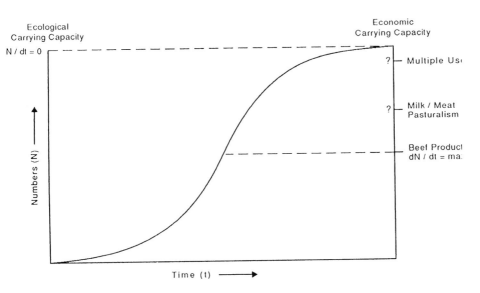

Figure 5.4 Relationships between ecological and economic carrying capacities (adapted from Scoones, 1989)

approaches. Expressed in another way, the different stocking possibilities fall between the extremes of an ecological carrying capacity and an economic carrying capacity (Scoones, 1989; see Figure 5.4).

Increasing opportunities to produce livestock in drylands have been linked to the sinking of boreholes and wells to tap groundwater supplies. A major consequence of this has been to place continual pressure on a restricted area of rangeland around each watering point, zoning vegetation use and grazing into circular zones known as piospheres (Lange, 1969). As cattle need to drink every second day the piosphere has a maximum radius that in theory is equivalent to one day's walk from the water source (Rapp, 1974). Hanan et al., (1991) and Perkins (1991) note that piospheres have been seen as synonymous with desertification, with radii of 30 km (Glantz, 1977) or even 50 km (Rapp et al., 1976) being cited for degraded areas around individual wells and boreholes.

McCabe's (1990) study suggested that problems only begin to arise when external factors upset traditional systems. Boreholes might be one such factor, because they could be seen as improving the chances of large livestock herds surviving through droughts. However, in such circumstances shortage of grazing probably leads to herd decline through starvation rather than water shortage, which is a further feedback mechanism that regulates additional environmental pressure. This has been termed a tracking strategy by Sandford (1983), where one way or another livestock numbers track rainfall and biomass fluctuations.

Overcultivation

Some authorities believe that overcultivation is the principal cause of dryland degradation (Woods, 1984; Warren and Agnew, 1988). The World Bank (1992) considers that such degradation has led to declining yields of staple food crops, especially in Sub-Saharan Africa and some South American countries (Figure 5.5). Overcultivation is a consequence of changes in the application of traditional dryland rainfed agricultural methods and the introduction of inappropriate methods developed in other environments.

Several attributes of cultivation are seen to create problems. Shorter fallow periods lead to nutrient depletion which is a serious problem in African drylands (Thomas and Middleton, 1993). This lowers the potential for production and reduced yields result. Soil erosion by wind and by water may result from the weaker soil structure (Grainger, 1990) but more significant in this respect may be the growth of mechanised agriculture with its attendant large fields and the ability to deep plough, further damaging soil structure. Lewis and Berry (1988) report the results of field experiments in Nigeria which show the soil erosion trade off that is the price paid for increased crop yields from different land management strategies (Table 5.3). High erosion rates are not just due to the direct effects of deep ploughing but also to increased runoff caused by surface compaction by machinery. The number of imported tractors in Iran increased by a factor of ten from 1962 to 1972 (Schulz, 1982) with easy access to machinery for farmers and villagers (Ganji and Farzaneh, 1990).

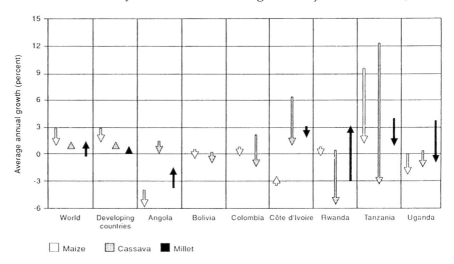

Figure 5.5 Changes in the yields of staple crops in selected countries, 1970–90 (after World Bank, 1992)

Table 5.3. Soil erosion rates and maize yields from differently managed plots, Ibadan, Nigeria (adapted from Lee and Berry, 1988)

Method	Erosion (ton/ha)	Runoff (mm)	Yield (ton/ha)
Manual			
Traditional clearing trees remain	0.01	2.6	0.5
Manual clearing, no tillage	0.4	15.5	1.6
Manual clearing and tillage	4.6	54.3	1.6
Mechanical			
Shear blade, no tillage	3.8	85.7	2.0
Tree pusher/root rake, no tillage	15.4	153.1	1.4
Tree pusher/root rake and tillage	19.6	250.3	1.8

In Sudan, tractor numbers trebled in six years up to 1973 (Lee and Brooks, 1977) contributing to serious wind erosion on the lands subject to mechanised methods in the east of the country (Warren and Agnew, 1988). The wind-liberated dust particles also lead to direct crop damage.

Dryland cultivated areas have increased in extent, particularly since the 1960s. This has proved to have a two-pronged detrimental effect in some places. It was noted above that one effect has been to reduce the areas available to livestock systems, to which can be added the displacement of subsistence farmers to new, more marginal lands in the face of expanding cash crop production (Timberlake, 1985) A second aspect of the quest for new lands to cultivate has been expansion on to steeper erosion-susceptible slopes, as in Kenya, Ethiopia and Lesotho and, particularly in Sahel countries, into areas that are extremely marginal in terms of rainfall, even for the production of staple crops such as sorghum and millet.

In Niger millet fields have appeared 100 km north of the official limit to cultivation (Mabbutt, 1989). Consequently, susceptibility to drought is increased as well as the potential for nutrient depletion. Crop yields from the new areas are not especially high, and in Niger the combination of drought and soil depletion during the 1970s meant that national yields were not increased and even barely maintained despite increases in the areas under production (Agnew and Anderson, 1992; see Figure 5.6). A similar picture exists for Rajasthan in India (Grainger, 1990). Overall, the World Bank (1992) suggests that the impact of erosion on crop yields is equivalent to the annual loss of 0.5–1.0 per cent of the Gross Domestic Product in Malawi, Mali and Mexico.

In practice it can be difficult to distinguish the impacts on yields of drought from those of mismanagement and inappropriate expansion, not

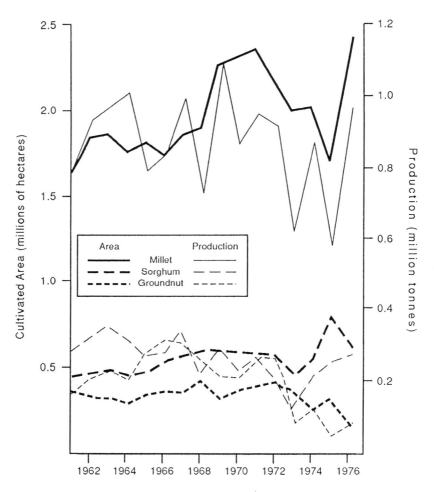

Figure 5.6 Crop production and areas of cultivation in Niger (adapted from Agnew and Anderson, 1992)

least because of inadequate data. Nonetheless one factor that has been regarded as significant is the expansion in crops grown for export (Ahlcrona, 1986), although again not all the evidence points in the same direction (see Chapter 6; IUCN, 1989). Grainger (1990), Agnew and Anderson (1992) and others note how cash crops, particularly the oft-cited case of groundnuts in Niger and Sudan, are very demanding on nutrients and rapidly contribute to soil depletion. In the context of desertification this can contribute to reduced ground cover through declining biomass. Even if fields are abandoned, natural vegetation can be slow to return because of the preceding nutrient depletion and top soil loss.

Degradation under rainfed cropping systems must not be seen simply as a feature of the developing drylands in the post-independence era. We have already discussed the Dust Bowl of the Great Plains (Chapter 2) and Heathcote (1983) eloquently considers a similar problem from the cash-cropped regions of Australia where dust from the eroding wheatfields coloured the sunsets of the eastern capitals and in the 1940s even reached the New Zealand snow-fields.

The Australian Government (1978) has produced data that present a gloomy picture of the extent of required soil conservation measures (Table 5.4). Soil erosion in the dry regions of Australia has increased since World War II, at least partly attributable to land use changes. In the Lower Namoi soil conservation area one survey has shown that the extent of erosion-affected lands increased from 47 per cent in 1967 to 69 per cent in 1975 (Aveyard, 1988), at least contributed to by the expansion of cultivation at the expense of rangelands.

Table 5.4 Soil conservation requirements in Australian rainfed croplands (arid and humid). Adapted from data in Heathcote 1983

Soil conservation measure	rainfed cropland	
	000 km²	%
Not necessary	140	31.6
Management changes	140	31.6
Restoration measures needed	149	33.6
Change of land use needed	0.5	0.1

Mismanagement of irrigation

Irrigation systems have been a feature of dryland agriculture for centuries and in some cases millenia, in effect offering the potential to overcome some of the problems that rainfall deficiencies in drylands pose for crop production. Not only are yields potentially increased but also the range of crops that it is possible to produce. It is not surprising therefore that irrigation schemes have dramatically increased in drylands, with a 34 per cent increase in the area of dryland irrigated cropland between 1961 and 1978 (Heathcote, 1983). Irrigation projects have been a popular target for aid schemes funded by the World Bank too (Grainger, 1990), yet their actual contribution to the economies of recipient nations has to be viewed in the light of the environmental problems that commonly accompany them.

Although food production from the irrigated lands of the Nile and Indus valleys is vital to the economies of Sudan, Egypt and Pakistan, the associated environmental problems are considerable. Similar problems exist in the San Joaquin basin in California. Irrigation schemes have contributed to very high productivity levels but over 800,000 ha are now lost each year to salinisation and associated problems in that area (Sheridan, 1981). The mismanagement and misuse of irrigation has in fact been called one of the 'seven paths to desertification' (Kassas, 1987) with the potential for irrigation schemes to become self-destructive (Hillel, 1982). One source has estimated that annually the equivalent of 12 per cent of the new area of drylands brought into irrigation is desertified (Dregne, 1983a).

There are several different types of irrigation system in use in drylands (see Weisner, 1970; Heathcote, 1983) that range from systems of canals and ditches taking water into fields from rivers, alluvial fans or over long distances via aqueducts to centre-pivot systems using water extracted from aquifers (Figure 5.7). The major problems associated with irrigation schemes are their wasteful use of water, with application rates exceeding possible plant uptake and leading to problems linked to salinisation and alkalinisation, the excess accumulation of sodium (Thomas and Middleton, 1993). Leakage from improperly-lined supply canals has been a major problem in the Punjab where the surrounding water table has risen by up to 9 m in 10 years (El-Hinnawi and Hashmi, 1982), but many difficulties arise from over-application of water, poor drainage and waterlogging. These, combined with the naturally high evaporation rates of drylands, result in the concentration of salts in the soil and at the soil surface. The salt tolerance of most cultivated plants is relatively low so that productivity rapidly declines. Wilcox (1955) recognised 16 classes of irrigation based on the relationship between the salinity and alkalinity hazards, of which all but one are damaging to crops and to the soil.

Degradation by salinisation is not only caused by irrigation, nor are salinisation and its attendant problems the only ones linked to irrigation. Salinisation has been widely reported to affect parts of the USA and Australia where natural vegetation has been removed for cultivation, reducing vegetative evapotranspiration leading to rising saline water tables (Brown et al., 1983; Malcolm, 1983; Bettenay, 1986; Berg et al., 1991). A further localised but significant cause of salinisation occurs in the Middle East where sea-water incursion has affected coastal drylands due to excessive groundwater pumping (Speece and Wilkinson, 1982).

Deforestation

Clearing forest and woodland to create agricultural and pasture land has been a human activity since time immemorial. It has been a characteristic of drylands too but in recent decades has accelerated in line with the

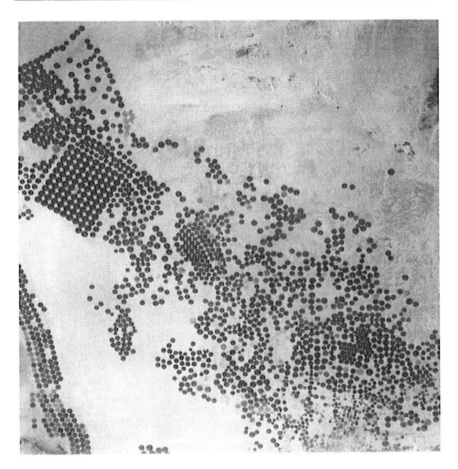

Figure 5.7 Space shuttle photograph of centre-pivot irrigation in Saudi Arabia

expansions of ranges and cultivated land described above. The scale of clearance has increased as modern agricultural methods have been implemented, both for mechanised ploughing, where large fields are most cost effective, and for the application of irrigation schemes. In Sudan, for example, previously planted shelter belts have been removed prior to the establishment of centre-pivot schemes, increasing the potential for wind erosion.

Naturally-forested upland areas are particularly susceptible to water erosion following clearance. The scale of clearance has been considerable: Mabbutt (1989) estimates that only 4–6 per cent of Ethiopia is now forested where 40 per cent once was. In Somalia, forest clearance has been notable as irrigation schemes have been established. Perhaps the principal cause of deforestation that leads to desertification is wood collection

Figure 5.8 Roadside firewood and charcoal sellers in Zambia

for domestic use. This includes extraction of timber for construction but is dominated by what has become known as the fuelwood crisis. The potential scale of the problem is all the more alarming when it is realised that in many Sahel countries fuelwood and charcoal account for over 90 per cent of all energy use (Eckholm *et al.*, 1984).

Wood has long been utilised as a source of fuel for heat and for cooking, but there are three factors which explain why a resource crisis has arisen. First, there is the simple factor of population growth and an increase in absolute demand. Second, high rates of rural–urban migration, a feature of virtually all dryland developing countries, creates spatial pressures of demand (Figure 5.8). The case of Khartoum in Sudan is often quoted, where hardly a tree survives within 90 km of the city (Grainger, 1982), but a similar picture applies to many other Sahel urban centres, for example Ouagadougou in Burkina Faso (Middleton, 1991a) and Dakar in Senegal (Courtant, 1991). Once the fuelwood reserve is exhausted, people may resort to burning dung which further deprives soils of nutrients. One study in Ethiopia estimated the fertiliser value of manure diverted from the field to the cooking stove as $123 million a year, which could increase grain harvests by 1–1.5 million tonnes annually (Newcombe, 1984). The third factor is that taking wood from living trees has often now replaced the traditional collection of dead wood. The consequences of this do not need spelling out, but the need to cut wood for fuel from living trees is in part due to the general reduction in woodland areas, resulting from clearance for cultivation, reducing the sustainable base for collection.

The World Bank (1985) has estimated the scale of the fuelwood problem in human terms for the Sudano–Sahelian region, suggesting an enormous resource shortfall (Table 5.5). It is difficult to translate this directly

Table 5.5 Population sustainability in relation to fuelwood availability, Sudano–Sahelian region (after World Bank, 1985)

Zone	Actual population (million)	Fuelwood sustainable population (million)
Saharan & Sahelo– Saharan	1.8	0.1
Sahelian	4.0	0.3
Sahelo–Sudanian	13.1	6.0
Sudanian	8.1	7.4
Sudano–Guinean	4.0	7.1
Total	31.0	20.9

into an assessment of ensuing desertification because over much of the area trees are part of mixed savanna vegetation systems. Areas where trees are removed or killed in the pursuit of fuel may well be stressed already through grazing pressure. This indicates both the difficulties of ascribing precise causes of land degradation and the way in which several human-resource-environment problems are entwined.

Many authorities have spoken of the need for reforestation programmes as a multifaceted step to dealing with several attributes of land degradation in drylands. Even where this is occurring the rate generally still falls well short of the annual rate of loss. In Somalia, 14 per cent of the country or 8.8 million ha were estimated to be under forest in the early 1980s (Orgut, 1983). At the end of the decade the World Resources Institute (WRI, 1989) gave an annual deforestation rate of 13,000 ha and afforestation at 1000 ha (IGAAD, 1990). For southern Africa, SADCC (1986:iii) reported that:

> deforestation for fuelwood, agriculture, industry and homecraft to a lesser extent, is increasing at an alarming rate and this is causing serious land degradation. Even though all SADCC member states are promoting afforestation, deforestation is going on at a faster rate than the former. Every member state promotes development of afforestation but the major constraints are inadequate funding and shortage of trained manpower to support the activity.

Urban and industrial activities

Waste disposal and pollution from industrial activities are not major causes of land degradation in drylands but they can take on local significance, for example in the Middle East and in the oil producing states of central Asia. Urbanisation has been a major feature of drylands in the new and old worlds since World War II and is likely to continue apace (Beaumont, 1989; Warren et al., 1993). The physical expansion of built land reduces or totally removes the biological production of the land and is therefore strictly a desertification process. Several authors have also noted the deleterious effects of recreational vehicle use by urban dwellers on the desert environment, by damaging vegetation and destabilising soil surfaces (Cooke et al., 1993). Similar effects have been noted during desert military campaigns (Middleton, 1991a).

The indirect effects of growing urban populations on demand for food and fuel are very significant factors in rural land use change and processes. This has contributed to the need for practices such as irrigation, notably in the drylands of the USA, Mexico, Egypt and the Indian subcontinent but also increasingly in Africa. Waste disposal is a particular problem for dryland industries and urban centres (Beaumont, 1989). Salinisation can occur through the direct dumping of wastes onto soil, a procedure that has been used for brackish waters pumped from oil wells in the Americas and Middle East (Kovda, 1980). The persistence of impacts caused by oil spills is unclear, but the magnitude of events such as the damage done to oil installations during the Iraqi invasion of Kuwait in 1990 may lead to significant environmental damage. Quarrying, for example for construction materials to supply growing urban areas, has had significant impacts on the environment in the Middle East, where one gravel quarry in Kuwait is over 20 km long (Khalaf, 1989).

Conclusion

People cause desertification. The ways in which the environment is used in drylands can cause degradation and these causes of desertification can be identified and classified. Having this information will not in itself lead to the desertification problem being solved: it is necessary to know the circumstances that cause unfriendly actions to be put into practice. It is not usually the specific land-use activities that cause degradation either. Rather, it is their intensity, the specific localities that they affect and their occurrence relative to other environmental attributes that lead to degradation. To understand this, the political, social and demographic underpinnings of land-use pressure require consideration.

6 Why does desertification occur?

... there is a need to find ways to bring together natural and social scientists more effectively to address the central question of why 'land managers' ... are so often unwilling or unable to prevent ... accelerated degradation. (Blaikie and Brookfield, 1987:xvii)

Root causes: society, economics and politics

Desertification, like all environmental problems, is a detrimental consequence of people's efforts to use natural resources. If viable solutions are to be found to the problems of desertification, the focus of attention must be on human actions. Irrespective of whether human action or nature, or some combination of the two, is believed to be responsible for desertification, it is the human role that we have the ability to modify, since as yet we are unable significantly to control such natural phenomena as drought.

In the search for solutions, analysis of the human role can be made at a practical level, in terms of the specific actions and land-use practices that directly result in degradation, or at a deeper level by examining the structures in social, economic and political systems that enable, encourage or force these practices to be employed. Both levels of analysis are important; the former for identifying specific methods of resource use which are inappropriate in a particular environment at a particular time, the latter for identifying the driving forces behind degradation.

It can be argued, however, that long-term, permanent solutions to specific desertification problems and areas can only be sought and implemented if the driving mechanisms are identified and changed. Identification and interpretation of these issues lie in the realms of social scientists, economists and governments. Table 6.1 gives an indication of the sorts of underlying structural forces at work. The issues include poverty and population growth (Blaikie, 1985; Eiker, 1986; Warren and Agnew, 1988; Scoging, 1991) which have been linked to many social and environmental issues at a range of spatial scales; structural themes such as land ownership, the use of common resources (Darkoh, 1986) and local political and organisational controls (Swift, 1977); and economic

Table 6.1 Suggested root causes of land degradation (modified after Barrow, 1991)

Natural disasters	Degradation due to bio-geophysical causes or 'acts of God'.
Population change	Degradation occurs when population growth exceeds environmental threshold (Neo-Malthusian) or decline causes collapse of adequate management.
Underdevelopment	Resources exploited to benefit world economy or developed countries, leaving little profit to manage or restore degraded environment.
Internationalism	Taxation and other forces interfere with the market, triggering overexploitation.
Colonial legacies	Trade links, communications, rural–urban linkages, cash crops and other 'hangovers' from the past promote poor management of resource exploitation.
Inappropriate technology and advice	Promotion of wrong strategies and techniques which result in land degradation.
Ignorance	Linked to inappropriate technology and advice above: a lack of knowledge leading to degradation.
Attitudes	People's or institutions' attitudes blamed for degradation.
War and civil unrest	Overuse of resources in national emergencies and concentrations of refugees leading to high population pressures in safe locations.

issues such as international trade and the demand for agricultural products (Gigengack *et al.*, 1990).

Without changes in the way in which these underlying mechanisms operate, attempts to address the specific and direct causes of desertification can only be viewed as short- or intermediate-term remedies. For if pressure from underlying driving mechanisms is not relieved then long-term or permanent solutions may not be feasible. Yet these are the very problems that are the most difficult to tackle, as they may be just one part of a broader and complex economic cost–benefit issue, such as in Blaikie's (1985) analysis of the political economy of soil erosion and Biot's (1992) consideration of soil loss and economic gains in Botswana. The resolution of some of these issues, such as those relating to the pressures of world trade and debt may require major international efforts and cooperation at a level above the platitudes present at international inter-governmental meetings and conferences, and as yet so far unseen.

Some of the factors cited above require a clearer level of understanding. For example, it is relatively simple to say that population growth increases pressure on marginal lands and that the use of common land resources encourages abuse of the environment because of the lack of accountability. However, it is quite another matter to demonstrate a link between these supposedly clear-cut root causes and desertification. Nevertheless, guarded and thorough analysis can shed more light on the interpretation of the roles that some of these factors play in the desertification problem.

Why are pastoral lands abused?

Overgrazing is frequently cited as a significant desertification cause, often linked to excessive livestock numbers. In Chapter 5 we have touched on some of the problematic issues related to the idea of excessive numbers and varying pasture 'carrying capacities', and further investigation of related ecological issues will be made in Chapter 8. Here we will consider overgrazing in the way it has usually been presented in the desertification literature.

The reasons for supposedly excessive numbers of livestock being grazed on a particular pasture may be divided into a number of basic categories. The number of livestock may have increased or the state of the grazing may have deteriorated (Figure 6.1). This could be because the mobility of livestock has been curtailed, or that new, less nutritious pastures are being used.

In some parts of the world's drylands it has been suggested that over-grazing is the result of a change in the approach to range utilisation: from a flexible strategy typical of traditional pastoralists' responses to the

Figure 6.1 Large herds have been seen as contributing to desertification, as in this example from central Botswana. The simple assumptions behind such views are now being questioned by advances in understanding of both sociological and ecological aspects of dryland herding

vagaries of the natural environment which are made by changing herd composition and by moving from pasture to pasture, to a more constrained westernised ranching approach which may delimit a set range and use it in a less flexible way, by keeping just cattle, for example. The reasons for the replacement of traditional pastoralism by ranching, such as in the middle belt of Nigeria, or the spread of ranching into previously ungrazed territory, as in parts of the Kalahari, are numerous. These trends have partly arisen through the desire to 'westernise' in the post-independence period, partly through the reapportionment of traditional grazing lands to a new political elite (Blench, 1985) and also due to entry into world meat markets, with their strict disease controls and subsidies from the west demanding modifications to traditional systems (Taylor and Martin, 1987).

Problems do not only arise when transferring western ideas on livestock management to dryland areas in developing countries. Similar overexploitation has occurred within developed countries when practices appropriate to more temperate environments have been used in national dryland pastures. Examples include the spread of sheep farming in Australia (Moore, 1959), and cattle grazing in the dryland southwest of the USA (Harris, 1966).

In all cases it is tempting to discern that the central theme is the conflict between a culture which demands a constant supply of a predictable commodity – meat – and an environment which is unable to support constancy simply due to its inherent natural variability. Approaches to resource use designed for a less variable environment inevitably lead to problems when applied to the more dynamic dryland scene.

The expansion of borehole water supplies, a notable trend in African drylands in recent decades, is another way in which moves to stabilise and regularise supplies of one resource have led to pressure on others. In Botswana, boreholes were first sunk in the Kalahari to provide drought relief in the 1930s. The programme was intensified in the 1950s and increased considerably after independence in 1966, so that between 1965 and 1976 both livestock numbers and the realisable grazing resource increased by perhaps two-and-a-half times (Sandford, 1977). Similar drought-relief programmes have been carried out in Sahelian countries (Mabbutt and Floret, 1980), with one organisation alone sinking 600 new boreholes and wells over a five-year period in Mauritania, Mali, Burkina Faso and Niger (Grainger, 1982). Boreholes have contributed to the utilisation of new areas for pastoralism, as in the case of government ranches in the Kalahari of Botswana, displacing hunter–gather groups (Cooke, 1985; Thomas and Shaw, 1991). In other areas they have permitted year-round grazing in regions where mobility was previously a prerequisite for survival during the dry season (Beaumont, 1989). In many cases, deliberately or otherwise, this has sedentarised previously mobile groups of people and animals, as in the case of the Khashm-el-Girba scheme in Sudan (Mabbutt, 1989).

The drilling of boreholes is often just one factor in a complicated equation which results in the sedentarisation of nomadic or transhumant pastoralists. It is an example of the sort of external influence which can be the all-important factor in upsetting traditional systems, leading to degradation. Sedentarisation of mobile pastoralists has occurred in many parts of the world for a range of reasons. It is often encouraged by central governments for political reasons, to make control of the population easier, to modernise practices, to make education and medical facilities more easily available, and to bring the pastoralists' products into the wider economy in a manageable way. These were the motives behind the forced collectivisation of nomadic herders in Mongolia in the 1950s, for example (Bawden, 1989). Throughout Africa and the Middle East the nomadic pastoralist way of life has suffered from suppression of raiding and protection, the imposition of political boundaries, the decline of caravan traffic, the loss of many favoured pastures and the general neglect and disapproval of authorities.

The interplay of factors is often complex. In Saudi Arabia, nomadic pastoralists have been encouraged to settle throughout this century for political and religious reasons, and government policies in this direction have been aided by drought in northern Arabia in the 1955–63 period and the steady fall in demand for dromedaries from the beginning of the century as pumps have replaced ancient lifting devices, and trucks supplanted caravans. Surviving pastoralists have changed their herds in response, and the more limited range of sheep, plus the increased provision of secure water points by government, has led to environmental pressure around boreholes (Beaumont et al., 1988).

Another important pressure on nomadic pastoralism has been competition for land which reduces the areas available for livestock. In parts of the Sudano–Sahelian ecozone in Senegal (FAO, 1988) and Niger (Blench, 1985) pastures have been lost to the expansion of cropland, as in Rajasthan, India where the growth of rainfed cropping has contributed to a 75 per cent increase in livestock densities on the remaining pastureland (Grainger, 1990). In East Africa, the Masai lost a large part of their traditional grazing lands under British rule and were reduced to living in a small reserve, while the Samburu cattle herders of northern Kenya have been compressed into about 60 per cent of their early twentieth century range by pressure from surrounding peoples and by land lost to a national park and private ranches to the south (Stiles, 1987).

Overstocking by traditional groups on a decreasing range or on existing ranges has been attributed to the social structure of some societies, where wealth and status may be measured in terms of livestock numbers. The size of individual herds may therefore bear no relation to food requirements and offtake may be low. This situation has led some authorities to talk of 'irrational herders', but this view has been challenged by Livingstone (1991), Abel and Blaikie (1989) and others through consideration of the total package of factors which affect the judgement of pastoralists in traditional east and southern African societies. The decision to retain animals can also be a form of insurance. In Saudi Arabia, Bedouin herders only sell female livestock when they are too old to reproduce as they represent the potential to generate wealth through breeding (Al-Sharif, 1990). Economic factors also contribute and Grainger (1990) notes how wet periods tend to coincide with low market prices, discouraging the sale of livestock and leading to growth in herd sizes. In Botswana, preferential access to the protected European beef market allowed by agreements under the Lomé Convention and provided by the EC as part of development aid, has encouraged herd sizes to grow (Thomas and Shaw, 1991). Again it seems that traditional management methods only begin to break down in the face of external influences.

The number of herds and their sizes have also increased in many areas in response to high rates of human population growth. In the five countries of the western Sahel (Senegal, Mauritania, Mali, Burkina and Chad), the annual increment in human population of 1.5 million exceeds, by six times, the total death toll during the famine and drought of the early 1970s (Grainger, 1990). With great social importance attached to livestock, it is not surprising that their numbers have also risen. Between 1938 and 1961 the cattle population of Niger rose by 450 per cent and by a further 30 per cent in the next ten years (Grainger, 1990). Estimates of the livestock population of Somalia in 1967 gave 1.4 million cattle, 2 million camels and 7 million sheep and goats. By 1988 the cattle population had risen 3.2-fold, camels 3.1 and sheep and goats 4.5 (IGAAD, 1990). Similar trends apply to many other dryland countries. In Mongolia, the national sheep herd grew from 12.6 million in 1950 to 15.1 million in 1990, while cattle numbers increased by more than 40 per cent to 2.8 million over the same period (Middleton, 1993).

Other factors which have encouraged the growth in animal numbers in traditional societies in recent decades include improved animal husbandry and veterinary methods (Salih, 1991; Yassin and Alshanfari, 1991); the eradication of pests such as the Tsetse fly (Thomas and Shaw, 1991); and the reduction in intertribal strife (Drabbs, 1967), though at the time of writing this situation had ceased in Ethiopia, Sudan and Somalia.

Why do people overcultivate?

An increasing demand for food is the most common root cause of over-intensive cultivation in drylands (Figure 6.2). Population growth, at

Figure 6.2. In Kenya rural lands including steep slopes are intensively cultivated due to the high demand for food

between two and three per cent a year in many developing countries means more mouths to feed. More food can be obtained either by increasing the area under cultivation or by increasing yields, the latter approach usually being the more expensive of the two.

In the Sahel, for example, a study of ten countries by IUCN (1989) over the period 1960–87, indicated that population had increased from 60 million to 107 million, with growth rates accelerating over the period. Although food production had not kept pace with the population increase (Omara-Ojungu, 1992), it had also grown, despite continuing rainfall deficits, decreasing soil water and periodic droughts, and this growth in production had been achieved primarily by increasing the area under cultivation.

Cultivation of virgin territory, leading to degradation because the techniques or crops are unsuitable for the newly cultivated areas, has been effected in many parts of the world, not always solely in response to pressure from increasing populations. Ideology and fears over food security played a prominent role in the expansion of cereal cultivation into the grasslands of northern Kazakhstan, western Siberia and eastern Russia in the 1950s (Eckholm, 1976) and in a copycat programme carried out in the Mongolian steppes in the 1960s (Middleton, 1991a). Deep ploughing, which removed the stubble from the previous year's crop, left soils exposed to wind erosion. Similar sorry catalogues of inappropriate agricultural machinery being applied to semi-arid former grasslands were experienced by French pioneer settlers in the Maghreb in the nineteenth century (Dresch, 1986), and European migrants into the Great Plains of the USA in the 1930s (Worster, 1979). The economic catalyst of high wheat prices which helped to drive the Great Plains settlers in the 1930s, was repeated in a slightly modified version, with equally disastrous results from the environmental point of view in the 1970s. The Federal Wheat Disaster Assistance Program, an essentially geopolitical economic tool, drove Plains farmers into another period of extensification with consequent widespread problems of wind erosion (see Chapter 2).

The expansion of rainfed barley cultivation into the Jezira area north of the River Euphrates in Syria was also largely a response to a changing geopolitical situation: the outbreak of World War II meant a need to provide more food domestically. But the adoption of mechanised methods was a function of the low population of farmers who arrived in the area from the more moist Aleppo area (Beaumont et al., 1988). Large tracts of the Jezira area lie beyond the rainfall limit for successful barley cultivation, and serious wind erosion, with attendant problems of sand accumulation has been the result (Ilaiwi et al., 1992). The exploitation of remote areas in Syria, as in other dryland countries, was also tied up with national development in terms of better communications enabling agricultural produce to reach urban markets.

Another oft-quoted reason for overcultivation in many developing countries stems from the cash-cropping legacy that many have inherited from colonial history and are forced to continue in a world economic order which leaves little alternative. A major expansion of groundnut cultivation occurred in the West African state of Niger during the 1950s and 1960s, partly as a response to American attempts to move in on the European market in vegetable oils. Producers in Niger, a French territory until 1960, were encouraged by France's guarantee of an artificially high price which protected producers against shifts in the world market price. The area under groundnut cultivation increased from 142,000 hectares in 1954 to 349,000 hectares in 1961. By 1968 the area had increased to 432,000 hectares (Grainger, 1990).

In the 1960s, farmers were becoming increasingly reliant upon the income from groundnuts, but the prices they received began to decline, spurring them to cultivate areas which would otherwise be fallow, and to push the areas of cultivation into more marginal lands. Similar patterns of events have been reported from many other Sahelian countries, although this trend seems to have stopped since IUCN (1989) indicate that cash crops as a proportion of total agricultural production had not increased in the Sahel between 1961 and 1987.

An important influence on subsistence farmers, who still account for a very high proportion of rainfed cropping activity in many countries, is the need to earn income from off-farm activities. Millington et al. (1989) report that 50 per cent of rural farms in Kenya depend on off-farm income which is more often than not earned in urban areas by male members of families. The resulting depletion of labour in rural areas has significant repercussions for planting, productivity and the maintenance of terraces, bunds and other erosion-preventing measures on steeper slopes which can then fall into disrepair (Millington et al., 1989; see Figure 6.3). A similar pattern of events occurred on a larger scale in the former Yemen Arab Republic during the 1970s when massive emigration of labour to neighbouring oil-rich states left domestic agricultural systems to stagnate and decline (Carapico, 1985), while in Oman depletion of the rural work-force was caused by the domestic oil industry's demand for labour (Dutton, 1983; see Figure 6.4). Poor agricultural practices may also be one result of the decline or debilitation of labour caused by poverty, malnutrition or diseases such as AIDS (Barrow, 1991).

Problems in irrigation management

Irrigated agriculture using traditional methods has long been practiced in drylands. Hand-built tunnels to extract groundwater have been used in Oman, where they are known as *qanats*, for nearly 3000 years. In modern times some dryland countries have little option but to irrigate

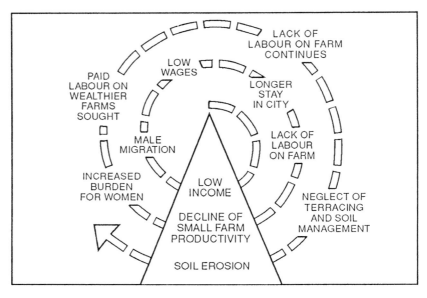

Figure 6.3 The implications of rural–urban migration for subsistence farming (after Millington *et al.*, 1989)

new areas in the face of rising food demands and a small national cultivable area. Just three per cent of the national land area in Egypt and Libya, for example, is cultivable, and in the case of Egypt most of this area is only obtained with irrigation. But the complex water laws and tenure systems developed to regulate water use in traditional systems have often not been successfully reproduced in large-scale irrigation schemes set up in modern times, usually by governments. An inadequate degree of attention to the involvement of local farmers in schemes, poor planning, design and management, and bureaucratic inefficiency all combine to contribute to degradation problems on irrigated cropland.

The sorts of problems which all too commonly plague large-scale irrigation schemes are well-illustrated on the Bura Irrigation Settlement Project on the Tana River in Kenya, initiated in 1979 for cotton cultivation, an important export crop and foreign exchange earner. Financial constraints, inexperienced management, maintenance problems, and shortages of spare parts and fuel have all compromised the success of the scheme (Adams and Hughes, 1990).

Administrative and technical problems also plagued the Greater Mussayeb Project on the Mesopotamian Plain south of Baghdad, established by the Iraqi government in the 1950s. The project's small supervisory unit was unable to prevent siltation and weed growth in the drainage canals through lack of the necessary authority, funds and

Figure 6.4. Successful cultivation of steep slopes requires the use of labour-intensive soil erosion prevention techniques. These terraces are an example from the Jabal Akdar, Oman

equipment for proper canal maintenance, and salinity problems resulted without effective drainage. The situation was further exacerbated by the fact that one-third of the land was distributed to people with no previous agricultural experience, resulting in the abandonment of many plots (Iraq, 1980).

Experience gained in a subsequent rehabilitation project showed clearly that the general welfare of the settler population was a key element in explaining the problems of overirrigation and salinisation. The need for continuing education through extension services able to advise and train farmers in language they could understand was deemed essential, and it was realised that such efforts would be less than satisfactory without adequate provision of credit and marketing facilities. A good understanding of the factors which can motivate project staff members and farmers was considered crucial to the success of the scheme:

> The adoption of a system which relies on the combined presence of special managerial skills, a well-organised administration, teams of engineers, researchers, economists, technicians, and social workers, and – last but not least – a farmer population receptive to new methods and advice, often means a revolutionary change in life-style for technical personnel as well as for the farmer population. (Iraq, 1980:212)

Like many irrigation schemes, one of the root causes of the degradation problems was a function of introducing modern technological methods to areas with predominantly traditional farming populations.

A lack of foresight or inadequate planning can also lead to degradation problems away from the irrigation scheme itself. The potential for degradation offsite due to overuse of a source of irrigation water is no better illustrated than by the ecological devastation caused around the Aral Sea, a direct function of irrigation schemes on the Amu-Darya and Syr-Darya in the central Asian countries of Uzbekistan and Kazakhstan (Kotlyakov, 1991). Inadequate knowledge of the hydrological workings of the water source can also lead to problems: the failure of the South Chad Irrigation Project due to the fall of the lake level of Lake Chad is a classic example (Kolawole, 1987).

Why cut down too many trees?

The cutting and felling of trees for fuelwood, to clear land for cultivation, for fodder and various other uses such as construction is at its most critical around dryland urban areas in developing countries.

Urban populations tend to use more fuelwood per capita than their rural counterparts. About 34 per cent of the total population of Senegal lives in urban areas, for example, but they use 54 per cent of the wood

(Floor and Gorse, 1988), and in Burkina Faso, Ougadougou accounts for no less than 95 per cent of national forest consumption.

The rapid growth of urban areas in many dryland developing countries has put increasing strains on the ability of the local environment to provide increasing amounts of wood. Drought in the Sahel has pushed rural inhabitants towards cities in the hope of finding employment and food. Rural military insecurity has been an additional push factor in several countries in recent times, including Sudan, Ethiopia and Somalia. The resultant growth in some dryland cities has been phenomenal. In Mauritania, Nouakchott's population, which stood at 4000 in 1959, exploded to more than 500,000 in the early 1990s, mainly due to the influx of environmental refugees. The urban demand for fuelwood is rapidly depleting forests and woodlands on the Senegal River. In Mauritania as a whole fuelwood consumption is eight times higher than the natural growth of accessible forests (Mauritania, 1986).

The (largely urban) fuelwood crisis in the Sahel is intimately linked to several important underlying causes. They include poverty and aspects of land and resource ownership. The problem will continue as long as fuelwood continues to be the cheapest fuel option, both in absolute terms and in terms of the investment needed to change to gas or kerosene stoves for example. This much appears clear, but the economic forces behind deforestation for fuelwood are only poorly understood. A simple economic analysis would suggest that as accessible fuelwood supplies decline, the urban price should rise. However, the small amount of evidence available for African cities does not show increases in real fuelwood prices over time (Leach and Mearns, 1988). Ownership of the trees cut down to supply urban fuelwood needs is another key issue, and in many cases the resultant degradation is an illustration of Hardin's (1968) 'tragedy of the commons' principle.

Conclusion

The foregoing overview of the underlying reasons behind people's overuse of the environment, leading to desertification, throws up a number of common themes, as summarised in Table 6.1. Ignorance, poor planning based on inadequate understanding of the dryland environment, and the adoption of inappropriate techniques go a long way towards explaining many of the examples of degradation described above, such as the Dust Bowl of the American Great Plains and the Greater Mussayeb Irrigation Project in Iraq. Although some authors (e.g. Warren and Agnew, 1988) have pointed out that ignorance is too easy a scapegoat to blame for degradation, we believe that it is appropriate enough to explain cases of desertification which are essentially examples of people or institutions who are learning by trial and error about how to operate in a new environment, applying ideas from their more temperate homelands and seeing them fail in drylands.

More worrying in these situations are instances of the same errors being made in the same areas at a later date. These may be a result of poor memory, either in individual farmers or in institutions, but in the wider perspective such repeated ecological blunders are a function of the low or non-existent value put on environmental resources compared to other priorities. The example of repeated wind erosion episodes in the American Great Plains comes to mind here. It is to be hoped that the rise of environmental economics and the current tentative moves towards sustainable development may offer some more ecologically sensible alternatives to such repeated mistakes in the future.

A more complex situation is faced when trying to understand degradation in societies which have been inhabiting dryland environments for many generations. Ignorance and misguided approaches may have some bearing in situations where people, through force of circumstances, are impelled to change their traditional lifestyles within drylands. But for societies who have been living off the land in the same way for a long time this explanation is clearly lacking. Traditional approaches to land management fail when external influences change the circumstances in which they operate. Such external influences include nomadic pastoralists being settled or squeezed into smaller territories, for political, economic or natural environmental reasons such as drought. Similarly, arguments based on common ownership (the 'tragedy of the commons') and people's lack of control over their own resources or in a wider perspective their own destiny, only appear to apply when societies are under stress from changed circumstances. Again, such circumstances may be based in economics, local, national or global, politics or environment, and the role of an increasing human population is certainly relevant here.

It should not be surprising that approaches to resource use and societal organisation which have developed over centuries are found wanting, with degradation the result, in an era of such rapid change as the twentieth century. Hence, serious efforts to solve desertification problems must strike at the heart of society itself, by attempting to help people through rapidly changing social and cultural environments in their attempts to adjust to new ways of organising themselves and using the resources of the natural environment. In doing so, however, it is important to remember that peoples who have inhabited drylands for many generations have as much to offer in the search for solutions as anyone, since it is they who understand how dryland environments work.

7 Unravelling the myth

It has even been questioned whether desertification is actually occurring and the word 'myth' has been mentioned. (Hellden, 1991:372)

Science and politics

Environmental degradation of one sort or another is clearly a worldwide issue. It might even be the case that much of the earth is already degraded, suffering from current degradation processes, or is under threat from them (Barrow, 1991). Concern for this degradation is clearly no longer the preserve of a fringe element of society or of parts of the scientific community. In the western world during the 1980s environmental awareness gained political credibility with both the left and right, though this can sometimes appear as nothing more than a skin deep convenience, evidenced by comments from President Bush of the USA in the 1992 presidential election campaign, who castigated the opposition's Vice-presidential candidate as 'Mr Ozone', more concerned with owls than job creation.

Desertification was unavoidably admitted to the world of political values and approaches in the late 1970s by the UN. As previous chapters have documented this took the form of institutionalisation of the issue. This may have created several advantages, for example it contributed to the direct concern of national governments in affected countries and in potential aid-donor states, and it gained a level of representation within the UN and its constituent bodies that other equally meritorious environmental issues did not gain so readily. In effect desertification became an 'ecological taboo' according to Riebsame (1986), controlling political actions on a prima facie basis, without close examination of the context or the underlying issues. Therefore the politicisation process also created difficulties. Desertification became a common word, representing an environmental and social problem of serious dimensions, long before it had the appropriate scientific and social understanding. At UNCOD in 1977, the control and eradication of desertification was placed on the agenda with a timetable that was born out of the rhetoric common to politicians and bureaucrats rather than from scientific reason. A day might be a long time in politics, so the target year of 2000 for the solution of the desertification problem could have seemed generous at UNCOD.

However, it took scant account of how little was really known at the time about the desertification phenomenon; by 1984 this target was officially being seen as unrealistic and unfeasible (see Chapter 3). The very politicisation of desertification, involving the interests of state élites and organisations that wield considerable influence, also led to the omission of politics from the conceptualisation and perception of the problem (Schulz, 1982). Rather, it was simpler to view the issue primarily in an environmental light, avoiding the need to address the role that land-use policies and agricultural interests played in the desertification process.

A further aspect of the initial institutional representation of desertification that we have previously noted was the inclusion of many general statements concerning the problem, its attributes and extent. At its worst this manifested itself in dramatic representations of the nature of desertification, as embodied and illustrated in the 'marching desert' concept, while playing down the complexity of the measures any solutions would entail. Such representation could possibly be seen as justifiable if it galvanised institutions, governments and NGOs into action, but it also needs to be viewed in the light of its negative affects. For example, seemingly it gave environmental support for actions such as settling, encouraging settlement, or moving social groups with supposedly detrimental land-use practices (e.g. Kaya, 1991) and, as we have noted in Chapter 1, the need to give priority to anti-desertification measures was used in 1985 by the President of Niger as a reason to delay the instigation of democratic elections.

Oversimplification of the desertification issue was probably at least partially due to the relative lack of detailed research into many aspects of the environmental and social systems embroiled within it, prior to its birth as a major environmental issue. This undoubtedly contributed to some of the factors that have been discussed in earlier chapters, for example the debate and confusion over definitions, the nature and extent of desertification and even to what the solutions might be.

Since UNCOD, perhaps because of it, scientific investigations and advances have occurred that provide clarification and understanding to many aspects central to the desertification debate and which have resulted in considerable rethinking in some areas vital to a clear representation of the problem, its causes and characteristics. In this chapter we will examine some key general issues: desertification in the broader context of land degradation, the characteristics and delimitation of drylands and monitoring desertification.

Land degradation and desertification

It is not easy to make a case on scientific grounds for desertification being a particularly special form of land degradation. In terms of the actual physical processes, desertification is not unique either. In Chapter 1 we considered definitions of desertification and noted that they have tended not to include specifically details of the physical processes of degradation. Instead, they have defined the issue in terms of an outcome, particularly the reduced biological productivity of the land (e.g. FAO/UNEP, 1984; Mainguet, 1991), and an environment or group of environments where this occurs: the susceptible drylands (e.g. Nelson, 1988; UNEP, 1992). There has also been a tendency to specify desertification being caused or triggered by human actions rather than simply by natural events, succinctly expressed by Grainger (1990) as degradation caused by poor land use.

The actual physical processes of degradation by desertification, which reduce the productivity of the land, are ultimately very important to understand if control or remedial measures are to be implemented. These are usually regarded as involving changes in soil properties or attributes, loss of soil through erosion and in some definitions loss of vegetation. There are considerable scientific problems with the inclusion of the last of these. This will be addressed in Chapter 8 but difficulties arise partially because ephemeral ecosystem changes are an inherent natural component of dryland system variability. These have sometimes been confused with the changes that desertification induces, which are effectively permanent, at least on the scale of human lifetimes, unless remedial or restorative action is implemented. To appreciate this issue it will be necessary, in Chapter 8, to explore further the inherent characteristics of dryland ecosystems and some significant recent scientific advances.

A further example of the obstacles preventing scientific clarity in the definition of desertification comes from the World Bank (1992). In this document desertification is viewed as representing loss of vegetation cover and plant diversity, and 'more widespread than desertification, if less dramatic, is the gradual deterioration of agricultural soils, particularly in dryland areas' (World Bank, 1992:55). The document then goes on to say that soil deterioration includes erosion and internal soil changes and cites UNEP sources that treat soil degradation as desertification for its information on this topic! The World Bank clearly appears to be acting unilaterally in regarding vegetation change as desertification and soil changes as something completely separate, illustrating the difficulties in getting uniform recognition of what the problem constitutes among policy-makers and donor agencies.

If desertification is viewed as primarily due to the processes associated with soil erosion, soil change and even vegetation loss, with the precise processes being considered dependent on the definition adopted, then it cannot be viewed as a unique form of land degradation in terms of the actual processes through which it takes effect. Soil degradation occurs in all environments, 'affecting developed and developing countries from the Equator to the poles' (Barrow, 1991:179), with human actions frequently and perhaps increasingly as the cause. In the case of desertification, some specific processes such as salinisation and wind erosion might be more prevalent in drylands than in other environments, but the physical principles are the same and their solution requires the same physical remedies (e.g. Goudie, 1990).

On this basis desertification is only a distinct form of land degradation by spatial definition (i.e. its confinement to specified environments). It may seem rather difficult to some to regard this alone as an adequate reason for giving it special status and concern, but two other points require consideration in this context.

First, dryland environments have been seen as having attributes that make them particularly vulnerable to degradation. Dryland ecosystems have been viewed as delicate, fragile systems that are highly susceptible to disturbance and degradation (e.g. Blair Rains and Yalala, 1972; Lal, 1988; UN, 1992). They are also subject to natural phenomena, particularly drought, which induce stresses in plant, animal and human populations alike. Drylands have therefore been seen as harsh regions where the danger of serious environmental damage is very real (UNCOD, 1977b). However, it is worth bearing in mind that most of these comments are made from the viewpoint of authorities brought up in the relatively stable environments of the mid-latitudes.

Second, drylands, particularly those that specifically brought desertification to the fore in the 1970s, contain societies that, for a range of social, political and technical reasons, are especially vulnerable to disturbances in the environment. The Sudano–Sahelian region contains many of the world's poorest nations (Warren and Khogali, 1992), which are subject to high rates of population growth. In this region and in other developing world drylands, desertification is part of a complex of factors incorporating drought, famine and also war which cause instability in social and ecological systems. From the perspective of the people who experience the consequences of desertification in these areas, it is just one part of a tangled web of factors causing social upheaval, food shortages and frequently death. To reiterate a point raised in Chapter 3, UNCOD was initially triggered by a more general concern for environmental and social problems in the Sahel region, but desertification in a global context ended up as the focal point of the meeting.

While recognising the possible links with other issues, there are pragmatic reasons why desertification needs to be both separated from them and considered in a broader context. As it is defined in a dryland context, it is not a degradation issue that only affects developing nations. Related issues of human-induced environmental degradation also occur in drylands in the economically-developed world, for example in Australia and in the USA. Indeed, the so-called Dust Bowl of the American mid-west was perhaps the first well-documented case of human mismanagement contributing to dryland degradation. A further factor is that on social and environmental grounds, desertification requires solutions to be attempted and remedial measures to be implemented. As such, clarity of cause and of process are required for appropriate social, land-management and scientific actions to be taken. The problems caused by different phenomena require different levels of solution (Warren and Khogali, 1992); drought may warrant short-term relief measures while a more complex package of social changes and engineering measures may be necessary to tackle the causes and consequences of desertification. A rigorous understanding of desertification is therefore not simply an academic issue, but a practical one too.

Desertification and attributes of dryland environments

Although there has been a widespread move to apply the concept of desertification to human-induced degradation in drylands (see Chapter 1) caused by the activities outlined in Chapter 5, it cannot be divorced from certain aspects of dryland environments which may increase their vulnerability to human actions. Just as there has been a tendency to over-simplify the actual desertification process, it is also possible to play down or ignore the complex array of environmental conditions that exist in drylands, the range of vegetation systems they possess and the range of environments and geomorphological processes that shape them (see Thomas, 1989). It is not within the scope of this volume to address these aspects in depth, but it is important to note that any attempted control or rehabilitation measures need specifically to address local conditions rather than simply implement centrally determined procedures. There are, however, a number of issues relating to moisture availability that are important to consider, which directly impinge on human utilisation of drylands and that affect the manner which apparent changes in other aspects of the environment should be interpreted.

Drought

If aridity, defined as a lack of moisture relative to average climatic conditions (Kemp, 1991; Agnew and Anderson, 1992) is the underlying factor that gives drylands their principal characteristics then drought is a periodic reduction in moisture availability below average conditions. Drought does not just affect drylands – witness the British drought of 1976 – but its impact can appear greatest in these already water-stressed regions, especially if the environment and its occupants are already under pressure from intensive use and growing populations. It is an increasingly apparent human tragedy that the same regions are susceptible to both drought and desertification (Figure 7.1), either of which may contribute to food shortages for the incumbent population. Drought may be a precursor to desertification in certain situations (Dregne, 1983a) and desertification may eventually contribute to drought through feedback mechanisms (Charney *et al.*, 1975; Hulme, 1989) but the two are distinct phenomena that frequently appear to be confused.

Drought can be defined in different ways with the distinction between meteorological and agricultural drought, sometimes in terms of the moisture requirements of specific crops, being a useful one. There are many definitions of meteorological drought (see Wilhite and Glantz, 1985; Agnew and Anderson, 1992) which range from the general such as 'a prolonged period of below normal rainfall' (Dracup *et al.*, 1980) to the more specific 'less than 80 per cent of normal levels' (Dhar *et al.*, 1979) or 'two or more years with rainfall substantially below the mean' (Warren and Khogali, 1992). In many cases the latter type of definition are useful for investigative purposes with, for example, Agnew (1990) using the Dhar *et al.* (1979) definition in an analysis of spatial and temporal aspects of drought in Niger. It is another matter to determine which definition is most appropriate, scientifically or otherwise, with the problems of establishing a norm against which to compare trends providing a further difficulty.

Whatever way drought is defined, it is an indisputable fact that drylands are especially susceptible to it. This is due to the nature and vagaries of the climate systems responsible for their rainfall and because of high interannual rainfall variability, which is frequently in excess of 30 per cent (e.g. Nicholson, 1980; Thomas and Shaw, 1991). Put simply, the lower the mean annual total, the more significant the failure of any single rainfall event will be to the resultant annual total.

Though drought is a normal rather than an unusual feature of dryland environments, increasing human utilisation has raised the potential for detrimental and even disastrous impacts to occur. Traditional dryland societies have many adaptations to cope with periodic water shortages; mobility on a seasonal basis in response to normal patterns of rainfall during the year and in response to droughts on a more *ad hoc* basis is the obvious one, with more subtle ecological and social adaptations also important (Legesse, 1989). Larger populations, changes in land use, sedentarisation and the enforcement of political boundaries have in many regions turned this norm into a process warranting concern and its practitioners into refugees. This human component of drought has been aptly expressed by Heathcote (1983:27) who states that:

> The occurrence of drought in many ways reflects the over-optimistic human appraisal of the moisture availability of an area as a component of its resource potential.

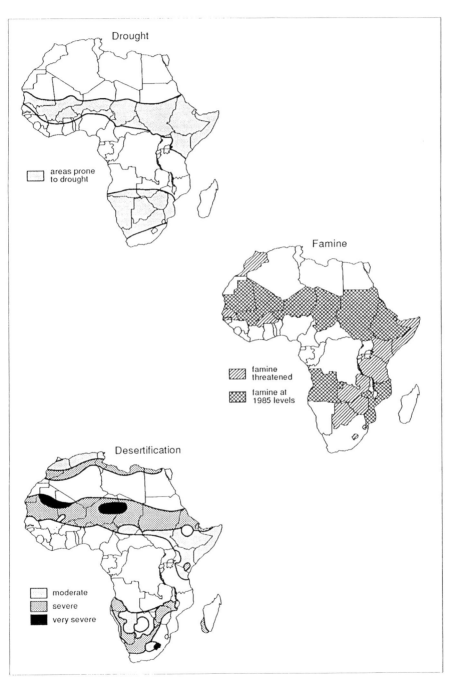

Figure 7.1 Drought, desertification and famine-susceptible areas in Africa (adapted from Canadian International Development Agency, 1985)

Meteorological drought appears, regardless of the details of definition, to have been a notable characteristic of the Sahel region in the decades of the 1960s, 1970s and 1980s (Chapter 2) and also of other drylands such as northeast Brazil, the Kalahari, central Australia and parts of the southwestern USA in the 1980s. The impact of these events has sometimes been seen to be regional in extent, but spatial analysis reveals a more complicated picture. Even without considering drought, dryland rainfall is known for its 'spottiness' or uneven distribution (e.g. Cooke and Warren, 1973; Thomas, 1989; Goudie, 1990). Analyses of rainfall data for Sudan (Hulme, 1987) and Niger (Agnew, 1990) show that there are considerable sub-regional variations in the distribution of meteorological shortfalls in moisture (Figure 7.2). Although meteorological droughts are therefore not necessarily region-wide events this does not undermine the likelihood that the social and economic effects are because of the knock-on impact on food production and on demands for resources such as grazing land.

Agricultural drought

Agricultural drought is a useful term, particularly with the expansion of rainfed cropping in drylands, as it is a way of assessing the impact of a moisture deficit on production systems. Agricultural drought can be considered to be the soil moisture deficit during the growing season (Wigley and Atkinson, 1977). This can be analysed using precipitation, potential evapotranspiration and soil moisture data together with coefficients reflecting the moisture requirements of different crops (Agnew, 1982). The drought thresholds of individual crops can then be calculated and the impacts of meteorological drought years on actual crop production assessed. In a study employing this approach Palutikof *et al.* (1982) demonstrated how the replacement of millet with maize as the staple crop in parts of Kenya has increased the likelihood of food production being reduced during meteorological droughts because of the higher water demands of maize. Another important aspect of agricultural drought is that an absolute annual or seasonal deficit of precipitation may not necessarily be the problem, since the timing of the rains is also of crucial importance.

Desiccation

Warren and Khogali (1992) consider desiccation to be a further useful term to describe environmental fluctuations in drylands. Desiccation can be defined as the process of longer-term reductions in moisture availability resulting from a dry period at the scale of decades (Hare, 1987). Goudie (1990) has noted how the view once persisted that the world, or

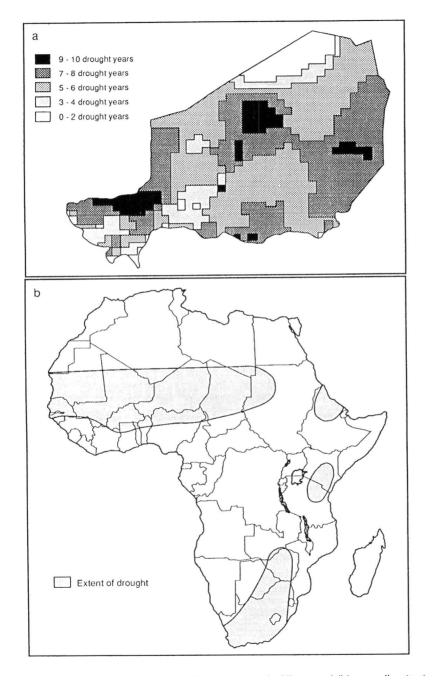

Figure 7.2 (a) Spatial variation of drought years in Niger and (b) overall extent of drought in Africa, 1972 (data from Agnew and Anderson, 1992 and Glantz, 1989)

specific regions of it, was progressively desiccating. Although for the Sahel desiccation as defined by Hare (1987) has persisted for much of the period since 1968 and the view that a climatic enhancement of aridity is occurring has arisen (e.g. Bryson, 1973; Lamb, 1974) others argue that there is no categorical evidence for a singular drying trend (Hare, 1984; Wijkman and Timberlake, 1985).

Periods of long-term rainfall deficit can clearly have major implications for production systems and degradation. Walsh *et al.* (1988) note that in Sudan rainfed cereal production declined by 14 per cent between 1970 and 1980 with a further estimate of a 50 per cent drop in the land area recently cultivated between 1959 and 1980. A significant aspect of rainfall decline was the reduction in high intensity storms, and in some parts of the country this far outweighed any tendency for increased runoff to occur as a consequence of land degradation.

One outcome of decade-scale rainfall fluctuations is that defining and delimiting the extent of drylands using simple climatic measures is complex, given the inherent variability that appears to occur in these systems. Meteorological evidence from many drylands suggests that runs of years with above average and below average rainfall may be a normal phenomenon of these environments (Figure 7.3), with Nicholson (1981) showing that several prolonged dry periods have occurred in the Sahel during the last 400 years. In southern Africa, Dutch colonists reported periods of rainfall deficiency after 1652 (Kenworthy, 1990). Tyson and Dyer (1975) and Tyson (1979 and 1986) have identified a statistically significant 18-year cycle of rainfall fluctuations in the summer rainfall zone that extends back at least to the 1840s. The cycle effectively contains drought and abundance decades (Figure 7.3) and Tyson (1986) relates the development of atmospheric circulation conditions responsible for southern African rainfall fluctuations to Southern Oscillation events. Though the manner in which links occur are not always clear, droughts and extended dry periods in the Sahel, Australia and northeast Brazil have also been attributed to sea surface temperature anomalies (Parry and Carter, 1988).

Delimiting drylands

The occurrence of droughts and related phenomena in drylands raises major questions about climatic norms and the delimitation of dryland regions which have both academic and practical implications. At the academic level, there are implications for mapping the distribution of drylands. Although drylands may be delimited with reference to features such as drainage systems and soils (see Thomas, 1989) it has become

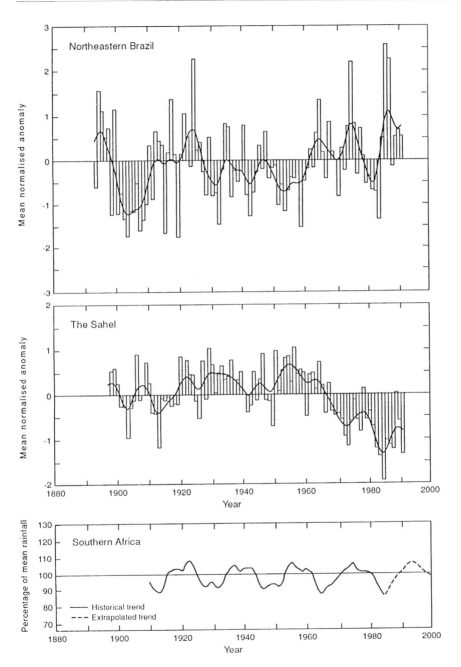

Figure 7.3 Normalised rainfall distributions in the Sahel and Northeastern Brazil and rainfall cycles in southern Africa (adapted from UNEP, 1992; Tyson, 1986; Bhalotra, 1985; and Thomas and Shaw, 1991)

usual for some form of aridity index based on climatic data to be utilised. The different schemes may incorporate the measurement of, for example, evapotranspiration in different ways (e.g. Meigs, 1953; UN, 1977d; UNEP, 1992), using either the Thornthwaite or Penman method, but they all rely on the principle of defining drylands in a manner that reflects deficits in available moisture.

The aridity index used by UNEP (1992) to determine the extent of the susceptible drylands (Figure 7.4) is the simple measure P/PET where P is mean annual precipitation and PET is mean annual potential evapotranspiration calculated using the Thornthwaite method (Hulme and Marsh, 1990). The different aridity zones as defined by the index and their extent are shown in Table 7.1.

Table 7.1 The global extent of dryland zones and their derivation (after data in UNEP, 1992)

	Aridity index (P/PET)	Million ha	% world land area
1. Dry-subhumid	0.50 - <0.65	1294.7	9.94
2. Semi-arid	0.20 - <0.50	2305.3	17.72
3. Arid	0.05 - <0.20	1569.1	12.06
4. Hyper-arid	<0.05	978.2	7.52
Susceptible drylands (=1+2+3)	0.05 - <0.20	5169.1	39.72

At a more practical level, determining the nature and extent of drylands and their climatic characteristics has implications for long-term planning, for example in the implementation of aid and agricultural schemes. Agricultural planning can go hopelessly awry if it is based on assumptions about conditions that are in fact abnormal in the long run but are apparently normal at the time of implementation. This may in turn contribute to environmental degradation if an agricultural system that is inappropriate for the environment is set in motion. In this respect Walsh et al. (1988) make the case that many agricultural development schemes implemented in Sudan in the late-colonial and early-independence period were based on the assumption that the wet conditions of the mid-twentieth century were the norm rather than the exception, whereas the converse may turn out to be the case. Such mistaken assumptions were and still are both a function of a poor understanding of dryland environments and a lack of long-term data on which to base such understanding.

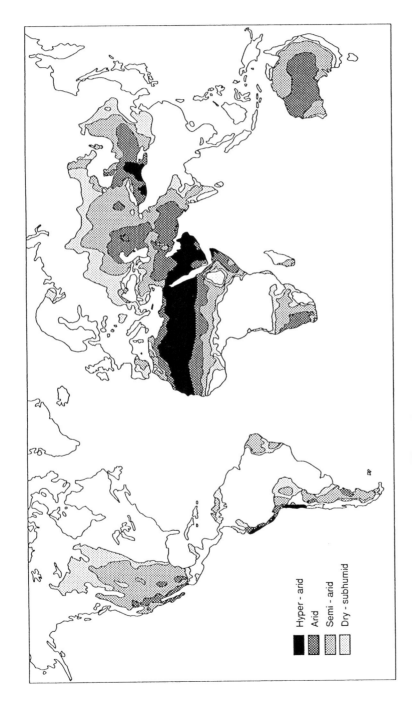

Figure 7.4 The world's drylands (after UNEP, 1992)

Hyper - arid
Arid
Semi - arid
Dry - subhumid

The literature on climatic trends in the Sahel is extensive and the debate on whether there is a move towards drier conditions is inconclusive (Agnew and Anderson, 1992). The importance of recognising drought and desiccation phenomena and climatic cycles has been addressed in Chapter 6, and from a planning perspective it is also valuable to note the analyses of Nicholson (1980; 1981; 1989). In effect, severe droughts can be noted to have occurred for at least several centuries in the Sahel. Walsh *et al.* (1988) go so far as to say that in the context of the last 100 or even 1000 years the mid-twentieth century wet spell was the anomaly, not the drought of the 1970s and 1980s. From the agricultural perspective, the character of rainfall events in the Sahel also differs now from that period, with the additional feature of an increase in rainfall breaks during the wet season.

Major droughts leading to famine are well represented in oral and written historical records for Ecuador back to the 17th century (Knapp and Canadas Cruz, 1988). Attempts to link the occurrence of drought to specific causative events have tended to focus on the so-called Southern Oscillation, which is a fluctuation in the intensity of intertropical atmospheric and hydrospheric circulations. In southern Africa, Lindsey and Vogel (1990) have linked drought periods from 1820 to the present with Southern Oscillation low-phase events. The relationship between Southern Oscillation extremes and periods of rainfall excess (El Niño events) or deficit (drought) are not always clear, as noted in the case of Ecuador by Rovere and Knapp (1988).

Unsurprisingly, drought prediction is therefore difficult (Lockwood, 1988; Nobre and Molion, 1988). Delimiting the extent of drylands is also problematic, as drylands defined using mean climatic data are obviously not going to be spatially static. Hulme (1992) has recently looked at Africa-wide rainfall changes between the periods 1931–60 and 1961–90. This study shows that the later period rainfall in tropical North Africa had decreased by 30 per cent and by 5 per cent in the tropical margins of southern Africa. Conversely, increases of 5 and 10 per cent were respectively identified for East Africa and the southern coast area of West Africa. Rainfall patterns are clearly dynamic.

Prior to UNEP (1992) the statistics that were used to calculate the extent and location of arid regions tended to be time-independent. Climatic data collection, particularly from meteorological stations in countries of the developing world, often commenced in the early or mid-twentieth century. The mean values calculated from these sources are therefore neither necessarily representative of long-term trends nor strictly comparable between stations because it may have been collected over different lengths of time. The 1977 UN aridity map (UN, 1977d) was based on information calculated from such 'timeless' data sets. Hulme and Marsh (1990) of the Climatic Research Unit (CRU) at the University of East Anglia have put forward an alternative approach whereby data are restricted to specific time periods. Thus, in the case of UNEP (1992) the delimitation of susceptible drylands utilised data for 1951–80 as the input to aridity index calculations. The CRU also produced comparative climatologies for 1930–59 and 1960–89 in terms of climatic surfaces for air temperature and annual precipitation (Hulme and Marsh, 1990; UNEP, 1992). The differences between aridity indices calculated from these two data sets are shown in Figure 7.5, and the changes in precipitation and temperature means within the UNEP-defined susceptible drylands in Figure 7.6. Most striking is the shift towards a moisture deficit in the Sahel, caused by changes in rainfall, and in southern Africa, caused by higher mean temperatures and therefore PET.

In the light of current concern about global warming, it can be asked whether the moisture deficits for African drylands identified in UNEP (1992) and Hulme (1992) are in any way related to this. The impacts of global warming caused by increased atmospheric greenhouse gases are uncertain. Rotmans and Den Elzen (1992) have suggested that the potential for global warming is less than that projected by the Intergovernmental Panel on Climatic Change (IPCC, 1991) and some authorities believe impacts are likely to be less in low latitudes than elsewhere (Parry and Carter, 1988; Parry, 1990). A 5–10 per cent decrease in low latitude rainfall may however be one outcome of global warming (Parry, 1990), possibly leading to the extension of susceptible drylands and an increase in rainfall variability. Hulme (1992) indicates that it is premature to link recent African rainfall changes to global warming, with Southern Oscillation and other sea surface temperature anomalies in the Atlantic and Indian Oceans a more likely explanation (Druyan and Hastenrath, 1991; Folland *et al.*, 1991) and likely to dominate rainfall variations in the low latitudes into the next century (Lockwood, 1988).

Interactions between desertification and moisture deficits

Both drought and desiccation in drylands may increase environmental susceptibility to human induced degradation, for example by reducing plant cover and raising the potential for soil erosion during cultivation. On the other hand increased human pressure on the environment, for example by people remaining in an area during drought because of the presence of a borehole water source, by reducing the length of fallow periods or by lowering the regional watertable, may reduce the ability of natural systems to withstand or recover from drought or desiccation. In practice and in the short term it may be very difficult to distinguish some of the impacts on the environment of human disturbance and natural moisture fluctuations, though attempting to do so is a vital component of successful management and the implementation of viable remedies.

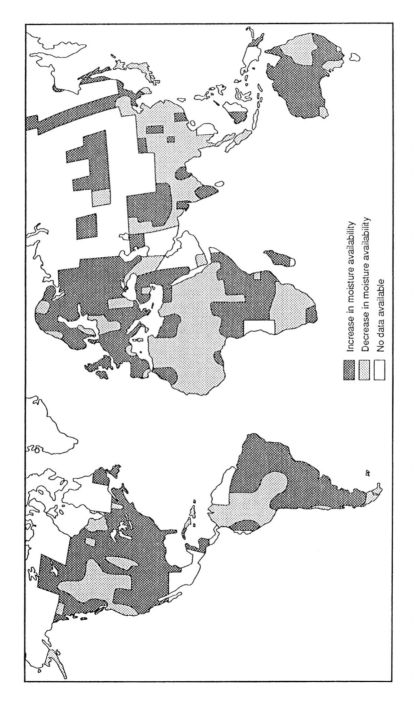

Figure 7.5 Summary of mean annual aridity index changes between 1930–59 and 1960–89 (after UNEP, 1992)

Increase in moisture availability

Decrease in moisture availability

No data available

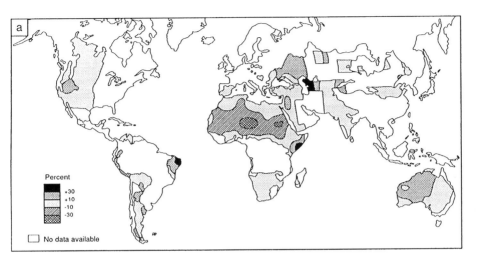

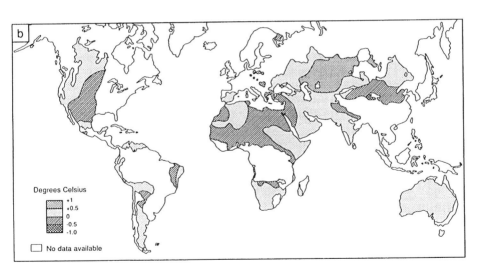

Figure 7.6 (a) Mean annual precipitation and (b) mean annual temperature changes between 1930–59 and 1960–89 (after UNEP, 1992)

As Warren and Khogali (1992) point out, drought demands short-term relief and desiccation needs a long-term strategy; desertification control may require major long-term planning, recovery and rehabilitation of the environment together with changes in land-use practices.

From a human perspective the nature and timing of drought require consideration (Glantz, 1989). It is not just whether rainfall occurs which is important but when it falls, because food shortages and famine have a seasonality too. Interactions between drought, famine and desertification are complicated. The timing of ploughing and sowing needs to be carefully geared to the onset of the rains in the highly seasonal drylands, and have an influence on potential degradation. Slopes are very erosion-susceptible in the period between ploughing and rainfall as the surface is bare and vulnerable to soil loss by wind erosion and by wash during the first rains. Seed stock can be lost by drying out, rotting or to pests if it is sown but germination subsequently fails, and unless further stock is available fields can remain uncultivated and vulnerable to erosion. If drought persists or desiccation ensues in one area then pressure can be created on others, either by direct migration to them or by the need to raise food production to supply people in the stricken area. This can intensify environmental pressures and lead to degradation (Glantz, 1989) in a 'societal positive feedback mechanism' (Scoging, 1991; Figure 7.7).

Desertification has been seen as enhancing drought via a hotly debated 'biophysical feedback mechanism' (Charney, 1975; Charney *et al.*, 1975; Figure 7.7). Charney and co-workers proposed that devegetated surfaces have a higher albedo than those possessing a natural vegetation cover. The albedo increase results in less short-wave energy being available to heat the lower atmosphere, encouraging air mass stability and therefore reducing convective rainfall. Although Laval (1986) has verified the workings of Charney's model and argues for the collection of field data to put it to the empirical test, there is in fact no conclusive evidence to show that the required albedo changes occurred during the period under consideration (Rasool, 1984; Hulme, 1989). The interactions between vegetation and rainfall have been developed further taking a range of factors into account. Walker and Rowntree (1977), Sud and Molod (1988) and others have examined the evapotranspirational contributions that plants make to atmospheric moisture in a semi-arid context and Rowntree (1988) has incorporated soil moisture and roughness effects. Though these studies demonstrate that vegetation does make a contribution to precipitation processes, the effects that changes in vegetation make to actual rainfall amounts remain unverified.

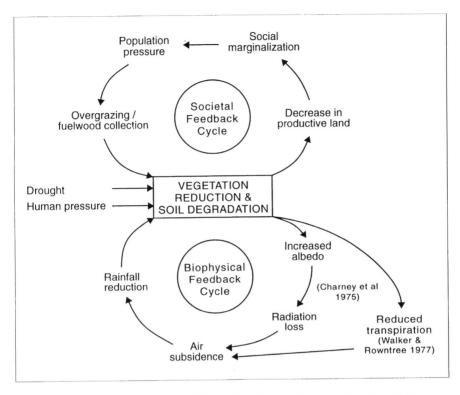

Figure 7.7 Social and biophysical desertification feedback cycles (based on Scoging, 1991 with considerable modifications)

Monitoring desertification

An improved understanding of desertification requires meaningful data on land degradation, but as Grainger (1990) and others have noted this has all too frequently been lacking. In Chapter 4 we considered some of the estimates that UNEP and its consultants have produced to give a global perspective on the issue, highlighting some of the shortfalls that these assessments possessed. The remainder of this chapter will examine several different approaches to collecting data on aspects of desertification, land degradation and vegetation change in drylands, considering both their rigour and practical aspects of their utilisation. Berry and Ford (1977) produced a list of possible indicators of desertification which in effect are embraced in Grainger's (1990) four-fold categorisation of indicators: ground conditions; climatic indicators; data on agricultural production; and socio-economic indicators. The various types of data which can be placed within this scheme embrace desertification and a range of related issues rather than land degradation alone. In the following discussion we will restrict ourselves to those with some bearing on assessing desertification *per se*.

There is a significant distinction between the information that it is desirable to have and that which it is practical to obtain. In part this is scale-dependent, Warren and Khogali (1992) noting that it is relatively simple to collect degradation data from individual fields but another matter to do so for whole regions or countries, yet both levels of data are necessary. Small-scale, case-specific information can be required before soil conservation and restoration practices are implemented with outside aid or with central government funds and may be gathered by expert consultants. It is certainly not always the case, however, that soil-loss data are needed before conservation measures are directly implemented by land users, and local knowledge and the incorporation of local people in conservation schemes may be far more effective than top-down engineering solutions (Roose, 1988; Bocco, 1990).

In this respect the measurements and perceptions of erosion problems by experts may differ markedly from those of the indigenous people who have to live with the problem and implement solutions, as Millington *et al.* (1989) have illustrated for Sierra Leone (Table 7.2). Furthermore, even at the field or erosion plot scale so favoured by soil scientists, it is not always straightforward to equate measurements of soil-erosion with land degradation, especially when it is desirable to distinguish natural changes from those caused by human actions. It is refreshing that Stocking (1984), a soil scientist with applied interests in the development field, has criticised the methods and approaches used in soil erosion studies both from an empirical perspective and from that of what the data really mean in determining the impact of degradation on production systems.

Assessing and monitoring desertification has to take practical as well as scientific factors into consideration. Mabbutt (1986) has provided a range of criteria and characteristics that indicators ought to have: being as specific as possible to desertification, sensitive enough to show changes over time, easily quantifiable from primary or secondary sources or available from published statistics, and recognisable without needing a high level of training. Meeting these goals is clearly a considerable task but one reflecting the need to strike a compromise between scientific rigour and practical needs. The need to compromise is probably greatest when assessing desertification at larger scales, where the logistical problems of collecting compatible field data from different areas are highest. The need to adopt as rigorous an approach as possible for this scale of monitoring was noted as early as 1975 by the United Nations (Stocking, 1987) with the first attempts at a methodology appearing four years later (FAO, 1979) and continuing through to the more recent GLASOD project.

Table 7.2 The severity of soil erosion risk in Sierra Leone Chiefdoms according to indigenous knowledge and scientific experts (after Millington et al., 1989)

	Ranking by indigenous knowledge	'Expert' estimated erosion
Lugbu	1	10
Tane	2	6
Toli	3	2
Njaluahun	4	11
Kunike Baarine	5	3
Gallinas Perri	6	8
Lei	7	4
Safroko Limba	8	1
Wara Wara Yagala	9	5
Ribbi	10	13
Small Bo	11	7
Dasse	12	14
Kori	13	15
Kapandakemo	14	9
Pejewa	15	12

Global monitoring: the GLASOD project

Recognising these problems and the need for better data on soil-related environmental degradation, the International Soil Reference Centre (ISRIC) commenced a programme in conjunction with UNEP for the Global Assessment of Soil Degradation (GLASOD) in 1987 (Oldeman, 1988). GLASOD utilises a Geographic Information System known as GRID, the Global Resource Information Database, which allows researchers to access data for different regions of the world and therefore degradation specific to susceptible drylands to be analysed at different scales, for specific processes and by cause. GLASOD forms the basis of the most recent UN studies of global land degradation (Oldeman et al., 1990) and desertification (UNEP, 1992).

We have previously noted how attempts to assess the extent of the desertification problem (UN, 1977c; UNEP, 1984 a; b) have been criticised for their vagueness of approach and lack of methodological rigour. For GLASOD, a consistent and replicable methodology was established (Oldeman, 1988; Oldeman et al., 1990). For practical purposes, the world was divided into 21 regions and for each of these a coordinator gathered published and unpublished data on land degradation.

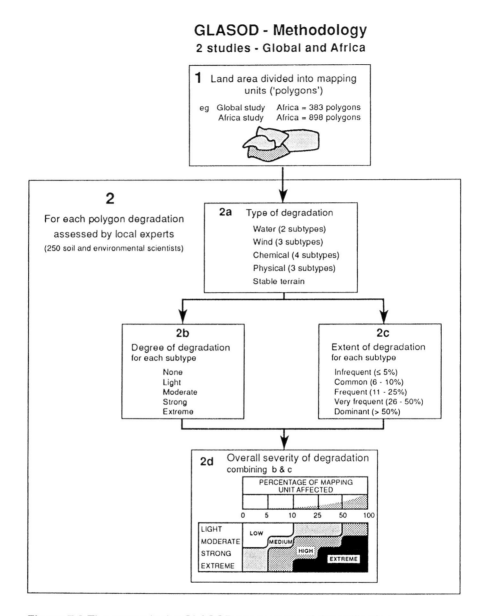

Figure 7.8 The stages in the GLASOD assessment of desertification

Additionally over 250 local experts were appointed for sub-areas of the regions, to evaluate critically existing information and to provide new data using a systematic methodology provided by ISRIC. The data covered degradation type, extent and degree, and human causes.

The manner of treating the data to give the global land degradation assessment is summarised in Figure 7.8. Each region of the world was divided into 'polygons': mapping units that corresponded to natural physiographic zones. For each polygon, human-induced soil degradation was classified into four categories, two covering soil erosion (by water and by wind) and two for soil *in-situ* change, by physical and chemical processes. Each of these categories was further subdivided into more specific mechanisms. Water erosion includes classes for loss of top soil and for terrain deformation (e.g. gullying) and wind erosion includes degradation by loss of top soil, by the creation of dunes and hollows and by the accretion of aeolian deposits. Chemical deterioration covers the loss of nutrients and organic matter, salinisation, acidification and pollution from industrial, urban and agricultural sources. Physical deterioration contains classes for compaction, sealing and crusting, for waterlogging and for the subsidence of organic soils such as peat (Oldeman *et al.*, 1990). This scheme is a development of that in FAO (1979) and FAO/UNEP (1984), recognising the same processes but classifying them in a slightly different manner.

In each polygon the present degree of degradation was assessed for each category (Figure 7.8), using classes of no degradation: light, representing suitability for local agricultural systems but with 'somewhat reduced agricultural potential' (Oldeman *et al.*, 1990) and restoration to full productivity possible through adjustments in the management system; moderate, which is land still suitable for agriculture but with productivity significantly reduced and major improvements necessary for restoration of the original biotic processes; strong, where original biotic functions are largely destroyed and major engineering works are necessary for restoration; and extreme where 'the terrain is not reclaimable and impossible to restore' (Middleton and Thomas, 1992). GLASOD also includes an assessment of the human activities responsible for degradation.

Five categories were used to quantify the extent of degraded land in the polygon from infrequent to dominant. Following this, degree and extent can be combined to give the overall severity of degradation, using the matrix in Figure 7.8. Severity has been used as the basis of mapping desertification at the global scale (Figure 7.9). This means that the most severe degradation present in a polygon is shown, so visually the impression is one of overestimation. Each class of severity can be derived from a range of combinations of degree and extent values: thus a polygon mapped with high severity degradation could contain 6–10 per

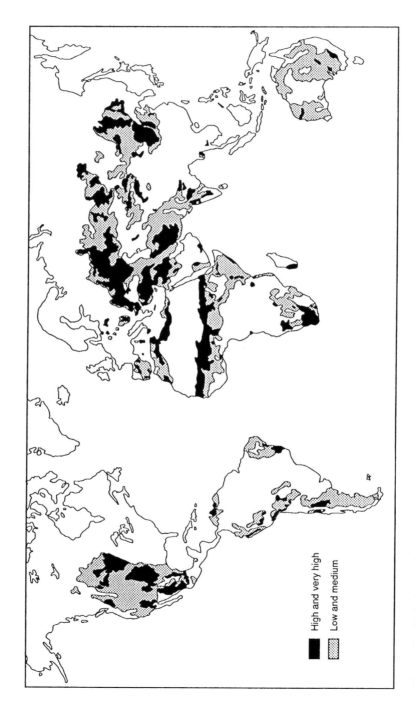

Figure 7.9 Global map of dryland human-induced soil degradation (after UNEP, 1992)

High and very high

Low and medium

cent of the area with extreme degradation or 51–100 per cent with light degradation. The overall database allows the extraction of more detailed information, which will be considered further in Chapter 8. In addition to the global study, one of a higher resolution was carried out for Africa based on a more refined base map with 898 polygons, as opposed to the 383 for Africa in the global study.

By assimilating data from a range of existing sources and utilising experts familiar with different areas, the GLASOD assessment draws widely on available information, though it is unclear how compatible and comparable the bases for different area data are when regions are compared and classified. The information which can be derived can appear as a quantified statement of desertification, though in fact it is ultimately a quantification of qualitative assessments. However, because of the compromises an approach such as GLASOD has to employ due to the absence of better primary data, it is easy to criticise it, but difficult to propose alternatives (Stocking, 1987). The database does not allow information to be produced for specific countries because of the physiographic basis of the mapping polygons, but it can be broken down for sub-regions and has been used in an analysis of salinisation in Africa by Thomas and Middleton (1993) and as a contribution to an assessment of desertification in the Sahel region by Warren and Khogali (1992).

Indirect measures of desertification

Indirect measures of desertification offer an alternative approach and are potentially attractive given the links between degradation and productivity decline, both in definitions and from the perspective of socio-economic concern. Yet this route to assessing desertification is beset by two significant difficulties, one scientific and one practical. First, although erosion and productivity are not exclusively independent, they are not simply linked either (Stocking, 1987). Productivity is affected by a range of extraneous factors related to the environment: weather, disease and so on, and to production systems and economic factors including the efficiency of individual farmers and market economic forces. Even without these complications, Larson et al. (1983) indicate that productivity decline is related to a range of soil factors, which to some extent depend on soil type (UNEPCOM-USSR, 1990) but are linked in a non-linear manner. Measurements of soil loss per unit area alone cannot be related to productivity decline in a simple manner (Stocking, 1987), as Scoones (1992) has well illustrated. In the communal lands of southern Zimbabwe measures of land degradation demonstrate that soil erosion is increasing, yet livestock production has not fallen. This is because both erosion and important pasture areas are spatially inconsistent, and erosion is principally from areas that are not important for grazing.

The second difficulty arises because data on productivity are both widely noted to be notoriously unreliable and in any case tend to be in the form of official statistics that at best are at a regional scale. While data at this scale can be valuable, in the case of productivity there are a range of factors that may have contributed to a change in output, including changes in the area under cultivation (Norton-Griffiths, 1989). Without additional information to evaluate such factors, desertification becomes just one of a number of possible causes.

Remote sensing

The various data sources that come under the umbrella of remote sensing offer the possibility of gaining environmental data over both large areas and relatively long time-periods. With appropriate ground data to permit correct interpretation of satellite imagery and aerial photography, this source has considerable potential for enhancing our understanding of dryland environments, including land degradation. It is not surprising therefore that considerable effort has be put into dryland remote sensing studies from within the UN (e.g. FAO, 1988), bodies such as the EC (e.g. Prince et al., 1990) and directly from scientific institutions, with one report suggesting that:

> satellite remote sensing is the only way to obtain systematic regional observations and to undertake spatially comprehensive monitoring of the Sahelian environment. (Prince et al., 1990:11)

Remote sensing has the potential to generate spatially extensive objective data (if interpretive ground data are available) relating to a range of physical and human features associated with desertification (Girard and Isavwa, 1990) and to date has contributed significantly to the revision of ideas about the nature of, for example, piosphere-related environmental changes (Hanan et al., 1991) and changes in the position of desert margins (e.g. Tucker et al., 1991). However, the information that can be gained is constrained by the characteristics of specific data sources and it is certainly just as true now as 20 years ago that remote sensing is not the panacea for all the environmental problems in areas such as the Sahel (Bale et al., 1974).

Two central issues affect the utility of remote sensing in this context: the resolution of the imagery concerned and the frequency of regional coverage. Clearly, resolution affects the scale of features and surface properties that can be identified and monitored while the frequency determines whether near-continuous monitoring, termed multi-temporal analysis or 'controlled observation' (Thornes and Brunsden, 1977) is possible or whether snap-shot or 'incidental monitoring' is all that is feasible. Vertical aerial photography has extremely high resolution but the frequency of government or commercial coverage is usually low, rarely better than once every five to ten years or even less frequent for some areas, unless a particular research investigation includes provision for light aircraft flights. Large numbers of photographs are produced and, while it is possible to digitise the information they contain and store it in a GIS, considerable manual input is necessary. The use of stereo pairs does, however, permit data such as the height of trees to be determined (e.g. FAO, 1988) but clearly this time-consuming analysis lends itself to detailed small-area or pilot studies rather than those of regional extent.

The resolution of data from different satellite sources is summarised in Table 7.3. Landsat multispectral scanner (MSS) imagery covering four radiation wavelength bands has a pixel resolution of 79 m x 79 m and a standard image covers an area in excess of 34,000 km². As Landsat satellites are polar orbiting they have passed over every part of the earth's surface with a fortnightly or better frequency virtually continuously since 1972. Not all imagery is preserved, however, due to the nature of the on-satellite storage facilities and the distribution of ground receiving stations, while others are night-time images or the earth's surface is obscured by cloud cover. Newer sensors have greater resolution but smaller standard image coverage. Thematic Mapper (TM) data have a higher pixel resolution of 30 m x 30 m, seven wavebands, and have been available from Landsat since 1984. The French SPOT satellite produces high resolution imagery which has been used by Guyot (1990) in a desertification context. Data from the Russian satellite Kosmos-1939 has also

Table 7.3 Resolution and other data affecting utilisation of satellite data in desertification studies

Satellite	Orbit (days)	Scene size (km²)	Resolution (m)	Minimum ident. unit size (ha)
Meteosat	30	15625 x 10	5000	15625
NOAA/AVHRR	3–9	5760000	1100	6250
Landsat/MSS	16	34225	80	40
Landsat/TM	16	34225	30	6.25
SPOT sensor a	9	3600	20	3.5
SPOT sensor b	9	3600	10	1.6

Source: FAO (1988) and Tucker *et al.* (1985a)

been evaluated for use in desertification studies (Kharin, 1990). The potential for abstracting data from imagery is also affected by whether hard copies of images are obtained or whether the original raw data on computer tape are available for processing. The latter clearly offers the greater possibilities for manipulation and investigation (e.g. Ringrose *et al.*, 1990), while the use of a computer-based GIS greatly assists in the manipulation of the large quantities of numerical data involved, as in Dalsted *et al.* (1982) and Dalsted's (1988) study of soil and vegetation conditions in Mauritania.

Perhaps the greatest use of satellite data to date in desertification studies has come as an indirect by-product of the network of the National Oceanographic and Atmospheric Administration of the USA (NOAA) weather satellites. Three of these polar orbiting satellites possess Advanced Very High Resolution Radiometer (AVHRR) sensors which gather data in a range of wavebands but only with the very coarse resolution of 1.1 km x 1.1 km. A by-product of the data output is a normalised vegetation index (NDVI) which combines near-infrared and red wavebands, but at a further reduced resolution equivalent to 15 km x 15 km at the equator and 25 km x 25 km at the poles (Justice *et al.*, 1985). This source has nonetheless been widely used to analyse biomass changes because of its high temporal resolution, as the combined output of the satellites produces sun-synchronous, twice-daily coverage of the entire earth (Dregne and Tucker, 1988).

NOAA also produce a weekly composite global vegetation index (GVI). Following considerable investigation of the waveband properties of the NOAA output by Tucker (1980) and Tucker *et al.* (1985a;b;c) and relationships with ground conditions, this source has proved to be a valuable, rapid tool for mapping green vegetation biomass at global and regional scales (Justice *et al.*, 1985) as the disadvantages of the low resolution are offset by the advantages of the spatial extensiveness of each individual image. NDVI studies have contributed significantly to the understanding of natural fluctuations in desert surface conditions (e.g. Tucker *et al.*, 1991) and will be considered further in Chapter 8, where a number of key advances that have improved understanding of the desertification phenomenon are explored.

Conclusion

Understanding desertification as an environmental issue has to be put in the context of the nature of dryland environments. Understanding and recognising it as a social problem also needs this context, as it provides some understanding of the risks and limits to human actions.

Any human activity in drylands that draws on the natural environment has to be set against a background in which drought is always likely to occur and prolonged periods of moisture deficiency are a possibility. Desertification and drought are not, however, the same thing, though they have often been confused as such. Famine may be caused by either, as well as by other events such as war, but alleviating the symptoms and consequences of famine requires a reasonable identification of the cause. It has been easy to blame famine on drought, because it is an 'act of God' without human causation, though actions can sometimes be taken to reduce the consequences. Desertification can also and has also been used as a scapegoat. If it has human triggers, then presumably solutions can be sought. However, these do not necessarily lie in the hands of those most intimately linked to the problem, but may well be due to wider social, economic and political circumstances.

Collecting accurate data on the scale of desertification is difficult due to the nature of the environments concerned and the phenomena under consideration. This is no excuse for the way some of the UNEP estimates have been used, however. More recent assessments may be better pictures but have their own drawbacks. Satellite imagery and data can contribute to a better understanding of desertification, but the data such studies yield have themselves to be placed in the context of important dryland characteristics. It is these that are discussed in the next chapter as we move on to consider a further component of the desertification myth.

8 Key environmental issues

The scientific disciplines of desertification, like all scientific disciplines, experience changes of paradigm. These changes cannot be ignored by planners, for their policies are inescapably founded on scientific models. (Warren and Khogali, 1992:vii)

Several key developments in the scientific understanding of drylands have major implications for the way in which desertification is perceived. These relate to the nature of dryland ecosystems and the spatial variability of desert conditions. Building on the issues addressed in the previous chapter, these will be analysed and their significance for the interpretation of desertification considered.

Ecosystem dynamics: ephemeral versus permanent changes

Variations in moisture availability in drylands at the seasonal, drought and decade scales have a particularly direct significance for the assessment of dryland degradation. The distinctions between long-term degradation, short-term changes and natural phenology in environmental conditions have already been discussed in relation to the definition and conceptualisation of desertification. Developments in the understanding of the ecological principles of dryland systems provide a scientific basis for interpreting environmental fluctuations in these areas and whether reductions in the productivity potential have taken place. These have in turn contributed to a paradigm shift in the way that dryland changes are perceived (Warren and Khogali, 1992).

Temporal changes in dryland ecosystems, whatever their cause, cannot be readily compared with a normal state or equilibrium; as Skarpe (1991:355) notes in a recent review of advances in savanna ecology, 'there is no such thing as a stable, typical savanna'. It is therefore inappropriate to have assumed, as Kharin (1990) and others have, that the risk of desertification is a factor of ecosystem stability, and the greater the instability, the higher the risk of desertification. A major driving force for dryland ecosystem changes or instabilities is the variability in moisture supply, whether seasonally or in relation to drought and desiccation phenomena (see Chapter 7). This can directly affect both plant communities and other components of systems that utilise plants. In a faunal context this ranges from large ungulates to insects, for example locusts, for which major population booms are reported rapidly to follow rainfall events (Barrow, 1991). Rather than being fragile, dryland ecosystems are in fact better regarded as robust, resilient and unstable, in the sense that there are typically considerable fluctuations in biomass and the sizes of plant and animal species' populations (Lewin, 1986). As well as moisture availability and herbivore pressure, the plant component of dryland systems also responds to fires, another natural feature which is a frequent, even annual, occurrence (Trollope, 1982; Walker, 1987).

Dryland ecosystems can be viewed as being event-dependent. Although in the desertification context livestock are often treated as a negative, disturbing influence on ecosystems, indigenous herbivores have been a natural, interactive part of system development. Thus, in Australia, trees of the mimosa family have not evolved thorns, while those in Africa have because of greater numbers of browsers during the evolutionary period (Cumming, 1982). Grazing may also have contributed to species composition and to the attributes of certain grass species. Climatic perturbations, fire and animal pressure can consequently all be viewed as natural features of dryland vegetation systems. It may also be questioned whether anthropogenic factors should be omitted from this list, given the length of time that humans have occupied the savannas of Africa, though it can be difficult to distinguish community-creating and community-maintaining processes in this respect (Goudie, 1981). What is different in potential degradation-creating situations and has been of concern in the desertification debate is the scale of livestock and human utilisation and the spatial patterns of such usage, notably the reduction and loss, enforced or otherwise, of nomadic habits.

The natural occurrence of disturbances in dryland ecosystems has led to a marked phenology in plant systems. Grass biomass is low during dry seasons but a rapid increase in leaf and shoot production follows the first rains (Walker, 1985). If the rains persist or soil moisture storage occurs, biomass levels soon stabilise during the rainy season. Herbaceous and woody species respond similarly, primarily through changes in leaf biomass (Tolsma et al., 1987). Natural seed banks in dryland communities may be as high as 5000 seeds/m^2 (Skarpe, 1991) so rapid recovery of annual species can follow droughts and even periods of desiccation, given the seeds' long dormancy periods. Even woody species can recover quickly (Laweson, 1991). Superimposed on these changes caused by variations in water availability are those caused by fire. Although this may be triggered by humans it also occurs naturally through lightning strikes and is now well recognised as a natural component of dryland ecosystem dynamics (Bourliere, 1983; Frost and Robinson, 1987). Fire removes plant litter and releases nutrients, triggers seed germination for annuals and encourages shoot production in perennials. The distribution of individual fire effects causes notable spatial variations in community conditions, imparting a mosaic-like appearance on the landscape.

Even with a growing literature proposing the ability of semi-arid and arid vegetation systems to recover from natural disturbance and indicating that disturbance may be a prerequisite for the success of these systems, the concepts need to be translated to situations where human-induced disturbances may occur before their relevance to desertification issues can be established. The most obvious situations are those where stocking levels are high, leading to what is usually called overgrazing in the literature. In a book which directly addresses the issue of herbivory, Crawley (1983) has noted that grasses subjected to grazing pressure may in fact increase shoot production and be enhanced in essential nutrients. Nutrient cycling is greater under grazed than ungrazed conditions, further encouraging plant growth in savannas (Hiernaux and Tiara, 1986; Georgiadis et al., 1989). However, some authorities suggest this may not result in an improvement or maintenance of range condition, with studies reporting the replacement of palatable with unpalatable species, for example the reduction of Cyprus conglometratus in the northern Sahel (Warren and Khogali, 1992) or the expansion of annuals at the expense of perennial grasses (Skarpe, 1986).

This simple picture requires further investigation, and it is therefore important to point out that Bosch (1989) and Perkins (1991) found that palatable species also expanded in some circumstances under grazing pressure. In the eastern Kalahari, Perkins (1991) identified that the highly palatable Digitaria eriantha increased significantly with high livestock use intensity. A further widely cited stage of the overgrazing process is that removal or reduction of perennial grasses lowers the overall year-round ground cover, allowing deeper penetration of rainfall and encouraging the expansion of the herbaceous layer. Bush encroachment may ensue (Noy-Meir, 1982; Tolsma et al., 1987; Skarpe, 1990) lowering livestock productivity by reducing the extent of the grazing resource, especially near boreholes where grazing pressure can be intense.

In South Africa, Roux and Verster (1983) considered the expansion of arid grass species and bush encroachment into more mesic communities to be part of the desertification process. These and similar vegetation community changes are undoubtedly going to be perceived as detrimental if and when they affect livestock productivity. But do they constitute desertification?

On a theoretical basis such changes may not constitute degradation because they are potentially reversible (Sandford, 1982; Abel and Blaikie, 1989), for example by reducing stocking levels. In any case and further to this, the persistence of these supposedly detrimental vegetation changes is at odds with the natural patterns of system dynamics. Livestock-induced changes, regardless of their precise character, need to be set against natural disruptions caused by drought and fire (Perkins and Thomas, 1993). Not only do these have the potential to reset the ecosystem clock through disturbing plant biomass and community composition, but drought also affects livestock directly, causing stock numbers to fluctuate in the manner identified in the previous chapter. To this effect, Warren and Khogali (1992) cite several studies indicating that disastrous stocking levels are rarely reached because under conditions of environmental stress the animals are frequently the first component of the system to fail.

It is nonetheless important to note that in some situations, for example where livestock systems are backed by significant economic resources, are part of integrated production programmes or are conducted on an intensive ranch style approach (which may be very uncommon in drylands), livestock numbers and pressure on the environment may remain high. This is hinted at in Bosch's (1989) examination of grassland degradation in South Africa, where in some circumstances the injudicious use of certain management practices may inhibit ecosystem recovery. If this leads to damage to the parts of the system (i.e. the soil) that support productivity, then desertification may indeed occur. However, spatial variability in the nature of ecosystem changes can complicate the picture further.

Spatial patterns of ecosystem change

An additional issue relates to the spatial arrangement of vegetation changes associated with livestock production in drylands, particularly in respect to boreholes. The occurrence of piospheres of change, introduced in Chapter 5, means that distinct zonations of disturbance can occur, radiating from the borehole (Glantz, 1977). These have been viewed as developing over time as foci of desertification (Rapp, 1974; Nechaeva, 1979), especially as borehole or well numbers increase over time (Figure 8.1). However, although it is a truism that the area of available grazing increases with distance from a point water source (Figure 8.2), this effectively causes spatial inequalities of impacts (Pickup and Chewings, 1988; Perkins and Thomas, 1993; Figure 8.3), although the use of preferred pathways by cattle can lead to livestock usage of the grazing resource being concentrated even at considerable distance from the watering point. Two widely recognised components of ecosystem changes associated with borehole- and well-focused grazing systems are bare or 'sacrifice' zones adjacent to the water source which are as much a consequence of trampling as of grazing (Figure 8.3) and bush-encroached zones that develop where grazing pressures are most concentrated.

The significance of these features needs to be set not only against the temporal ecosystem dynamics discussed above but also considered with

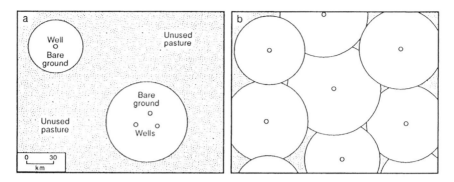

Figure 8.1. The idea of desertification spreading from around boreholes and wells (after Rapp, 1974)

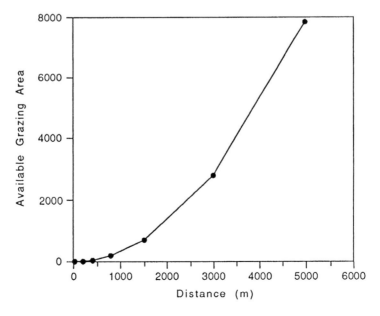

Figure 8.2. The change in available grazing area with distance from a point water source (after Perkins and Thomas, 1993)

Figure 8.3. Oblique low aerial photograph of a borehole-centred ranch in the central Kalahari

respect to the total range of changes taking place in the environment. Hellden (1984) and Hanan *et al.* (1991) have found that sacrifice zones, respectively in Sudan and Senegal, do not necessarily expand significantly over time in the manner typified by early reports (Rapp, 1974; Glantz, 1977). Sacrifice zone soils can in fact accrue enhanced levels of nutrients because of the concentration of dung and urine inputs around the watering point (Barker *et al.*, 1990; Perkins and Thomas, 1993; Figure 8.4). Although the bare zone may be susceptible to enhanced levels of wind erosion and even water erosion if trampling has compacted the surface (Nechaeva, 1979), the dung additions may balance out the negative impacts. Furthermore, as bush-enhanced zones are a feature of areas surrounding sacrifice zones they can provide a further obstacle to long-distance aeolian transport (Perkins and Thomas, 1993).

Although it is common to regard bush encroachment as a negative feature of grazing systems (e.g. Ringrose *et al.*, 1990), under certain circumstances the bush zone can itself be viewed as a resource for browsing, particularly for mixed herds (Figure 8.5) that include goats, and during drought years when even cattle will browse. In the Kalahari, Perkins (1991) further notes that grasses frequently exist in the shadow of bushes, protected from grazing and trampling, and can act as a species reserve and seed bank. Both the studies of Hanan *et al.* (1991) and Perkins (1991) demonstrate that simple interpretations of the consequences of dryland livestock systems are not always valid, with Hanan *et al.* (1991) and Valenza (1981) indicating that the grazing system is subordinate to rainfall variations as a determinant of vegetation productivity in the Ferlo area of Senegal.

Although caution should equally be exercised in the extrapolation of conclusions from these findings, with some studies such as Ringrose *et al.* (1990) from Botswana suggesting that there might still be circumstances when grazing-induced changes are supplanted on those caused by rainfall variation, they are further evidence of the need for care in assuming simple deleterious and progressive impacts of livestock systems on dryland ecosystems. The only obvious way in which such issues can be better resolved is by the collection of data over longer time-periods embracing successive climatic fluctuations.

Changes in desert boundaries: remote sensing and the desert front

At a greater spatial scale, major advances in understanding dryland ecosystem dynamics have come from analysis of remotely-sensed data, particularly from the NDVI by-product of the NOAA AVHRR system (see Chapter 7 for details of this source). Interpretations of biomass changes in the southern Sahara and Sahel zone have especially been enhanced, prompting the ensuing major re-evaluations of the principles involved in assuming environmental degradation and desertification on the basis of vegetation decline.

NDVI data have been used by Dregne and Tucker (1988) to compare biomass in the 1984 drought year with the wet year of 1985 in Sudan, by Tucker and Choudhury (1987) to chart changes between 1981 and 1986 and by Tucker *et al.* (1991) to look at Sahara-wide vegetation changes from 1980 to 1990. All these studies have demonstrated how biomass fluctuates seasonally and annually in response to rainfall, illustrating the dynamic nature of vegetation and that the concept of an advancing desert front, used to infer desertification and the spread of the Sahara (e.g. Lamprey, 1975) is incorrect. Put crudely, the size of the Sahara, as measured by green biomass, directly relates to interannual rainfall variability. For reasons of practical assessment Tucker *et al.* (1991) took the 200 mm isohyet as the southern limit of the Sahara and found both expansions and contractions of desert area to occur over the ten-year period covered by the study. Such changes do not necessarily display clear movements of a 'desert front' but more complex temporal and spatial patterns (Hellden, 1991) in response to patchy rainfall distribution. Hellden (1991:381) has summarised the changes in biomass thus:

> this is a normal phenomena [sic] that can be related to the normal variability of rainfall in the Sahel rather than to man's mismanagement of the natural resources.

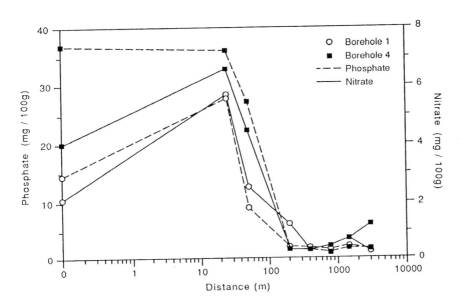

Figure 8.4. Spatial trends in phosphate and nitrate content of soils around boreholes in the central Kalahari (after Perkins and Thomas, 1993)

Figure 8.5. Mixed herds have long been a part of traditional livestock production in drylands, as in this scene from Mongolia's Gobi Desert. They offer the advantages that different species have varying susceptibilities to moisture availability and are able to exploit different ecological niches

Other remote-sensing sources have been put to good effect in combination with field-based investigations in Sudan by Hellden (1984; 1988); K. Olsson (1983; 1985) and L. Olsson (1983). Their use of air photograph analysis, Landsat MSS and TM sources, published records and field data have shown no trend at the decade scale for several parameters that might reflect the progressive spread of desertification (see Chapter 4). As Walsh *et al.* (1988) report, severe impacts of droughts on crop production and biomass were noted for the early and mid-1970s, but subsequent recovery of vegetation, marked by reduced albedo, occurred in the wet years at the end of the decade. In northern Kordofan province the extent of environmental changes around 77 villages was investigated and no systematic patterns were identified between 1962 and 1979, with Hellden (1988) observing that some changes in ground cover may have been the result of rotational cultivation patterns. Systematic advances in sand dune coverage was also dismissed by this study.

There is therefore a growing body of data that is indicating that earlier simple analyses of vegetation cover changes may have confused natural temporal and spatial variability imparted by drought with long-term degradation caused by human activities. This is not too surprising given the tendency for studies, such as Suliman (1988), to compare drought and pre-drought conditions, thereby attributing differences to human actions rather than climactic variability (Olsson, 1985; Hellden, 1991).

Changes in the soil system

Notwithstanding the limitations that exist in interpreting area assessments incorporating a large qualitative input, the GLASOD project described in the previous chapter does provide the opportunity to consider the extent and nature of soil degradation throughout the world's drylands. UNEP (1992) provides detailed coverage of the whole project and additionally Warren and Khogali (1992) utilise the data specifically for the Sahel region. The assessment here will therefore be restricted to a consideration of the salient points before we examine some important issues that impinge on the interpretation of the degradation–productivity relationship in the next section.

The extent of soils degraded by human action in susceptible drylands is shown by continent in Table 8.1. The data have been derived from information in UNEP (1992) and show that degradation is dominated by water and wind erosion and interestingly that a third of the dryland soil resource in Europe appears to be degraded, compared for example with a quarter in Africa. Worldwide, 9 per cent of the world's susceptible drylands are affected by human-induced water erosion (Figure 8.6), 8.3 per cent by wind erosion, 2 per cent by chemical degradation (salinisation, alkalinisation and nutrient loss) and just 0.7 per cent by physical processes (principally compaction and crusting).

Figure 8.6. An extreme example of the effects of water erosion: a 15-metre-deep gully cut in arable land in central Tunisia

Table 8.1. Soil degradation in the susceptible drylands by process and continent (million ha)

	Africa	Asia	Aust.	Eur.	N. Am	S. Am	Total
Water	119.1	157.5	69.6	48.1	38.4	34.7	467.4
Wind	159.9	153.2	16.0	38.8	37.8	26.9	432.4
Chemical	26.5	50.2	0.6	4.1	2.2	17.0	100.6
Physical	13.9	9.6	1.2	8.6	1.0	0.4	34.7
Total	319.4	370.5	87.4	99.6	79.4	79.0	1035.1
Area Suscept. dryland	1286.0	1671.8	663.3	299.7	732.4	516.0	5169.2
% degraded	24.8	22.2	13.2	33.2	10.8	15.3	20.0

Calculated from data in UNEP (1992)

This information can be distilled further, and it is important to note how GLASOD also classified the nature of degradation by its degree. In this respect, it can be recalled (Chapter 7) that the GLASOD methodology (ISRIC, 1988; Oldeman *et al.*, 1990) states that light degradation is when land 'has somewhat reduced agricultural suitability, but is suitable for use in local farming systems. Restoration to full productivity is possible by modifications of the management system. Original biotic functions are still largely intact'. An implication of this is that productivity has only been reduced in the context of introduced agricultural methods, and that only limited changes are necessary to restore conditions. At this level it may be additionally problematic to distinguish natural background levels of change, for example in water erosion, from those specifically induced by human actions.

If, due to these doubts, the light category is removed from the assessment, which Warren and Khogali (1992) have also done in their Sudano–Sahelian study, the data can be reconsidered. Table 8.2 indicates that degradation in the moderate, strong and extreme categories, which can be regarded as more certain degradation, affects about 12 per cent of the world's drylands, with Europe having lost more in terms of per area dryland productivity than other continents. This can perhaps be related to the intensity and length of utilisation of land, including those affected by severe soil erosion since the classical period in the eastern Mediterranean (Vita-Finzi, 1969) and the problems of erosion in the Murcia area of southeast Spain (Middleton and Thomas, 1992).

Table 8.2. Soil degradation in the susceptible drylands by process and continent, excluding degradation in the light category (million ha)

	Africa	Asia	Aust.	Eur.	N. Am	S. Am	Total
Water	90.6	107.9	2.1	41.7	28.1	21.9	292.3
Wind	81.8	72.7	0.1	37.3	35.2	8.1	235.2
Chemical	16.3	28.0	0.6	2.6	1.9	6.9	66.3
Physical	12.7	5.2	1.0	4.4	0.8	0.4	23.9
Total	201.4	213.8	3.8	86.0	66.0	37.3	617.7
Area Suscept. dryland	1286.0	1671.8	663.3	299.7	732.4	516.0	5169.2
% degraded	15.6	12.8	0.6	28.6	9.0	7.2	11.9

Calculated from data in UNEP (1992)

Table 8.3 Summary data for land degradation by dryland region in Africa (million ha)

	North	Sahel	South	Other	Total
(i) Extent					
Arid	98.1	348.6	54.1	2.7	503.5
Semi-arid	37.4	303.7	159.4	13.3	513.4
Dry subhumid	15.1	150.1	81.5	22.0	268.7
Total	150.6	802.4	295.0	38.0	1285.6
(ii) Degradation					
Light	25.6	109.8	6.4	2.4	144.2
Moderate	13.4	80.3	15.9	2.6	112.2
Strong	1.7	30.8	36.4	3.9	72.8
Extreme	0.0	3.1	0.0	0.0	3.1
Total (excl. light)	15.1	114.2	52.3	6.5	288.1
% of area	10.0	14.2	17.7	17.1	14.6
(iii) Cause (excl. light)					
Water	6.5	45.1	43.4	5.5	100.5
Wind	8.8	105.2	20.2	0.0	134.2
Chemical	1.7	13.8	0.3	1.8	17.6
Physical	1.0	12.0	5.2	2.8	21.0

Note: Area totals in (iii) can be greater than those in (ii) as land units can be affected by more than one type of degradation
Calculated from data in UNEP (1992)

The general pattern of degradation indicated by GLASOD can be examined more closely to give a regional perspective, particularly in the case of Africa where a second continent-specific data base has been produced (UNEP, 1992). One particular advantage of this is that it utilises a greater density of mapping units than for the same area in the global coverage; some 898 compared to 383 (Thomas and Middleton, 1993). The analysis of the African data set in UNEP (1992) by Middleton and Thomas (1992) treated the susceptible drylands in four regions: north of the Sahara, incorporating the Maghreb countries plus western Sahara and Cape Verde, the Sahel, southern Africa comprising the SADCC countries plus South Africa and other isolated dryland pockets including southwest Madagascar and parts of Tanzania and Mozambique. Table 8.3 summarises degradation data from this study. It should be noted that the total area of degraded land is not the same as the African total in the global study because of the distinct derivations of the two data bases.

With the light degradation category omitted for the previously explained reason it is interesting to note from Table 8.3 that on a percentage land area basis the southern region experiences more of a degradation problem than the Sahel, though if areas affected by light degradation had been included in this calculation this would not be the case. The experts contributing to this GLASOD study provided data that indicate water and wind erosion to be the principal causes of dryland degradation in African susceptible drylands. In southern Africa, water erosion is a significant problem, especially in South Africa and parts of Namibia (Figure 8.7). In the Sahel, degradation by water erosion is particularly severe in upland areas, notably in the Ethiopian Highlands (Warren and Khogali, 1992), where Brown and Wolf (1986) suggest that up to one billion tons of top soil are lost per annum.

The data in Table 8.3 suggest that, in terms of area affected, wind erosion makes a more significant contribution to Sahelian degradation than water. In fact, according to UNEP (1992), the southern provinces of Sudan and the central areas of Mali are notable for the severity (extent and degree combined in the matrix in Figure 7.8—see p.120) of wind erosion. The former area is the same one which was focused on in the remotely-sensed studies of biomass change discussed previously, where only rainfall – rather than degradation – induced changes were identified. This must raise an important doubt about the basis of the assessment used for the GLASOD data input in this region, particularly whether permanent and ephemeral changes have been confused. Warren and Khogali (1992) give a similar hint of scepticism for the GLASOD assessment of conditions in this area, while Suliman (1988) provides a further study from Sudan where changes in conditions caused by drought and human actions are not differentiated.

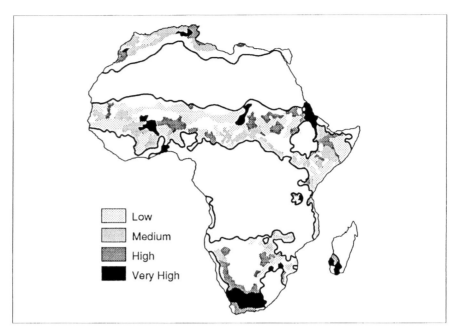

Figure 8.7. GLASOD map of water erosion severity in Africa (after UNEP, 1992)

The spatial variability of the nature of degradation processes is highlighted by the GLASOD data concerning chemical degradation. On a continental basis this is a particular feature of the Asian drylands, but greater scrutiny reveals its principal containment to individual drainage basins and irrigation schemes, notably in Iraq, Syria, central Asia and Pakistan. In the African context the salinisation problem reaches its greatest dimensions outside the susceptible drylands, because the 2.8 million hectares of irrigated land in the Nile Valley strictly fall in a hyper-arid region. A specific analysis of the African chemical degradation data by Thomas and Middleton (1993) indicates that at a continent-wide level the more insidious problem of soil degradation by nutrient depletion is a greater threat to productivity, affecting some 15 million ha (excluding light category) compared to just over 2 million ha for human induced salinisation.

The GLASOD data bases have considerable potential for yielding useful information on soil degradation, of which the above discussion has indicated but a part. Because of the inevitable limitations in such a spatially-extensive assessment, some of which have been indicated above, its greatest use is probably in the provision of the general overview, because as the scale of analysis is reduced, so problems of interpretation can arise.

The inadequate and problematic science of soil degradation

The GLASOD survey shows that soil degradation by water and wind erosion dominates over that by *in situ* changes (chemical and physical degradation) in the susceptible drylands. A frequent conclusion drawn from indicators of soil erosion is that they are evidence of a decline in potential productivity. In effect this is the link within the sustainability–desertification debate. It is however necessary to consider whether this relationship can automatically be assumed, and in this respect several studies provide interesting evidence for evaluation of this issue.

Wind erosion, particularly in the form of dust storms and the mobilisation and creation of sand dunes, has been a major illustrative component of publicity relating to desertification. There are situations where the effects of wind erosion have been on a large scale and have been lasting. The Dust Bowl of the United States described in Chapter 2 is the classic example, where the scale of renewed soil loss in the 1970s exceeded that of the 1930s (Lockeretz, 1978). In this case the nature of agricultural production systems, the wholesale clearance of natural vegetation and the creation of large fields for mechanised methods are undoubtedly the principal problems leading to erosion and degradation. Though parts of Iran and specific agricultural schemes in the Sahel region have been subjected to similar methods, the extensive nature of Dust Bowl erosion is still not the usual scale at which wind erosion occurs in the susceptible drylands and is therefore not a suitable model for the examination of the wind erosion issue in general.

While in many cases the encroachment of mobile sand dunes onto agricultural land can be locally very significant, as in the Tengger Desert of China (Zhu Zhenda *et al.*, 1992), in Rajasthan, India (Kaushalya, 1992) and in the Niger valley around Tombouctou in Mali, and major dust storms can emanate from cultivated drylands (Middleton, 1985), it has been suggested that the effects on long-term soil productivity are in fact probably minimal (Dregne, 1992). One reason for this is that the extent of aeolian erosion or accumulation is frequently localised, concentrated for example along the margins of river valleys because of their foci for human activities in water-deficient drylands. It is not necessarily the 'self fuelling mechanism' described by Kaushalya (1992). In the case of sand transport and dust storms off-site effects may be greater than the impacts in source areas due to encroachment onto communication routes and buildings by sand and because of the dispersive nature of fine silt or dust-sized aeolian sediment. Sources of deflation may be very specific (Warren and Khogali, 1992) and dust mobilisation strongly linked to drought events (Middleton, 1985).

The very low levels of natural fertility in many dryland soils that have a significant aeolian component, as in the case of the Quaternary dune sediments of the Kalahari (Skarpe and Bergstrom, 1986) and Australia

(Buckley, 1981) means that loss of soil by wind erosion may have a minimal impact in terms of nutrient depletion (Perkins and Thomas, 1993), although the deflation of fine particles can reduce soil moisture retention properties (Fryrear, 1981). Perhaps more significant than the loss of productivity potential are the severe difficulties that aeolian transport of sediment can cause for cultivation systems and for crop growth. Dune encroachment and the creation of blowouts and hummocky terrain can severely hinder mechanised agriculture. Most significant however is the damage that entrained sediment can do to plants through burial, particularly of young plants, and blasting. The problem of damage to seedlings may be enhanced by the winds with the greatest sediment transport potential occurring at the end of the dry season and onset of rains in some locations, notably central Australia (Brookfield, 1970), parts of the Sahel (Mainguet, 1991) and southern Kalahari (Thomas and Shaw, 1991).

The effects of sediment impacts on plant physiology have been the subject of several studies (e.g. Fryrear et al., 1973; Bubenzer and Weis, 1974). Of particular importance is the fact that abrasion of the surfaces of stems and leaves enhances evapotranspiration, causing plants to become desiccated with growth rates also being significantly retarded. This may be the most important factor in the decline in crop yields from soils subject to wind erosion, as reported for example from North American drylands (Lyles, 1977; Fryrear, 1981), rather than the common assumption that falling yields result from a drop in soil productivity.

Several methods exist for reducing the effects of wind erosion and restoring land that has been degraded by it (Watson, 1990; Middleton, 1990). Of particular importance in the agricultural context are the establishment of wind breaks and shelter belts which can both encourage deposition of entrained material and reduce wind velocities, thereby lowering the potential for sediment mobilisation. In some circumstances previously established wind breaks have been removed to facilitate larger fields for mechanised agriculture or the installation of centre-pivot irrigation schemes (McCauley et al., 1981; Warren and Agnew, 1988). Although nearly 2000 km of windbreaks were removed in the American west between 1970 and 1975, an average 3200 km of new ones have been established there each year since 1942 (Grainger, 1990). A key issue here in the context of regional soil loss is the comparative spatial distribution of the removal and addition of windbreaks.

Zhu Zhenda et al. (1992) demonstrate just how effective restoration and preventative measures can be. In the Shapotou area of the southeastern Tengger Desert of China the equivalent of 53 km^2 of shelterbelt were created in the 30 years prior to 1990. This, together with the laying of surface-protecting check boards, reduced wind erosion to the extent that soil organic content increased between 16- and 23-fold, silt and clay content by a factor of 12 and plant cover increased in areas subject to moving sand from 5 per cent to 20–40 per cent. Consequently agriculture has been re-established, increasing the area under cultivation from 210 km^2 to 285 km^2.

As in the case of wind erosion, simple links between soil loss through water action and productivity decline need to be treated with care. In part, problems arise from the very difficulty of measuring water erosion from agricultural land, especially in the translation and extrapolation of results from experimental plots to actual fields and hillslopes, and from short-term studies to longer time-periods (Stocking, 1987), particularly given the vagaries and variations in dryland rainfall events. Unlike in more temperate environments, high-magnitude, low-frequency rainfall events carry out the most geomorphic work in drylands (Wolman and Gerson, 1978) and therefore infrequent events may account for more erosional loss than a run of average magnitude storms. Indirect measures of sediment loss from land under production, such as the use of sediment loads in rivers may also present problems and can result in the misleading representation of the degradation problem. Mukinya (1990) provided data from three Kenyan rivers that suggest soil erosion has increased up to 10 ten times between 1965 and 1986. Yet much of the sediment load may come from bank erosion rather than from agricultural land throughout a catchment.

Rates of soil loss through erosion need to be balanced against natural rates of soil formation, as the seriousness of degradation may be related to the net rate of loss in this relationship (Abel and Blaikie, 1989). Although Warren and Khogali (1992) offer words of caution in making simple comparisons, Lal (1984) in Kenya and Mulugeta Tesfaye (reported by Warren and Khogali, 1992) in Ethiopia both found soil loss from agricultural land to be below or equal to rates of natural soil formation. Spatial variations in erosion patterns and rates particularly complicate the establishment of straightforward relationships. Sutherland and Bryan (1990) have studied runoff generation and sediment yield from a catchment in the semi-arid Baringo district of Kenya. They found both runoff and sediment generation to be unevenly distributed. Although the sediment yield in the basin was equivalent to an overall basin lowering of 4.0 mm per year, the actual loss was twice as much from lower slope colluvial sources than from higher up on hillslopes. The Kenyan government's soil rehabilitation scheme, involving establishing agroforestry schemes on steeper slopes, may well be inappropriate and is furthermore at odds with the pastoral land use dominant in the region (Sutherland and Bryan, 1990).

The picture is further complicated by studies in other locations that have found erosion to be concentrated on upper slopes, for example in a study in Mali by IGN France (1992). From this investigation Mainguet (1991) reports that in the Mourhia area of central Mali erosion on upper slopes has improved plant growth in valleys and gullies because of the increased arrival of sediment and runoff. IGN France (1992) note just how complex are the spatial patterns of erosion, vegetation change, land use and population dynamics. In southern Zimbabwe, Scoones (1992) has reported how increased indicators of land degradation have not been accompanied by a fall in livestock production. This is because gulley and rill erosion is focused on 'top lands' while grazing predominates in lower slope locations. The transfer of sediment from upper- to lower-slope and valley locations can actually give significant advantages for production because the latter are better locations for water retention and therefore cultivation, livestock production and human occupation (Ingram, 1991).

Soil erosion and livestock production systems: analyses from Africa

In the degradation debate, ultimately it is not possible to divorce environmental and economic aspects of the problem. This adds a further dimension, and a major difficulty, to the assessment of the significance of desertification, and may complicate the sustainability issue. It has been argued in some circles that slow rates of degradation can be acceptable under circumstances of economic gain and social benefit (e.g. Abel and Blaikie, 1989). This has been illustrated by studies in Botswana and Zimbabwe. In the hardveld of eastern Botswana, Biot (1988; 1992) has used an assessment of the vegetation productivity–soil resource relationship to calculate that at the current rate of net soil erosion the sustainability of the present livestock production system will only come into question in 300–500 years' time. If this calculation is correct and the long-term extrapolation of erosion rates which Biot uses is justifiable, which it may not be (see above), the environmental cost of maintaining the present land-use system may be within the bounds of acceptability, and any changes in usage to maintain sustainability only need be effected in several hundred years' time!

Abel and Stocking (1987) and Abel and Blaikie (1989) have explored the erosion–livestock relationship using data from Communal Areas in southeast Zimbabwe. The soil loss estimation model for southern Africa (SLEMSA) of Elwell and Stocking (1982) was used to predict the annual rate of soil loss (gross rather than net values) under different percentage vegetation covers on two Communal Areas (Figure 8.8). If vegetation cover is related at least in part to livestock stocking levels, also termed the herbivore use intensity, or HUI (e.g. Perkins, 1991) then the curve on the graph can be used to predict the reduction in soil loss that might occur if HUI is reduced through a destocking programme. Abel and Blaikie (1989) quote vegetation cover values in the range of 57–63 per cent on different management schemes, noting that because of the exponential shape of the curve a reduction in HUI leading to improved vegetation cover may have little impact on erosion rates. In effect, levels of destocking would have to be extremely high, incurring major negative social impacts, before a significant decrease in erosion is effected (Scoones, 1992). In any case, following from Biot's (1988) work, it may be difficult from a practical perspective to effect land-use changes or changes in stocking levels if erosion rates are not detrimental on the scale of human lifespans.

A limitation of these interesting studies is the assumption that the erosion estimates from short-term studies are adequate for making long-term projections. Livingstone (1991) also points out that the data from Zimbabwe were collected during a run of years with 'normal' rainfall, whereas the immediate post-drought period, when vegetation cover may have been further reduced by natural means, may be the critical time for vegetation cover. Using the Abel and Blaikie (1989) model in Figure 8.8 it can be seen that soil erosion in a 20 per cent vegetation cover year is almost five times greater than in a 'normal' 55 per cent cover year (Livingstone, 1991). Under these conditions, destocking may well reduce degradation because the ability of the vegetation to recover may be hindered by continued livestock pressure. However, livestock mortality during droughts (Abel and Blaikie, 1989; Perkins, 1990) may effectively act as a safety valve (Livingstone, 1991) in the system preventing undue pressure on the environment during the recovery period.

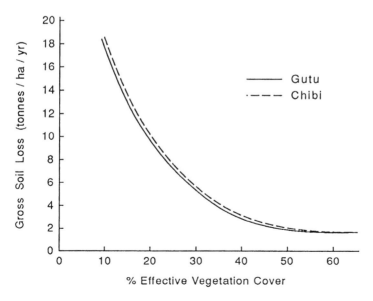

Figure 8.8. The relationship between gross soil erosion and vegetation cover from two Zimbabwean Communal Areas (after Abel and Blaikie, 1989)

Conclusion

Drylands are dynamic systems in which human-induced degradation needs to be set against natural variations in environmental parameters and the resilience of dryland ecosystems. The GLASOD programme has provided a more rigorous assessment of desertification than previous studies and has identified wind and water erosion as the main processes through which it occurs. Even here though, the nature of degradation needs to be set against a realisation of the nature, consequences and spatial dynamics of erosion. Many questions remain unanswered or unclear and point out the need for further research into the links between different system components. Almost all aspects of our understanding of degradation would be well served by longer-term monitoring of dryland ecosystem, erosion and climatic dynamics in order to facilitate a fuller consideration of the environmental components of the desertification debate.

The advances being made in dryland ecology indicate that natural variations in dryland plant communities cannot be described as desertification. While it may be difficult, in the short term, to distinguish between natural cyclic and human-induced changes in drylands, such difficulties must not be used to generate oversimplifications concerning the occurrence of desertification. Even though soil degradation can be difficult to monitor, desertification must not be represented in terms of previous, now discredited data, which reinforce past estimates that do not stand up to scientific scrutiny. The GLASOD data are likely to have many imperfections that arise from the underlying methodology. These are a challenge to future investigators, not an excuse to revert to past imperfections.

9 The future

... it is only by accumulating judgements based on empirical studies that environmentalist slogans can be replaced by more balanced evaluations. (Mortimore, 1989:157)

Monitoring

The importance of long-term monitoring of dryland environments has been discussed in this book. Monitoring is necessary to identify where desertification is occurring, and to give indicators as to how and why it is happening. Monitoring can also help to distinguish between impacts that can be attributed to human action and those that are a reflection of natural parameters. It also makes sense for such monitoring programmes to combine scientific observations with an understanding of social systems and their relationship to the environment. Although there have been few long-term desertification monitoring studies to date, the approach is well illustrated by Mortimore's (1989) study of the Manga grasslands in northern Nigeria over a period of 36 years.

Localised rejuvenation of formerly stabilised Quaternary dunes was observed over the period 1950–86, with mobile dunes increasing in extent across the rangelands (Figure 9.1). Mortimore (1989:184) observes that rangeland dunes 'began to develop under grazing pressure, but their growth in size and numbers accelerated, after 1969, under conditions of drought stress'. However, the environment's dynamism was also noted, demonstrating the great resilience of grasses under the pressures of grazing and drought. Recolonisation of deflation areas was observed over the period and in wetter years on the slopes of the dunes themselves. The fact that mobile dunes were also observed in the area in the 1930s suggests that such landforms are by no means a recent feature.

The adaptions of local human populations to their dynamic dryland environment are illustrated in the cases where village perimeters were threatened by mobile dunes. The dynamics of the dunes were closely dependent upon the growth and decline of human settlements. Grazing of village-based livestock at the eastern end of villages, the direction of dominant dry season winds, was directly responsible for the mobilisation of dunes which, if unimpeded, progressed around the north and

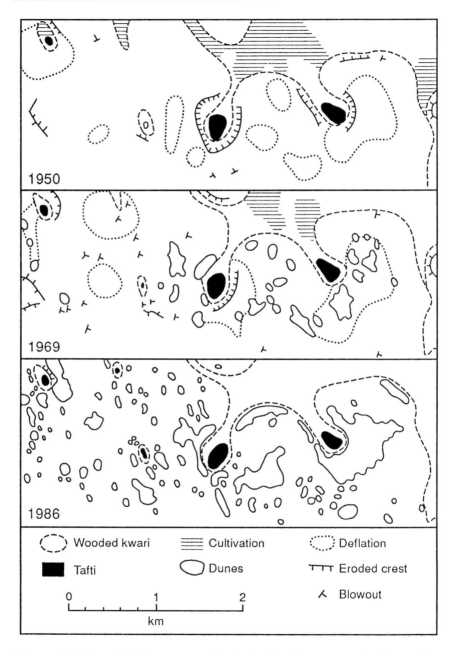

Figure 9.1 Rangeland dunes near Kaska in the Manga grasslands, northern Nigeria. The maps for 1950 and 1969 were produced from aerial photograph interpretation, that for 1986 from field traverses (after Mortimore, 1989)

south sides of villages to unite at the west. However, the inconvenience of the moving sands caused households to move, taking their livestock with them. Removal of the grazing pressure allowed grasses to recolonise the dunes from the windward side.

Mortimore's studies in northern Nigeria have also examined traditional social responses to drought and consequent food shortages, highlighting the reasons for people's failure to combat the horrors of the 1970s drought in the Sahel (Mortimore, 1987). The same failures of traditional social responses at times of environmental stress can be equally applied to the problems of desertification.

Adaptive responses to times of stress can be divided into strategies at home and strategies away from home. The most common home-based response from small farmers was to sell their labour to larger concerns to enable them to purchase food they were unable to grow themselves. Alternatively, their efforts would be turned to other money-earning activities such as mat- and rope-making, and the gathering of firewood and dung for sale. People also turned to famine foods, such as leaves, which are not a normal part of their diet.

The movement of males away from home to seek work in the south of the country or in nearby cities is common during good rainfall times, but the incidence and frequency of migration rises dramatically during times of drought and even extends to whole families. Labouring, begging and handicraft work were the commonest forms of occupation noted away from home, with the anonymity of unfamiliar locales providing some cover from the shame of begging.

These adaptive responses to drought, which are enacted when times become hard, are superimposed upon inbuilt approaches to preparing for drought which local inhabitants know will always return. Four main preparatory strategies are identified by Mortimore and shown in Table 9.1.

These traditional insurance strategies have been weakened by the changing political economy of the region, and the situation in northern Nigeria is illustrative of the changing scene faced by inhabitants of developing dryland communities the world over.

The possibilities for grain storage have been diminished by a combination of circumstances, including land scarcity and an increasing population. The colonial imposition of taxes payable in currency, the monetisation of the economy, and deteriorating terms of trade for rural communities have also driven producers from subsistence to export crop production and thereby into an increasing dependence upon a fickle market for essential foodstuffs: 'When the market has taken the place of the family granary in times of scarcity, it can dictate its own terms (or fail altogether)' (Mortimore, 1987:9).

The generation of savings from alternative applications of labour has

Table 9.1 Traditional indigenous insurance strategies against drought in northern Nigeria (after Mortimore, 1987)

Food storage	Store food during times of plenty, the oldest insurance system in history.
Monetary savings	Work hard at alternative opportunities – off-farm production and labouring at home.
Social insurance	Rely on the community network of extended families, supplemented by the moral responsibility under Islam of richer members of society to assist the poor in times of hardship.
Ecological insurance	Practice diversified farming and herding – intercropping, spatial fragmentation of holdings, diversification of livestock, grazing mobility – to give some protection against hazards specific to particular crops, animals or places.

also suffered from changing political policies. In 1984, for example, the new military government in Nigeria forcibly implemented a 'back-to-the-land' policy, repatriating members of the urban informal sector and banning itinerant traders from pavements and street corners. Within days of the start of the policy, 50,000 or more self-employed enterprises had disappeared from the streets of Kano alone. Further erosion of the monetary saving option has occurred due to high inflation and sudden changes in valuation of the national currency.

The drought of the 1970s and 1980s, combined with the continued growth in population numbers, meant that 'social insurance' suffered as people who could normally be relied upon to help out poorer relations did not have enough food for themselves. The advantages of 'ecological insurance' have also been eroded in colonial and more recent times, as specialisation has been the central theme of initiatives in the agricultural sector.

A loss of autonomy over their affairs lies at the heart of the consequent problems faced by farming and pastoral communities in developing country drylands. Such communities never had control over the natural variability of rainfall, but in more recent times the absorption of rural communities into centralised economies, started in colonial eras and continued in the post-independence period, has further eroded traditional abilities to cope with environmental stress (Figure 9.2). As a closed system, a village might survive the shock of a drought with an adequate grain surplus from normal years, but since the beginnings of incorporation into the market economy integration has had to be intensified for survival, even though it is conducted on unfavourable terms, increasing the village's vulnerability to forces beyond its control. Mortimore suggests that income from secondary production, labour circulation and migration are becoming crucial to the survival of rural communities in areas prone to drought.

Population growth

Although we have highlighted the fact that relationships between population density and desertification are by no means clear-cut, the rapid growth of populations in developing countries does play a part in the degradation issue. Ultimately, more people does mean more pressure on resources.

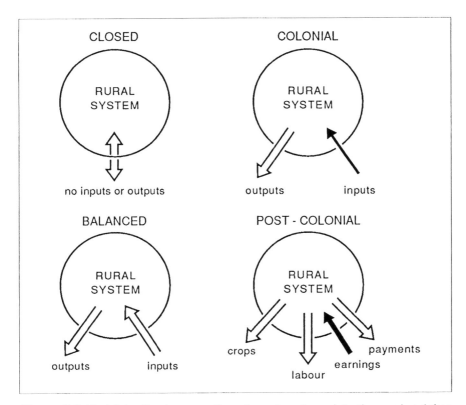

Figure 9.2 Model for the incorporation of rural systems into the market (after Mortimore, 1987)

Population increase in developing countries is undoubtably a function of improved medical facilities, disease prevention, education and a general access to better living standards. However, the reasons for an individual deciding to have more children can also be viewed in the light of a poor rural society's diminishing autonomy over their resources and their options for survival during times of stress such as drought and ultimately desertification (Mortimore, 1987).

When traditional responses to periods of environmental difficulty are eroded by changing socio-political environments, as outlined above, and financial, distribution and welfare systems available in richer societies are not an option for many inhabitants of poor countries, labour becomes the only factor of production which such a population has within its power to increase. When drought arrives, or desertification begins to bite, labour requirements grow. As yields are diminished, more cultivation is necessary; as available pasture is reduced, more foliage from trees becomes essential; as the journey for fuelwood becomes longer, more people are needed to collect it; as more family members spend time away from home, more hands are needed on the homestead. Unless appropriate, better techniques, crop strains or technology are available, the only way of improving agricultural productivity is through more labour.

The logical end-result of such a strategy continuing is environmental breakdown, which some suggest is already happening, and a Malthusian crash of population. Starvation and suffering are things that much of Western society regards as morally unacceptable. It is important to make the proviso 'Western', because in some other societies such events may ultimately be put down to the will of God, or a similar higher power. We could argue that such a resignation to greater powers is simply a sociological adaption to environmental realities. The life cycles of plant and animal populations in drylands are characterised by 'boom and bust' cycles in tune with a variable environment, and human populations may have adjusted in a similar manner under environmental stress in the past. When this occurs today, it is viewed from the West as unacceptable, and hence emergency aid, sometimes on a massive scale, is implemented. This emergency aid is, however, a markedly different phenomenon to long-term development aid, a more important input to the tackling of long-term problems of developing country drylands. The realities of the world today are such that the Western way of thinking and doing things, rightly or wrongly, is dominant. This being the case, we must search for acceptable alternatives to the deficiencies of development assistance.

Small-scale development

The dominant theme of desertification programmes in developing countries has been on large-scale approaches, a characteristic of development programmes in general. Hancock (1989) suggests that the UN Development Programme, for example, establishes about 100 new projects each year, at an average cost of $393,000. The lion's share of this money, Hancock notes, goes to the employment of consultants and experts, their fees and field work expenses. Too little reaches local communities, and all too often development programme failures have been put down to a lack of community participation.

The realisation that local people must be involved in the solution to environmental problems is a philosophy held by many NGOs and expressed by many involved in the environment and development debate (e.g. Timberlake, 1985). It is a reaction to the 'unsuccessful technological triumphalism of rural development practice' (Adams, 1990:169), and is now apparently being accepted in multilateral development aid circles (UNCED, 1992; World Bank, 1992). The chapter in Agenda 21 (UNCED, 1992) that deals with desertification and drought notes: 'the experience to date on the successes and failures of programmes and projects points to the need for popular support to sustain activities related to desertification and drought control' (UNCED, 1992:117). Since it is seen increasingly that additional funding is unlikely to be available from donor nations, a clear priority is to use the funds that are available more effectively. Small-scale participatory projects are increasingly recognised as being particularly effective, if not the only effective, means of improving local resource management (Cardy, 1993; Toulmin, 1993). Participatory approaches to projects aiming to resolve the desertification problem , as with other environmental problems, are regarded as offering three main advantages: they give planners a better understanding of local values, knowledge and experience; they win community backing for project objectives and community help with local implementation; and they can help resolve conflicts over resource use (World Bank, 1992).

There are drawbacks to popular participation. It tends to be expensive and can cause delays in implementation, while decentralisation of decision-making can easily reinforce the power of local elites and reinforce and widen income differentials (World Bank, 1992). Successful projects aiming to increase local participation must be carefully managed to avoid such pitfalls, although they can hardly be less effective than many large-scale environmental relief projects (e.g. Hancock, 1989; Timberlake, 1985). The incorporation of indigenous institutions and the harnessing of local voluntary groups can only help to improve the chances of project realisation.

Such approaches, however, should not be pursued to the detriment of consideration being given to wider issues of the political economy. Reform of national and international bodies also needs to be tackled, a task which in many cases will mean the overturning of practices and attitudes which are tuned to urban demands at the expense of rural needs.

This is one of the aims of many World Bank 'structural adjustment programmes', although in practice the harsh measures employed to achieve these aims have been criticised (e.g. George, 1988).

Desertification, drought or famine?

As we have outlined in Chapter 2, it was drought and famine in the Sahel in the late 1960s and early 1970s that triggered the projection of desertification onto the world stage. The spectre of famine rightly engenders a reaction to combat it. Famine being what it is – large numbers of people dying directly and indirectly due to food shortages – it provokes strong emotional reactions. But while an *in situ* shortage of food is undoubtably linked to drought, in that harvests are reduced and animals become thin and ultimately perish, the occurrence of famine is not so simply linked to natural environmental factors. Political instability and civil strife are important inputs to the famine equation, as is poverty (Sen, 1981). We need only point to the African countries which experienced serious famines in the 1980s and early 1990s – Sudan, Ethiopia, Mozambique and Somalia – to realise the contribution made by civil war. War disjoints economies, forces mass migrations of people away from land which they would otherwise be cultivating, and obstructs transport corridors. People fighting are not tilling the land but are still hungry, it is not for nothing that the Renamo guerillas in Mozambique were known to peasants as 'the locust people'. People deprived of their normal livelihoods are often reduced to poverty as a result and therefore cannot afford to buy what food is available. Even when foreign assistance brings food to countries in need, distribution is difficult in war-torn territories, and is sometimes even used as a weapon itself, as in Sudan and Ethiopia in the 1980s (e.g. Keller, 1992).

This is not to say that desertification cannot play an important part in the occurrence of famine. It can, but until desertification is demonstrated to be happening and to be a principal component of the causes of food shortages, it is an all too convenient scapegoat to take attention away from more important politico-economic causes. And when it comes to an event as emotive as famine, identification of the causes always comes secondary to attacking the problem. However, the USAID assistant administrator for Africa made a thought-provoking statement at a press conference in June 1991 when he said that he had been told that 'there has never been a famine in a country that had a democratic government, a free press, and free markets in history' (Spangler, 1991). Irrespective of any hidden political agendas that the US government aid agency might be accused of in making such a statement, this comment highlights the issue. And yet press reports from the early stages of negotiations over the UN convention on desertification suggest that famine is again being raised in conjunction with desertification (Chatterjee, 1993).

So long as governments continue to blame their own marginalised people for problems which are of their own or other governments' making, the true underlying causes of issues such as famine and indeed desertification itself will never be tackled.

The developed world

From the human perspective, desertification in developed countries is much less important than in poorer societies, since in richer countries social security safety nets and economic insurance packages are usually available for the victims of desertification to fall back on, while such backstops are simply not available in the developing world. In the developed world desertification should never be the potentially life and death matter which it could be in poorer countries. In the wider context of the well-being of society as a whole, the depletion of the soil resource from agricultural land is also less important since, given adequate economic resources, food can be grown with sufficient inputs of fertilizers.

The techniques for soil conservation are well known, and thus the reasons for not employing them must be sought out and tackled. Just as in the Sahel a farmer will only eat into his natural environmental capital when circumstances dictate, so too in the richer countries; degradation is the result of a cost-benefit analysis in which long-term environmental costs are perceived to be worth the short-term social benefits. But the question as to whether the true environmental costs are being entered into these mental equations is raised by the new discipline of environmental economics. As Pearce (1993:12) suggests: 'Demonstrating that "conservation pays" in economic development terms is a process that has really only just begun. But it is already possible to point to significant findings. Far from environmental and resource conservation being inimical to sustained economic development, it is in a great many cases integral to the development process'.

The role of science

It is interesting to note the differing roles that scientific uncertainty has been made to play in the desertification issue relative to its role in another major global environmental debate, that of global warming. Whereas in desertification circles the lack of scientific evidence has been continually played down and understressed, if not actually covered up, in the debate over the global warming outcomes of a human-enhanced greenhouse effect in the global atmosphere the lack of scientific certainty over the magnitude, location and nature of effects is continually being

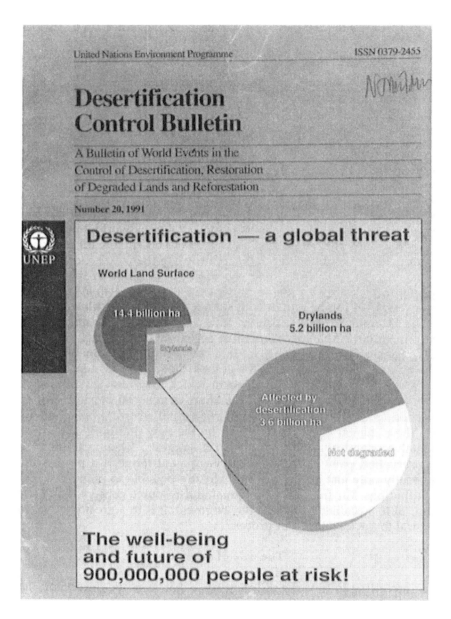

Figure 9.3 'Desertification - a global threat'. The cover of UNEP's Desertification Control Bulletin, Volume 20, 1991

highlighted and re-examined. The guardians of desertification study have had a long time to sort out the lack of scientific rigour in their data, and yet seemingly definitive statements about the threat continue (Figure 9.3). The dangers of crying wolf are well known, and questions are now being asked.

In a wider context, the difficulties that science and scientists are experiencing in dealing with the new breed of global environmental problems goes right to the heart of the very role of science itself. Science should be seen as a tool rather than an end in itself. Over-reliance on the 'techno-fix' has been found wanting, since without an appreciation of social, economic and political factors, technical solutions can only provide short-term relief. Concentration on changing the organisation of society and the forces of the political economy, both within nation states and between rich and poor countries, is therefore all the more relevant.

Epilogue

We started this book with a prologue (page xiii) proposing four parts to the desertification myth. In the preceding pages we have attempted to break down and analyse desertification into terms of how it has been commonly presented, how it has been turned into a global problem and how science and social science researchers and commentators have attempted to disentangle fact from fiction. We now return to the myth and summarise the evidence that leads us to confirm its four main parts.

1. According to United Nations data, desertification affects one third of the world's land area. It is a voracious process which rapidly degrades productive land, especially in drylands.

The bases for such data are at best inaccurate and at worst centred on nothing better than guesswork. Estimates of the global extent of desertification that may have been derived for guidance or as rough indicators became facts, almost carved in tablets of stone. These data have been widely used to publicise desertification and create a self-perpetuating institutional myth. Problems of estimating the extent of soil-degradation over large areas or regions and problems of separating natural variations in environmental conditions from those due to human actions make even the most guarded calculations nothing more than estimates. The advancing desert concept may have been useful as a publicity tool but it is not one that represents the real nature of desertification processes. It is however the myth that has commonly entered public and political imaginations.

2. Drylands are fragile ecosystems that are highly susceptible to degradation and desertification.

Ecological studies are indicating that dryland ecosystems commonly experience dramatic changes in character and biomass in response to natural climatic fluctuations. These changes are often reversible as the ecosystems appear to be well-adapted to cope with and respond to disturbance, demonstrating good recovery characteristics. Vegetation changes alone caused by human actions do not in themselves necessarily constitute degradation and may well be easily confused with natural changes. These changes are relatively easily identified compared with changes in soil systems and have commonly been treated as desertification. Changes in dryland soil systems can be harder to identify and are certainly harder to monitor, especially over large areas and using current satellite-based systems.

3. Desertification is a, if not the, primary cause of human suffering and misery in drylands.

Distinguishing the social outcomes of desertification and drought may be difficult. Drought and desertification together may have provided convenient explanations for general social maladies that may be due to political mismanagement and disadvantaging economic systems. People may cause desertification when traditional land-use systems are destroyed or pressurised, population pressure increases or developing nations have to participate in the world market economy.

4. The United Nations is central to attempts to understand and solve the desertification problem.

The United Nations has played a major role in conceptualising desertification since 1977. It could be considered to have created desertification, the institutional myth. It has been the source of publicity that has frequently had little reliable scientific foundation. The success of UN-derived anti-desertification measures have yet to be reliably demonstrated and, in many cases, appear to have had little relevance to affected peoples. Without the UN, desertification may not be as high on the environmental agenda as it is today.

Bibliography

Abel, N.O.J. and Blaikie, P.M., 1989 Land degradation, stocking rates and conservation policies in the communal rangelands of Botswana and Zimbabwe. *Land Degradation and Rehabilitation* **1**: 101–123.

Abel, N.O.J. and Stocking, M., 1987 A rapid method for assessing rates of soil erosion from rangeland: an example from Botswana. *Journal of Range Management* **40**: 460–466.

Abel, N.O.J., Flint, M.E.S., Hunter, N.D., Chandler, D. and Maka, G., 1987 *Cattle-keeping, ecological change and communal management in Ngwaketse.* International Livestock Centre for Africa, Addis Ababa, and Ministry of Agriculture, Gaborone.

Adams, W.M., 1990 *Green developement: environment and sustainability in the third world.* Routledge, London.

Adams, W.M. and Hughes, F.M.R., 1990 Irrigation development in desert environments. In A. S. Goudie (ed) *Techniques for desert reclamation.* Wiley, Chichester: 135–160.

Agnew, C.T., 1982 Water availability and the development of rainfed agriculture in S.W. Niger. *Transactions, Institute of British Geographers* NS7: 419–457.

Agnew, C.T., 1990 Spatial aspects of the drought in the Sahel. *Journal of Arid Environments* **18**: 279–293.

Agnew, C.T. and Anderson, E., 1992 *Water resources in the arid realm.* Routledge, London.

Ahlcrona, E., 1986 *Monitoring the impact of climate and man on land transformation.* Lunds Universitets Naturgeografiska Institution Report 66.

Ahlcrona, E., 1988 *The Impact of Climate and Man on Land Transformation in Central Sudan – Applications of Remote Sensing.* Doctoral thesis, Meddelanden Fran Lunds Universitets Geografiska Institution Avhandlingar No. 103.

Al-Sharif, A., 1990 The present rangeland situation in the northern region of Saudi Arabia. In R. Halwagy, F.K. Taha and S.A. Omar (eds) *Advances in range management in arid lands.* Kegan Paul, London: 113–118.

Anderson, D.M., 1984 Depression, dust bowl, demography and drought: the colonial state and soil conservation in East Africa during the 1930s. *African Affairs* **83**: 321–344.

Aru, A., 1986. Aspects of desertification in Sardinia, Italy. In R. Fantechi and N. S. Margaris (eds) *Desertification in Europe*. Reidel, Dordrecht: 194–198.

Aubreville, A., 1949 *Climats, forêts et désertification de l'Afrique tropicale*. Soc d'éditions géographiques maritimes et coloniales, Paris.

Australian Government, 1978 *A basis for soil conservation policy in Australia*. Resource Directorate Report 1. Department of the Environment, Housing and Community Development, Canberra.

Aveyard, J.M., 1988 Land degradation: changing attitudes–why? *New South Wales Journal of Soil Conservation* **44**: 46–48.

Bale, J.B., Conte, D., Goehring, D. and Simonett, D.S., 1974 *Remote sensing applications to resource management problems in the Sahel*. USAID, Department of State, Washington.

Barker, J.R., Thurow, T.L. and Herlocker, D.J., 1990 Vegetation of pastoralist campsites within the coastal grassland of Somalia. *African Journal of Ecology* **28**: 291–297.

Barrow, C.J., 1991 *Land degradation*. Cambridge University Press.

Bauer, P., 1988 Creating the third world. *Encounter* **80**: 66–75.

Bawden, C.R., 1989 *The modern history of Mongolia*. Kegan Paul International, London.

Beaumont, P., 1989 *Environmental management and development in drylands*. Routledge, London.

Beaumont, P., Blake, G.H. and Wagstaff, J.M., 1988 *The Middle East: a geographical study*. David Fulton, London.

Berg, W.A., Naney, J.W. and Smith, S.J., 1991 Salinity, nitrate and water quality in rangeland and terraced wheatland above saline seeps. *Journal of Environmental Quality* **20**: 8–11.

Berry, L. and Ford, R.B., 1977 *Recommendations for a system to monitor critical indicators in an area prone to desertification*. Unpublished, Clark University, Massachusetts.

Berry, L., Taurus, T. and Ford, R., 1980 *East African country profiles – Somalia*. Program for International Development, Clark University, Worcester.

Bertrand, M., 1985 *Some reflections on reform of the UN*. Joint Inspection Unit of the UN, Geneva.

Bettenay, E., 1986 Salt affected soils in Australia. *Reclamation and Revegetation Research* **5**: 167–179.

Bhalotra, Y.P.R., 1985 *Rainfall maps of Botswana*. Department of Meteorological Services, Gaborone.

Binns, T., 1990 Is desertification a myth? *Geography* **75**: 106–113.

Biot, Y., 1988 *Forecasting productivity losses caused by sheet and rill erosion. A case study from the communal areas of Botswana*. Unpublished PhD. thesis, University of East Anglia, Norwich.

Biot, Y., 1992 How long can high stocking densities be sustained? In R. Behnke and I. Scoones (eds) *Rethinking range ecology: new directions for range management in Africa.* IIED/ODA, London.

Blake, J.W. (ed) 1941–1942 *Europeans in West Africa 1450-1560.* Hakluyt Society, London.

Blaikie, P., 1985 *The political economy of soil erosion in developing countries.* Longman, Harlow.

Blaikie, P., 1989 Explanation and policy in land degradation and rehabilitation for developing countries. *Land Degradation and Rehabilitation* **1**: 23–37.

Blaikie, P. and Brookfield, H., 1987 *Land degradation and society.* Routledge, London.

Blair Raines, A. and Yalala, A.M., 1972 *The central and southern state lands, Botswana.* Land Resources Study 11. Land Resources Division, Foreign and Commonwealth Office, ODA, London.

Blench, R., 1985 Pastoral labour and stock alienation in the sub-humid and arid zones of West Africa. *Pastoral Network Paper* 19e. ODI, Cambridge.

Bocco, G., 1990 Traditional knowledge for soil conservation in central Mexico. *Journal of Soil and Water Conservation* **46**: 346–348.

Born, M., 1965 Zentralkordofan-Bauern und nomaden in savennengebieten des Sudan. *Marburger Geographische Schriften* **25**.

Bosch, O.J.H., 1989. Degradation of the semi-arid grasslands of southern Africa. *Journal of Arid Environments* **16**: 165–175.

Bourliere, F., 1983 (ed) *Ecosystems of the world 13: Tropical savannas.* Elsevier, Amsterdam.

Bovill, E.W., 1921 The encroachment of the Sahara on the Sudan. *Journal of the Royal African Society* **20**: 175–185, 259–269.

Bovill, E.W., 1929 The Sahara. *Antiquity* **3**: 4–23.

Breman, H. and de Wit, C.T., 1983 Rangeland productivity and exploitation in the Sahel. *Science* **221**: 1341–1347.

Bremaud, O. and Pagot, J., 1968 Grazing lands, nomadism and transhumance in the Sahel. *UNESCO Arid Zone Research* **18**: 311–334.

Brookfield, M., 1970 Dune trends and wind regime in central Australia. *Zeitschrift für Geomorphologie Supplementband* **10**: 121–158.

Brown, J.C., 1875 *Hydrology of South Africa or details of the former hydrological conditions of the Cape of Good Hope and of causes of its present aridity.* Kirkaldy.

Brown, P.L., Halvorson, A.D., Siddoway, F.H., Mayland, F.H. and Miller, M.R., 1983 *Saline seeps diagnosis, control and reclamation.* US Department of Agriculture Conservation Research Report 30.

Brown, R.B. and Wolf, E.C., 1986 *Restoring African soils.* World Watch Paper 65, World Watch, Washington DC.

Brown, R.H., 1948 *Historical geography of the United States.* Harcourt Brace, New York.

Bryson, R.A., 1973 Drought in Sahelia: who or what is to blame? *Ecologist*

3: 336–370.

Bubenzer, G.D. and Weis, G.G., 1974 Effects of wind erosion on production of snap beans and peas. *Journal of the American Society of Horticultural Science* **99**: 527–529.

Buckley, R., 1981 Parallel dunefield ecosystems – southern Kalahari and central Australia. *Journal of Arid Environments* **4**: 287–298.

Canadian International Development Agency, 1985 *Food Crisis in Africa*. CIDA, Hull.

Carapico, S., 1985 Yemeni agriculture in transition. In P. Beaumont and K. McLachlan (eds) *Agricultural development in the Middle East*. Wiley, Chichester: 241–254.

Cardy, F., 1993 *Protect the land that feeds us*. Remarks presented at the opening of the First Substantive Session of the Intergovernmental Committee for the Negotiation of a Convention to Combat Desertification. Nairobi, 24 May, 1993. UNEP, Nairobi.

Charney, J.G., 1975 Dynamics of deserts and drought in the Sahel. *Quarterly Journal of the Royal Meteorological Society* **101**: 193–202.

Charney, J. G., Stone, P.H. and Quirk, W.J., 1975 Drought in the Sahara: a biophysical feedback mechanism. *Science* **187**: 434–435.

Chatterjee, P., 1993 Sands running out – and out. *The Guardian*, London, 12 April: **16**.

Chepil, W.S. and Woodruff, N.P., 1963 The physics of wind erosion and its control. *Advances in Agronomy* **15**: 211–302.

Chepil, W.S., Siddoway, F.H. and Armbrust, D.V., 1963 Climatic index of wind erosion conditions in the Great Plains. *Proceedings of the Soil Science Society of America* **27**: 449–451.

Chile, Government of, 1980 Desertification in the region of Coquinbo, Chile. In UNESCO/UNEP/UNDP *Case studies on desertification*. Natural Resources Research Series XVIII. UNESCO, Paris: 52–114.

Coching, C., 1926 Climatic pulsations during historic times in China. *Geographical Review* **16**: 274–282.

Cooke, H.J., 1983 The struggle against environmental degradation – Botswana's experience. *Desertification Control Bulletin* **8**: 9–15.

Cooke, H.J., 1985 The Kalahari today: a case of conflict over resource use. *Geographical Journal* **151**: 75–85.

Cooke, R.U. and Warren, A., 1973 *Geomorphology in deserts*. Batsford, London.

Cooke, R.U., Warren, A. and Goudie, A.S., 1993. *Desert geomorphology*. UCL Press, London.

Courtant, J.J., 1991 Le Sénégal à l'assaut des forêts de ses voisins. *Club du Sahel, Bulletin de Liason* **10**: 9–10.

Cousins, B., 1987 *A survey of current grazing schemes in the communal lands of Zimbabwe*. Centre for applied Social Science, University of Harare, Zimbabwe.

Crawley, M.J., 1983 *Herbivory, the dynamics of animal-plant interactions.* Blackwell, Oxford.

Cumming, D.H.M., 1982 The influence of large herbivores on savanna structure in Africa. In B.J. Huntley and B.H. Walker (eds) *Ecology of tropical savannas.* Springer-Verlag, New York: 217–245.

Dalsted, K.J., 1988 The use of a Landsat-based soil and vegetation survey and graphic information system to evaluate sites for monitoring desertification. *Desertification Control Bulletin* **16**: 20–26.

Dalsted, K.J., Andrawis, S., Falconi, J., Seefeldt, S., Stewart, C. and Westin, F., 1982 *Resource inventory of southwestern Mauritania.* USAID contract AID/afri-c-1619. Remote Sensing Institute, South Dakota State University, Brookings.

Darkoh, M.B.K., 1986 Combatting desertification in Zimbabwe. *Desertification Control Bulletin* **13**: 17–245.

DECARP, 1976 *Sudan's Desert Encroachment Control and Rehabilitation Programme.* The General Administration for Natural Resources, Ministry of Agriculture, Food and Natural Resources and the Agricultural Research Council, National Council for Research in collaboration with UNEP, UNDP and FAO.

Dhar, O.N., Rakhecha, P.R. and Kulkani, A.K., 1979 Rainfall study of severe drought years in India. In *Proceedings, symposium on the Hydrological Aspects of Droughts.* Indian National Committee for the International Hydrology Programme, New Delhi.

Drabbs, R.J., 1967 *Report to the government of Saudi Arabia on improving range production.* Report TA2397, FAO, Rome.

Drakup, J., Lee K. and Paulson, E., 1980 On the definition of droughts. *Water Resources Research* **16**: 297–302.

Dregne, H.E., 1977 *The status of desertification. World map at a scale of 1:25,000,000.* United Nations UNCOD A/CONF.74/31.

Dregne, H.E., 1983a *Desertification of arid lands.* Harwood Academic Publishers, London.

Dregne, H.E., 1983b *Evaluation of the implementation of the Plan of Action to Combat Desertification.* Unpublished report to UNEP.

Dregne, H.E., 1984 Combating desertification: evaluation of progress. *Environmental Conservation* **11**: 115–121.

Dregne, H.E., 1985 Aridity and land degradation. *Environment* **27**: 16–20, 28–33.

Dregne, H.E., 1987 Reflections of the PACD. *Desertification Control Bulletin* **15**: 8–11.

Dregne, H.E., 1989 Informed opinion: filling the soil erosion data gap. *Journal of Soil and Water Conservation* **44**: 303–305.

Dregne, H.E., 1992 Erosion and soil productivity in Asia. *Journal of Soil and Water Conservation* **47**: 8–13.

Dregne, H.E., Kassas, M. and Rozanov, B. 1991 A new assessment of the world status of desertification. *Desertification Control Bulletin* **19**: 6–18.

Dregne, H.E. and Tucker, C.J., 1988 Desert encroachment. *Desertification Control Bulletin* **16**: 16–19.

Dresch, J., 1986 Degradation of natural ecosystems in the countries of the Maghreb as a result of human impact. In USSR Commission for UNEP *Arid land development and the combat against desertification*, UNEP, Moscow: 65–67.

Druyan, L.M. and Hastenrath, S., 1991 Modelling the differential impact of 1984 and 1950 sea-surface temperatures on Sahel rainfall. *International Journal of Climatology* **11**: 367–380.

Dutton, R.W., 1983 Introduction, overview and conclusions. In the scientific results of the Royal Geographical Society's Oman Wahiba Sands Project. *Journal of Oman Studies*, special report **3**: 1–17.

Eckholm, E.P., 1976 Two costly lessons: the Dust Bowl and the Virgin Lands. In E.P. Eckholm (ed) *Losing ground*. Pergamon, Oxford: 46–57.

Eckholm, E.P., Foley, G., Barnard, G. and Timberlake, L., 1984 *Fuelwood: the energy crisis that won't go away*. Earthscan, London.

Eiker, C.K., 1986 Transforming African Agriculture. *The Hague Project Papers* 4. The Hague Project, San Francisco.

El-Hinnawi, E. and Hashmi, M., 1982 *Global environmental issues*. UNEP/Tycooly, Dublin.

Elwell, H.A. and Stocking, M.A., 1982 Developing a simple, yet effective method of soil loss estimation. *Tropical Agriculture* **59**: 43–48.

Evenari, M., Shanan, L. and Tadmor, N., 1971 *The Negev: the challenge of a desert*. Harvard University Press, Cambridge, Massachusetts.

Fage, J.D. and Verity, M., 1978 *An atlas of African history*. 2nd edition. Edward Arnold, London.

Fantechi, R. and Margaris, N.S. (eds) 1986 *Desertification in Europe*. D. Reidel, Dordrecht.

FAO, 1979 *A provisional methodology for soil degradation assessment*. FAO, Rome.

FAO, 1988 *Inventory and monitoring of Sahelian pastoral ecosystems. Senegal*. GEMS Sahel Series Technical Report AG:EP/SEN/001. FAO, Rome.

FAO, UNESCO and WMO, 1977a *World map of desertification at a scale of 1:25,000,000. Explanatory note*. UN Conference on Desertification, A/CONF. 74/2, UN, New York.

FAO, UNESCO and WMO, 1977b *Status of desertification in the hot arid regions, climatic aridity index map and experimental world scheme of aridity and drought probability, at a scale of 1:25,000,000. Explanatory note*. UN Conference on Desertification, A/CONF. 74/31, UN New York.

FAO/UNEP, 1977 *Map of desertification hazards, explanatory note*. FAO, Rome.

FAO/UNEP, 1984 *Provisional methodology for assessment and mapping of desertification*. FAO, Rome.

Field, D.I., 1977 *Potential carrying capacity of rangeland in Botswana*. Unpublished report. Land Utilisation Division, Ministry of Agriculture, Gaborone.

Field, D.I., 1978 *A handbook of basic ecology for range management in Botswana*. Unpublished report. Land Utilisation Division, Ministry of Agriculture, Gaborone.

Floor, W. and Gorse, J., 1988 Household energy issues in West Africa. In *Desertification control and renewable resource management in the Sahelian and Sudanian zones of West Africa*. World Bank Technical Paper **70**: 72–98.

Folland, C.K., Owen, J.A., Ward, M.N. and Colman, A.W., 1991 Prediction of seasonal rainfall in the Sahel using empirical and dynamical methods. *Journal of Forecasting* **10**: 21–56.

Forse, B., 1989 The myth of the advancing desert. *New Scientist*, February: 31–32.

Franke, R. and Chasin, B.H., 1981 Peanuts, peasants, profits and pastoralists. *The Ecologist* **11**: 156–168.

Frost, P.G.H. and Robertson, F., 1987 The ecological effects of fires in savannas. In B.H. Walker (ed) *Determinants of tropical savannas. IUBS Monograph Series* **3**. IUBS, Paris: 93–140.

Fryrear, D.W., 1981 Long-term effect of erosion and cropping on soil productivity. In T.L. Péwé (ed) *Desert dust: origins, characteristics and effects on man*. Geological Society of America Special Paper **186**: 253–259.

Fryrear, D.W., Stubbendieck, J. and McCully, W.G., 1973 Grass seedling response to wind and windblown sand. *Crop Science* 113: 622–625.

Ganji, M.R. and Farzaneh, A., 1990 Desertification and its control in Islamic Republic of Iran. In *Desertification revisited: proceedings of an ad hoc consultative meeting on the assessment of desertification*. UNEP DC/PAC, Nairobi: 319–326.

Garduno, M.A., 1977 Technology and desertification. In UN, 1977b: 319–448.

George, S. 1988 *A fate worse than debt*. Penguin, London.

Georgiadis, N.J., Ruess, R.W., McNaughton, S.J. and Western, D., 1989 Ecological conditions that determine when grazing stimulates grass production. *Oecologia* **81**: 316–322.

Gigengack, A.R., Jepma, C.J., MacRae, D. and Poldy, F., 1990 Global modelling of dryland degradation. In J. A. Dixon, D.E. James and P.B. Sherman (eds) *Dryland management: economic case studies*. Earthscan, London: 330–349.

Girard, M-C. and Isavwa, L.A., 1990 Remote sensing of arid and semi-arid regions: the state of the art. *Desertification Control Bulletin* **18**: 13–18.

Glantz, M.H., 1977 Water and inappropriate technology: deep wells in the Sahel. In V.P. Nanda (ed) *Water needs for the future*. Westview

Press, Boulder: 305–318.

Glantz, M.H., 1989 Drought, famine and the seasons in sub-Saharan Africa. In R. Huss-Ashmore and S.H. Katz (eds) *African food systems in crisis. Part one: micro perspectives.* Gordon and Breach, New York: 45–71.

Glantz, M.H. and Orlovsky, N., 1983 Desertification: a review of the concept. *Desertification Control Bulletin* 9: 15–22.

Goldschmidt, W., 1981 The failure of pastoral development projects in Africa. In J.G. Galaty, D. Aronson, P.C. Saltzman and A. Chouinard, (eds) *The future of nomadic peoples.* International Development Research Centre, Ottawa.

Goldsmith, E. and Hildyard, N., 1988 *The earth report.* Mitchell Beazley, London.

Goudie, A.S., 1972 *The concept of post-glacial progressive desiccation.* School of Geography, University of Oxford, Research Paper 4.

Goudie, A.S., 1981 *The human impact: mans role in environmental change.* Blackwell, Oxford.

Goudie, A.S., 1990 Desert degradation. In A.S. Goudie (ed) *Techniques for desert reclamation.* John Wiley, London: 1–33.

Grainger, A., 1982 *Desertification: how people make deserts, how people can stop and why they don't.* Earthscan, London.

Grainger, A., 1990 *The threatening desert.* Earthscan, London.

Grove, A.T., 1977 Desertification. *Progress in Physical Geography* 1: 296–310.

Grove, A.T., 1986 The scale factor in relation to the processes involved in 'desertification' in Europe. In R. Fantechi and N.S. Margaris (eds) *Desertification in Europe.* D. Reidel, Dordrecht: 9–14.

Guyot, L., 1990 Development of a new method for assessment and monitoring of desertification in Sahelian and Sudanian regions (1957-1987): presentation of the results obtained on the first transect: Mauritania–Mali. In *Desertification revisited: proceedings of an ad hoc consultative meeting on the assessment of desertification.* UNEP DC/PAC, Nairobi: 295–297.

Hadley, R.F., 1977 Evaluation of land-use and land-treatment practices in semi-arid western United States. *Philosophical Transactions, Royal Society of London* B278: 543–554.

Hanan, N.P., Prevost, Y., Diouf, A. and Diallo, O., 1991 Assessment of desertification around deep wells in the Sahel using satellite imagery. *Journal of Applied Ecology* 28: 173–186.

Hancock, G., 1989 *Lords of poverty.* Macmillan, London.

Harden, D., 1963 *The phoenicians.* Fredrick A. Praeger, New York.

Hardin, G., 1968 The tragedy of the commons. *Science* 162: 1243–1248.

Hare, F.K., 1977 Climate and desertification. In UN, 1977b: 63–167.

Hare, F.K., 1984 Recent climatic experience in the arid and semi-arid lands. *Desertification Control Bulletin* **10**: 15–22.

Hare, F.K., 1987 Drought and desiccation: twin hazards in a variable climate. In D. Wilhite and W. Easterby (eds) *Planning for drought.* Westview Press, London: 3–10.

Harris, D.R., 1966 Recent plant invasions in the arid and semi-arid southwest of the United States. *Annals of the Association of American Geographers* **56**: 408–422.

Harrison, M.N. and Jackson, J.K., 1958 Ecological classification of the vegetation of Sudan. *Forests Bulletin* **2**, Khartoum, and the *Vegetation Map of Sudan.* Sudan Survey Department, Khartoum, Topo No S: 625–40.

Heathcote, R.L., 1983 *The arid lands: their use and abuse.* Longman, Harlow.

Hedin, S., 1940 *The wandering lake.* Routledge, New York.

Hellden, U., 1984 Drought impact monitoring – a remote sensing study of desertification in Kordofan, Sudan. *Rapporter och Notiser* 61. Lund Universitetes Natugeografiska instituten.

Hellden, U., 1988 Desertification monitoring: is the desert encroaching? *Desertification Control Bulletin,* 17: 8–12.

Hellden, U., 1991 Desertification – time for an assessment? *Ambio* **20**, 372–383.

Hiernaux, P. and Diarra, L., 1986 Savanna burning, a controversial technique for rangeland management in the Niger floodplains of central Mali. *Proceedings, Second International rangeland Congress, Australia.* Cambridge University Press, Cambridge: 238–243.

Hillel, D., 1982 (ed) *Advances in irrigation.* Academic Press, London.

Hogg, R., 1987 Development in Kenya: drought, desertification and food scarcity. *African Affairs* **86**: 47–58.

Horowitz, M.M., 1979 *The sociology of pastoralism and African livestock projects.* USAID Discussion Paper 6. USAID, Washington.

Hubert, H., 1920 Le désséchement progressive en Afrique Occidentale française. *Bulletin Comité d'études Historiques et Scientifiques de l'Afrique Occidentale Française,* 1920: 401–437.

Hulme, M., 1987 Rainfall in central Sudan: an asset or a liability? *Geoforum* **18**: 321–331.

Hulme, M., 1989 Is environmental degradation causing drought in the Sahel? An assessment from recent empirical research. *Geography* **74**: 38–46.

Hulme, M., 1992 Rainfall changes in Africa: 1931-60 to 1961-90. *International Journal of Climatology* **12**: 685–699.

Hulme, M. and Marsh, R., 1990 *Global mean monthly humidity surfaces, for 1930-59, 1960-89 and projected for 2030.* Report to UNEP/GEMS/GRID. Climatic Research Unit, University of East Anglia, Norwich.

Huntington, E., 1907 *The pulse of Asia.* Constable, London.

IADIZA (Instituto Argentino de Investigaciones de las Zonas Aridas),

1992 Desertification hazard mapping of central-western Argentina. In UNEP *World Atlas of desertification*. Edward Arnold, Sevenoaks: 50–53.

IGAAD (Intergovernmental Authority on Drought and Development), 1990 *Forum on environmental protection and development of subregional strategy to combat desertification*. IGAAD/NORAGRIC.

IGN France (Institut géographique National) 1992 Mali: a methodology for the assessment of desertification south of the Sahara. In UNEP *World atlas of desertification*. Edward Arnold, Sevenoaks: 62–65

Ilaiwi, M., Jabour, E. and Abdelgawad, G., 1992 Syria: human-induced soil degradation. In UNEP *World atlas of desertification*. Edward Arnold, Sevenoaks: 42–45.

Ingram, J., 1991 Soil and water processes. In I. Scoones (ed) *Wetlands in drylands: the agroecology of savanna systems in Africa*. IIED, London.

IPCC, 1991 *Climate change: the IPCC response strategies*. IPCC Working Group III. UNEP/WMO.

Iraq, Government of, 1980 Desertification in the Greater Mussayeb Project, Iraq. In UNESCO/UNEP/UNDP *Case studies on desertification*. Natural Resources Research series XVIII. UNESCO, Paris: 176–213

ISRIC, 1988 *Guidelines for general assessment of the status of human-induced soil degradation*. Working Paper and Preprint 88/4. ISRIC, Wageningen.

Issar, A. and Tsoar, H., 1987 Who is to blame for the desertification of the Negev, Israel? In *The influence of climate change and climatic variability on the hydrologic regime and water resources*. Proceeding of the Vancouver Symposium. IAHS Publication No. 168: 577–583.

IUCN, 1989 *The IUCN Sahel studies*. IUCN, Nairobi.

Jacks, G.V. and Whyte, R.O., 1939 *The rape of the earth: a world survey of soil erosion*. Faber and Faber, London.

Jacobsen, T. and Adams, R.M., 1958 Salt and silt in ancient Mesopotamian agriculture. *Science* **128**: 1251–1258.

Jahnke, H.E., 1982 *Livestock production systems and livestock development in tropical Africa*. Kieler Wissenschaftsverlag Vauk.

Jodha, N., 1987 A case study of the degradation of common property resources in India. In P.M. Blaikie and H. Brookfield, *Land degradation and society*. Routledge, London: 196–207.

Jones, B., 1938 Desiccation and the West African colonies. *Geographical Journal* **91**: 401–423.

Jordan, Government of, 1988 *National Plan of Action to Combat Desertification*. Jordan.

Justice, C.O., Townshend, J.R.G., Holben, B.N. and Tucker, C.J., 1985 Analysis of the phenology of global vegetation using meteorological satellite data. *International Journal of Remote Sensing* **6**: 1271–1318.

Kassas, M., 1987 Seven paths to desertification. *Desertification Control Bulletin* **15**: 24–26.

Kassas, M., Ahmad, Y.J. and Rozanov, B., 1991 Desertification and drought: an ecological and economic analysis. *Desertification Control Bulletin* **20**: 19–29.

Kates, R.W., Johnson, D.L. and Johnson Haring, K., 1977 Population, society and desertification. In UN, 1977b: 261–317.

Kaushalya, R., 1992 Monitoring the impact of desertification in western Rajasthan using remote sensing. *Journal of Arid Environments* **22**: 293–304.

Kaya, G.A., 1991 Alternative policies and models for arid and semi-arid lands in Kenya. In P.T.W. Baxter (ed) *When the grass is gone: development interactions in African arid lands.* Scandinavian Institute of African Studies, Uppsala: 73–89.

Keller, E.J., 1992 Drought, war, and the politics of famine in Ethiopia and Eritrea. *Journal of Modern African Studies* **30**: 609–624.

Kemp, R., 1991 *Global environmental issues: a climatological approach.* Routledge, London.

Kenworthy, J., 1990 The recognition and interpretation of recurrent drought in Africa. In G.J. Stone (ed) *Pastoralists responses to drought.* Aberdeen University Press, Aberdeen.

Khalaf, F.I., 1989 Desertification and aeolian processes in Kuwait. *Journal of Arid Environments* **12**: 125–145.

Kharin, N.G., 1990 Recommendations on application in the Sahelian zone of the FAO/UNEP provisional methodology for desertification assessment and mapping. In *Desertification revisited: proceedings of an ad hoc consultative meeting on the assessment of desertification.* UNEP DC/PAC, Nairobi: 179–238.

Khogali, M.M., 1983 The grazing resources of the Sudan. In Ooi Jin Bee (ed) *Natural resources in tropical countries.* Singapore University Press, Singapore: 326–345.

Knapp, G. and Canada Cruz, L., 1988 Introduction: vulnerability to climatic variations. In M.L. Parry, T. R. Carter and N.T. Konijn (eds) *The impact of climatic variations on agriculture* (Part IV: The effects of climatic variations on agriculture in the Central Sierra of Ecuador). Kluwer, Dordrecht: 389–398.

Kokot, D.F., 1955 Desert encroachment in South Africa. *African Soils* **3**: 404–409.

Kolawole, A., 1987 Environmental change and the South Chad Irrigation Project. *Journal of Arid Environments* **13**: 169–176.

Kotlyakov, V.M., 1991 The Aral Sea basin. *Environment* **33**: 4–9, 36–38.

Kovda, V.A., 1980 *The problem of combatting salinization of irrigated soils.* UNEP, Nairobi.

Kropotkin, P., 1904 The desiccation of Eur-Asia. *Geographical Journal* **23**: 722–741.

Lal, R., 1984 Soil erosion from tropical arable lands and its control.

Advances in Agronomy **37**: 183–248.

Lal, R., 1988 Soil degradation and the future of agriculture in sub-Saharan Africa. *Journal of Soil and Water Conservation* **43**: 444–451.

Lamb, H.H., 1974 The earth's changing climate. *Ecologist* **4**: 10–15.

Lamprey, H.F., 1975 *Report on the desert encroachment reconnaissance in northern Sudan, October 21–November 10, 1975.* National Council for Research, Ministry of Agriculture, Food and Resources, Khartoum. (Reproduced in *Desertification Control Bulletin*, 17 [1988]: 1–7).

Lamprey, H.F., 1983 Pastoralism yesterday and today: the overgrazing problem. In F. Bouliere (ed) *Ecosystems of the world. 13. Tropical savannas.* Elsevier, Amsterdam.

Lange, R.T., 1969 The piosphere: sheep track and dung patterns. *Journal of Range Management* **22**: 396–400.

Laprade, K.E., 1957 Dust storm sediments of Lubbock area, Texas. *Bulletin of the American Association of Petroleum Geologists* **41**: 709–726.

Larson, W.E., Pierce, F.J. and Dowdy, R.H., 1983 The threat of soil erosion to long-term crop production. *Science* **219**: 458–465.

Laval, K., 1986 General circulation model experiments with surface albedo changes. *Climatic Change* **9**: 91–102.

Laweson, J., 1991 *Aspects of woody vegetation in Sahel.* Unpublished report to the SAREC workshop on the 'Impact of grazing on savanna ecosystems'.

Leach, G. and Mearns, R., 1988 *Bioenergy issues and options for Africa.* Report to the Norwegian Ministry of Development Cooperation. International Institute for Environment and Development, London.

Lee, F.A and Brooks, H.C., 1977 *The economic and political development of Sudan.* Westview Press, Boulder.

Legesse, A., 1989 Adaptation, drought and development: Baran and Gabra pastoralists of northern Kenya. In R. Huss-Ashmore and S.H. Katz (eds) *African food systems in crisis. Part one: microperspectives.* Gordon and Breach, New York: 261–279.

Le Houérou, H.N., 1968 La désertification du Sahara septentrional et des steppes limitrophes. *Annales Algériennes de Géographie* **6**: 2–27.

Le Houérou, H.N. and Grenot, C.J., 1986 The grazing lands ecosystems of the African Sahel: state of knowledge. In R.T. Coupland (ed) *Ecosystems of the world. Vol. 8: Natural grasslands.* Elsevier, Amsterdam.

Lewin, R., 1986 In ecology, change brings stability. *Science* **234**: 1071–1073.

Lewis, L.A. and Berry, L., 1988 *African environments and resources.* Unwin Hyman, Winchester, MA.

Lindsay, J.A. and Vogel, C.H., 1990 Historical evidence for Southern Oscillation – Southern African rainfall relationships. *International Journal of Climatology* **10**: 679–689.

Livingstone, D., 1857 *Missionary travels and researches in South Africa.* J. Murray, London.

Livingstone, I., 1977 Economic irrationality among pastoral peoples: myth or reality. *Development and change* **8**: 209–230.

Livingstone, I., 1991 Livestock management and 'overgrazing' among pastoralists. *Ambio* **20**: 80–85.

Lockeretz, W., 1978 The lessons of the dust bowl. *American Scientist* **66**: 560–569.

Lockwood, J.G., 1988. Climate and climatic variability in semi-arid regions at low altitudes. In M.L. Parry, T.R. Carter and N.T. Konijn (eds) *The impact of climatic variations on agriculture (Part I The impact of climatic variations on agriculture: introduction to the IIASA/UNEP case studies in semi-arid regions)*. Kluwer, Dordrecht: 85–120.

Lowdermilk, W.C., 1935 Man-made deserts. *Pacific Affairs* (University of British Columbia) **8**: 409–419.

Lyles, L., 1977 Wind erosion: processes and effect on soil productivity. *Transactions of the American Society of Agricultural Engineers* **20**: 880–884.

Mabbutt, J.A., 1978 The impact of desertification as revealed by mapping. *Environmental Conservation* **5**: 45–56.

Mabbutt, J.A., 1984 A new global assessment of the status and trends of desertification. *Environmental Conservation* **11**: 103–113.

Mabbutt, J.A., 1985 Desertification of the world's rangelands. *Desertification Control Bulletin* **12**: 1–11.

Mabbutt, J.A., 1986 Desertification indicators. *Climatic Change* **9**: 113–122.

Mabbutt, J.A., 1987a A review of progress since the UN Conference on Desertification. *Desertification Control Bulletin* **15**: 12–23.

Mabbutt, J.A., 1987b Implementation of the Plan of Action to Combat Desertification. *Land Use Policy* **4**: 371–388.

Mabbutt, J.A., 1989 Desertification: the public record. In R. Huss Ashmore and S.H. Katz (eds) *African food systems in crisis. Part one: microperspectives*. Gordon and Breach, New York: 73–109.

Mabbutt, J.A. and Floret, C., 1983 *Etudes de cas sur la désertification*. Natural Resources Research XVIII. UNESCO, Paris.

McCabe, J.T., 1990 Turkana pastoralism: a case against the tragedy of the commons. *Human Ecology* **18**: 81–103.

McCauley, J.F., Breed, C.S., Grolier, M.J. and Mackinnon, D.J., 1981 The US dust storm of February 1977. In T.L. Péwé (ed) *Desert dust: origins, characteristics and effects on man*. Geological Society of America Special Paper **186**: 123–147.

McNaughton, S.J., 1976 Serengeti migratory wildebeest: facilitation of energy flow by grazing. *Science* **191**: 92–94.

Macdonald, W., 1914 *The conquest of the desert*. Laurie, London.

Mace, R., 1991 Overgrazing overstated. *Nature* **349**: 280–281.

MacMichael, H.A., 1911 The Kheiran. *Sudan Notes and Records*, III(4).

Mainguet, M., 1991 *Desertification. Natural background and human mismanagement*. Springer-Verlag, Berlin.

Malcolm, C.V., 1983 Wheatbelt salinity, a review of the salt land problem in southwestern Australia. *Western Australia Department of Agriculture Technical Bulletin* **52**.

Mali, Republic of, 1987 *National programme to combat desertification.* Ministry of Natural Resources and Livestock, Republic of Mali.

Mauritania, Islamic Republic of, 1986 Master plan to combat desertification. *National plan of action to combat desertification, Volume I.* Department for Protection of Nature, Islamic Republic of Mauritania.

Meigs, P., 1953 World distribution of arid and semi-arid homoclimates. *Arid zone hydrology.* UNESCO Arid Zone Research Series **1**: 203–209.

Mendoza, M., 1990 Global assessment of desertification: world atlas of thematic indicators of desertification: proposal document. In *Desertification revisited: proceedings of an ad hoc consultative meeting on the assessment of desertification.* UNEP DC/PAC, Nairobi: 289–294.

Meyer, J.F., 1980 Etude des systèmes de production d'élevage au Sénégal; volet zoo-économie, 1ère année. IEMVT, Paris.

Middleton, N.J., 1985 Effect of drought on dust production in the Sahel. *Nature* **316**: 431–434.

Middleton, N.J., 1990 Wind erosion and dust-storm control. In A.S. Goudie (ed) *Techniques for desert reclamation.* Wiley, Chichester: 87–108.

Middleton, N.J., 1991a *Desertification.* Oxford University Press, Oxford.

Middleton, N.J., 1991b Dust storms in the Mongolian People's Republic. *Journal of Arid Environments* **20**: 287–297.

Middleton, N.J., 1993 *Mongolia: restructuring for a market economy.* Industrial development review series. UN Industrial Development Organisation, Vienna.

Middleton, N.J. and Thomas, D.S.G., 1992 *World atlas of desertification.* Edward Arnold/UNEP, Sevenoaks.

Millington, A.C., Mutiso, S.K., Kirby, J. and O'Keefe, P., 1989 African soil erosion – nature undone and the limits of technology. *Land Degradation and Rehabilitation* **1**: 279–290.

Moore, P.D., 1987 Mobile resources for survival. *Nature* **325**: 198.

Moore, R.M., 1959 Ecological observations on plant communities grazed by sheep in Australia. In A. Keast, R.L. Crocker and C.S. Christian (eds) *Biogeography and ecology in Australia.* Junk, The Hague: 500–513.

Mortimer, M., 1988 Desertification and resilience in semi-arid West Africa. *Geography* **73**: 61–64.

Mortimore, M., 1987 Shifting sands and human sorrow: social response to drought and desertification. *Desertification Control Bulletin* **14**: 1–14.

Mortimore, M., 1989 *Adapting to drought, farmers, famines and desertification in West Africa.* Cambridge University Press, Cambridge.

Mukinya, J., 1990 Kenya: environment and national efforts. In IGAAD *Forum on environmental protection and development of subregional strategy to combat desertification. Volume II Country reports.* IGAAD/NORA-

GRIC: 196–279.

National Research Council, 1981 *Environmental degradation in Mauritania*. Board on Science and Technology for International Development. National Academy Press, Washington DC, USA.

National Research Council, 1983 *Environmental change in the West African Sahel*. Board on Science and Technology for International Development. National Academy Press, Washington DC, USA.

Nechaeva, N.T., 1979 Effect of the management regime on the vegetation productivity in the Kara Kum. *Problems of Desert Development* **6**: 8–18.

Nelson, R., 1988 Dryland management: the 'desertification' problem. *Environment Department Working Paper* 8. World Bank, Washington.

Newcombe, K., 1984 *An economic justification for rural afforestation: the case of Ethiopia*. World Bank, Energy Department Paper 16, World Bank, Washington.

Nicholson, S.E., 1980 The nature of rainfall fluctuations in sub-tropical west Africa. *Monthly Weather Review* **108**: 473–478.

Nicholson, S.E., 1981 Rainfall and atmospheric circulation during drought periods and wetter years in west Africa. *Monthly Weather Review* **109**: 2191–2208.

Nicholson, S.E., 1989 Long term changes in African rainfall. *Weather* **44**: 46–56.

Nobre, C.A. and Molion, L.C.B., 1988 The climatology of droughts and drought prediction. In M.L. Parry, T.R. Carter and N.T. Konijn (eds) *The impact of climatic variations on agriculture. Part 3. The effects of climatic variations on agriculture in Northeast Brazil*. Kluwer, Dordrecht: 305–323.

Norton-Griffiths, M., 1989 *Food and agricultural production*. IUCN Sahel Studies, Nairobi: 53–82.

Noy-Meir, I., 1982 Stability of plant-herbivore models and possible application to savanna. In B.J. Huntley and B.H. Walker (eds) *Ecology of tropical savannas*. Springer-Verlag, Berlin.

Odingo, R.S., 1990a The definition of desertification and its programmatic consequences for UNEP and the international community. *Desertification Control Bulletin* **18**: 31–50.

Odingo, R.S., 1990b Review of UNEP's definition of desertification and its programmatic implications. In R.S. Odingo (ed) *Desertification revisited, proceedings of an ad hoc consultative meeting on the assessment of desertification*. UNEP-DC/PAC, Nairobi: 7–44.

O'Hara, S.L., Street-Perrot, F.A. and Burt, T.P., 1993 Accelerated soil erosion around a Mexican highland lake caused by prehispanic agriculture. *Nature* **362**: 48–51.

Oldeman, L.R. (ed) 1988 *Guidelines for general assessment of the status of human-induced soil degradation*. Working Paper and Preprint 88/4. ISRIC, Wageningen.

Oldeman, L.R., Hakkeling, R.T.A and Sombroek, W.G., 1990 *World map* of the status of human-induced soil degradation. An explanatory note. ISRIC/UNEP, Wageningen.

Olsson, K., 1984 Long term changes in the woody vegetation in N. Kordofan, the Sudan. Rapporter och Notiser 60. Department of Physical Geography, University of Lund, Sweden.

Olsson, K., 1985 Remote Sensing for Fuelwood Resources and Land Degradation Studies in Kordofan, the Sudan. Doctoral thesis, Meddelanden Fran Lunds Universitets Geografiska Institution Avhandlingar No C.

Olsson, L., 1983 Desertification or climate? Investigation regarding the relationship between land degradation and climate in the central Sudan. Lund series in Geography series A, 60.

Omara-Ojungu, P.H., 1992 Resource management in developing countries. Longman, Harlow.

Orgut, A., 1983 Supply of charcoal and fuelwood to urban centres. National Range Agency, Somali Democratic Republic, Mogadishu.

Palutikof, J.P., Farmer, G. and Wigley, T.M.L., 1982 Strategies for the amelioration of agricultural drought in Africa. Proceedings of the Technical Conference on the Climate of Africa. WMO, Geneva: 222–248.

Parry, M.L., 1990 Climatic variability and agriculture. Earthscan, London.

Parry, M.L. and Carter, T.R., 1988 The assessment of effects of climatic variation on agriculture. A summary of results from studies in semi-arid regions. In M.L. Parry, T.L. Carter and N.T. Konijn (eds) The impact of climatic variations on agriculture. Volume 2. Assessments in semi-arid regions. Kluwer, Dordrecht: 9–60.

Paylore, P., 1976 Desertification; a world bibliography. Office of Arid Lands Studies, Tuscon.

Pearce, D., 1993 Economic values and the natural world. Earthscan, London.

Pearce, F., 1992 Few grains of truth in the shifting sands. The Independent on Sunday, London, 26 April: 48–49.

Perkins, J.S., 1990 Drought, cattle-keeping and range degradation in the Kalahari, Botswana. In G.J. Stone (ed) Pastoralists responses to drought. Aberdeen University Press, Aberdeen.

Perkins, J.S., 1991 The impact of borehole dependent cattle grazing on the environment and society of the eastern Kalahari sandveld, Central District, Botswana. Unpublished PhD thesis, University of Sheffield.

Perkins, J.S. and Thomas, D.S.G., 1993 Environmental responses and sensitivity to permanent cattle ranching, semi-arid western central Botswana. In D.S.G. Thomas and R.J. Allison (eds) Landscape sensitivity. John Wiley and Sons, Chichester: 273–286.

Perrier, G., 1986 Limiting livestock pressure on public rangeland in Niger. Pastoral Development Network paper 21d, ODI, London.

Peters, P., 1987 Embedded systems and rooted models. In B. McCay and J. Acheson (eds) The question of the commons. University of Arizona Press, Tuscon.

Picardi, A. and Siefert, W., 1976 A tragedy of the commons in the Sahel. *Technology Review* **78**: 42–51.

Pickup, G. and Chewings, V.H., 1988 Soil erosion in arid lands from Landsat MSS data. *International Journal of Remote Sensing* **9**: 1469–1490.

Prince, S.D., Justice, C.O. and Los, S.O., 1990 *Remote sensing of the Sahelian environment: a review of the current status and future prospects.* Technical Centre for Agricultural and Rural Cooperation, ACP/CEE Lomé Convention, EC, Brussels.

Purvis, J.C., 1977 *Satellite photos help in dust episode in South Carolina.* Information Note 77/8. US National Weather Service. Natural Environment Satellite Service, Satellite Applications.

Rapp, A., 1974 *A review of desertization in Africa - water, vegetation and man.* Secretariat for International Ecology, Stockholm.

Rapp, A., 1976 Sudan. In A. Rapp, H.N. Le Houérou and B. Lundholm (eds) Can desert encroachment be stopped? A study with emphasis on Africa. *Ecological Bulletin* **24**. Swedish Natural Science Research Council, Stockholm.

Rapp, A., Le Houérou, H.N. and Lundholm, B., 1976 Can desert encroachment be stopped? A study with emphasis on Africa. *Ecological Bulletin* **24**. Swedish Natural Science Research Council, Stockholm.

Rasool, S.I., 1984 On dynamics of desert and climate. In J.T. Houghton (ed) *The global climate.* Cambridge University Press, Cambridge: 107–120.

Renner, G.T., 1926 A famine zone on Africa: the Sudan. *Geographical Review* **16**: 583–596.

Richardson, E.R., 1984 *Evaluation of institutional and financial arrangements.* Unpublished report for UNEP.

Riebsame, W.E., 1986 The dust bowl: historical image, psychological and ecological taboo. *Great Plains Quarterly* **6**: 127–136.

Riley, J., 1817 *Sufferings in Africa: Captain Riley's narrative.* Reprinted 1965. Clarkson N. Potter, New York.

Ringrose, S., Matheson, W., Tempest, F. and Boyle, T., 1990 The development and causes of range degradation features in southeast Botswana using multi-temporal Landsat MSS imagery. *Photogrammetric Engineering and Remote Sensing* **56**: 1253–1262.

Roose, E., 1988 Soil and water conservation lessons from steep slope farming in French speaking countries in Africa. In W.C. Moldenhauer and N.W. Hudson (eds) *Conservation farming on steep lands.* Soil and Water Conservation Society, Ankeny, Iowa: 129–139.

Rotmans, J. and Den Elzen, M.G.J., 1992 A model-based approach to the calculation of global warming potentials (GWP). *International Journal of Climatology* **12**: 865–874.

Roux, P.W. and Vorster, M., 1983 Vegetation change in the Karoo.

Proceedings of the Grassland Society of Southern Africa **18**: 25–29.

Rovere, O. and Knapp, G., 1988 Selection of the climatic scenarios. In M.L. Parry, T.R. Carter and N.T. Konijn (eds) *The impact of climatic variations on agriculture (Part IV: The effects of climatic variations on agriculture in the Central Sierra of Ecuador).* Kluwer, Dordrecht: 399–412.

Rowntree, P., 1988 Review of general circulation models as a basis for predicting the effects of vegetation change on climate. *Proceedings, United Nations University workshop on forest, climate and hydrology.* UNU, Tokyo.

Rozanov, B.G., 1990 Global assessment of desertification: status and methodologies. In *Desertification revisited: Proceedings of an ad hoc consultative meeting on the assessment of desertification.* UNEP-DC/PAC, Nairobi: 45–122.

Rozanov, B.G., Targulian, V.O. and Orlov, D.S., 1989 Global trends in soil changes. *Pochvovedenie* **5**: 5–18.

Sabadell, J.E., Risley, E.P., Jorgenson, H.T. and Thornton, B.S., 1982 *Desertification in the United States.* Department of the Interior, Bureau of Land Management, Washington DC.

SADCC, 1986 *Land degradation and desertification control in the SADCC region.* Soil and Water Conservation and Land Utilization Programme Report 5. SADCC, Maseru.

SADCC, 1990 *Plan of Action for the Kalahari–Namib region.* Soil and Water Conservation and Land Utilization Unit, SADCC, Maseru.

Salih, M.A.M., 1991 Livestock development or pastoral development? In P.T.W. Baxter (ed) *When the grass is gone: development interactions in African arid lands.* Scandinavian Institute of African Studies, Uppsala: 37–57.

Sandford, S., 1977 *Dealing with drought and livestock in Botswana.* ODI, London.

Sandford, S., 1982 Pastoral strategies and desertification: opportunism and conservation in dry lands. In B. Spooner and H.S. Mann (eds) *Desertification and development: dryland ecology in social perspective.* Academic Press, London: 61–80.

Sandford, S., 1983 *Management of pastoral development in the third world.* ODI and John Wiley, London.

Schulz, A., 1982 Reorganizing deserts: mechanisation and marginal lands in southwest Asia. In B. Spooner and H.S. Mann (eds) *Desertification and development: dryland ecology in social perspective.* Academic Press, London: 27–41

Schwarz, E.H.L., 1919 The progressive desiccation of Africa: the cause and the remedy. *South African Journal of Science* **15**: 139–190.

Schwarz, E.H.L., 1923 *The Kalahari or thirstland redemption.* Masker Miller, Cape Town.

Scoging, H., 1991 Desertification and its management. In R. Bennet and

R.Estall (eds) *Global change and challenge. Geography for the 1990s.* Routledge, London: 57–79.

Scoones, I., 1989 *Economic and ecological carrying capacity: implications for livestock development in the dryland communal areas of Zimbabwe.* ODI Pastoral Network Paper 27b. London.

Scoones, I., 1992 Land degradation and livestock production in Zimbabwe's Communal Areas. *Land Degradation and Rehabilitation* **3**: 99–114.

Sen, A., 1981 *Poverty and famines: an essay on entitlement.* Clarendon Press, Oxford.

Sheridan, D., 1981 *Desertification in the United States.* Council for Environmental Quality, Washington.

Skarpe, C., 1986 Plant community structure in relation to grazing and environmental changes along a north-south transect in the western Kalahari. *Vegetatio* **68**: 3–18.

Skarpe, C., 1990 Shrub layer dynamics under different herbivore densities in an arid savanna, Botswana. *Journal of Applied Ecology* **27**: 873–885.

Skarpe, C., 1991 Impact of grazing in savanna ecosystems. *Ambio* **20**: 351–356.

Skarpe, C. and Bergstrom, R., 1986 Nutrient content and digestability of forage plants in relation to plant phenology and rainfall in the Kalahari, Botswana. *Journal of Arid Environments* **11**: 147–164.

Smith, S.E., 1986 Drought and water management: the Egyptian response. *Journal of Soil and Water Conservation* **41**: 297–300.

Spangler, S. 1991 verbatim quote at USAID press conference. Washington DC, 5 June.

Speece, M. and Wilkinson, M.J., 1982 Environmental degradation and development of drylands. *Desertification Control Bulletin* **7**: 2–9.

Spooner, B., 1982 Rethinking desertification: the social dimension. In B. Spooner and H.S. Mann (eds) *Desertification and development: dryland ecology in social perspective.* Academic Press, London: 1–24.

Spooner, B., 1987 The paradoxes of desertification. *Desertification Control Bulletin* **15**: 40–45.

Spooner, B., 1989 Desertification: the historical significance. In R. Huss-Ashmore and S.H. Katz (eds) *African food systems in crisis. Part one: microperspectives.* Gordon and Breach, New York: 111–162.

Spooner, B. and Mann, H.S. (eds) 1982 *Desertification and development. Dryland ecology in social perspective.* Academic Press, London.

Stebbing, E.P., 1935 The encroaching Sahara: the threat to the West African colonies. *Geographical Journal* **85**: 506–519.

Stebbing, E.P., 1938 The advance of the Sahara. *Geographical Journal* **91**: 356–359.

Stein, A., 1938 Desiccation in Asia: a geographical question in the light of history. *Hungarian Quarterly*, 1938: 13.

Stiles, D., 1987 Camel vs cattle pastoralism: stopping desert spread. *Desertification Control Bulletin* **14**: 15–21.

Stiles, D. and Sangweni, S.S., 1984 Summary of the activities and output of the General Assessment of Progress in the implementation of the Plan of Action to Combat Desertification, 1978-1984. *Supplement, Desertification Control Bulletin* **10**: 12–17.

Stocking, M.A., 1984 *Erosion and soil productivity: a review*. Consultants' working paper 1. Land and Water Development Division, FAO, Rome.

Stocking, M.A., 1987 Measuring land degradation. In P.M. Blaikie and H.C. Brookfield *Land degradation and society*. Routledge, London: 49–63.

Sud, Y.C. and Molod, A., 1988 A GCM simulation study of the influence of Saharan evapotranspiration and surface–albedo anomalies on July circulation and rainfall. *Monthly Weather Review* **116**: 2388–2400.

Suliman, M.M., 1988 Dynamics of range plants and desertification monitoring in the Sudan. *Desertification Control Bulletin* **16**: 27–31.

Sutherland, R. and Bryan, R.K., 1990 Runoff and erosion from a small semi-arid catchment, Baringo district, Kenya. *Applied Geography* **10**: 91–109.

Swift, J., 1977 Pastoral development in Somalia: herding cooperatives as a strategy against desertification and famine. In M.H. Glantz (ed) *Desertification. Environmental degradation in and around arid lands*. Westview Press, Boulder CO: 275–305.

Syria, Government of, 1987 *National Plan of Action to Combat Desertification*. Syria.

Taylor, R.D. and Martin, R.B., 1987 Effects of veterinary services on wildlife conservation in Zimbabwe. *Environmental Management* **11**: 327–334.

Thomas, D.S.G., 1989 (ed) *Arid zone geomorphology*. Belhaven, London.

Thomas, D.S.G. and Middleton, N.J., 1993 Salinization: new perspectives on a major desertification issue. *Journal of Arid Environments* **24**: 95–105.

Thomas, D.S.G. and Shaw, P.A., 1991 *The Kalahari environment*. Cambridge University Press, Cambridge.

Thompson, M., 1988 Uncertainty and its uses. In P.M. Blaikie and T. Unwin (eds) *Environmental crisis in developing countries*. Developing Areas Research Group monograph 8. Institute of British Geographers, London: 125–141.

Thompson, M., Warburton, M. and Hatley, T., 1986 *Uncertainty on a Himalayan Scale*. Milton for Ethnographia Press, London.

Thornes, J.B. and Brunsden, D., 1977 *Geomorphology and time*. Methuen, London.

Timberlake, L., 1985 *Africa in crisis*. Earthscan, London.

Tolba, M.K., 1987 The tenth anniversary of UNCOD. *Desertification Control Bulletin* **15**: 3–7.

Tolsma, D.J., Ernst, W.H.O. and Verwey, R.A., 1987 Nutrients in soil and vegetation around two artificial waterholes in eastern Botswana. *Journal of Applied Ecology* **24**: 991–1000.

Toulmin, C., 1993 *Combatting desertification: setting the agenda for a global convention*. IIED Drylands Network Programme, Paper 42. IIED, London.

Trollope, W.S.W., 1982 Ecological effects of fire in South African savannas. In B.J. Huntley and B.H. Walker (eds) *Ecological studies* **42**. Springer-Verlag, Berlin: 292–306.

Tucker, C.J., 1980 A critical review of remote sensing and other methods for non-destructive estimation of standing crop biomass. *Grass and Forage Science* **35**: 115–182.

Tucker, C.J. and Choudhury, B.J., 1987 Satellite remote sensing of drought conditions. *Remote Sensing of Environment* **23**: 243–251.

Tucker, C.J., Dregne, H.E. and Newcomb, W.W., 1991 Expansion and contraction of the Sahara Desert from 1980 to 1990. *Science* **253**: 299.

Tucker, C.J., Hielkema, J.U. and Roffrey, J., 1985a The potential of satellite remote sensing of ecological conditions for survey and forecasting desert locust activity. *International Journal of Remote Sensing* **6**: 127–138.

Tucker, C.J., Townshend, J.R.G. and Goff, T.E., 1985b African land-cover classification using satellite data. *Science* **227**: 369–375.

Tucker, C.J., Vanprae, C.L., Sharman, M.J. and Van Ittersum, G., 1985c Satellite remote sensing of total herbaceous biomass production in the Senegalese Sahel: 1980-1984. *Remote Sensing of Environment* **17**: 233–249.

Tunisia, Government of, 1985 *National plan of action to combat desertification*. Tunis.

Tyson, P.D., 1979 Southern African rainfall: past, present and future. In M.T. Hinchley (ed) *Proceedings of the Symposium on Drought in Botswana*. Botswana society, Gaborone: 45–52.

Tyson, P.D., 1986 *Climatic change and variability in southern Africa*. Oxford University Press, Cape Town.

Tyson, P.D. and Dyer, T.G.J., 1975 Mean annual fluctuations of precipitation in the summer rainfall region of South Africa. *South African Geographical Journal* **57**: 104–110.

UN, 1977a *Desertification, its causes and consequences*. Pergamon Press, Oxford.

UN, 1977b *Draft plan of action to combat desertification*. UN Conference on Desertification, Nairobi, 29 August–9 September 1977. Document A/CONF.74/L.36. UNEP, Nairobi.

UN, 1977c *World map of desertification*. UN Conference on Desertification,

Nairobi 29 August–9 September 1977. Document A/CONF.74/2.

UN, 1977d *Status of desertification in the hot arid regions, climatic aridity index map and experimental world scheme of aridity and drought probability, at a scale of 1:25,000,000. Explanatory note.* UN Conference on Desertification. A/CONF. 74/31. UN, New York.

UN, 1992 *Report of the UN Conference on Environment and Development. Malaysia draft resolution.* UN General Assembly, 47th session, second committee, agenda item 79, 20 November.

UNCED, 1992 *Earth summit '92.* The UN Conference on Environment and Development, Rio de Janeiro.

UNEP, 1981 News from UNEP. *Desertification Control Bulletin* **4**: 16–20.

UNEP, 1982a Review of the implementation of the Plan of Action to Combat Desertification. *Desertification Control Bulletin* **6**: 34–47.

UNEP, 1982b Additional measures to finance the Plan of Action to Combat Desertification. *Desertification Control Bulletin* **6**: 20–25.

UNEP, 1984a *Activities of the United Nations Environment Programme in the Combat Against Desertification.* Report prepared by the Desertification Control/Programme Activity Centre, UNEP, Nairobi.

UNEP, 1984b *General assessment of progress in the implementation of the plan of action to combat desertification 1978-84.* UNEP, Nairobi.

UNEP, 1987 *Sands of change.* UNEP Environmental Brief No 2.

UNEP, 1988 News from UNEP. *Desertification Control Bulletin* **16**: 32–40.

UNEP, 1990a News from UNEP. *Desertification Control Bulletin* **18**: 51–70.

UNEP, 1990b Global assessment of land degradation/desertification – GAP II. *Desertification Control Bulletin* **18**: 24–25.

UNEP, 1991 *Status of desertification and implementation of the United Nations plan of action to combat desertification.* Report of the executive director to the governing council, third special session, Nairobi.

UNEP, 1992 *World atlas of desertification.* Edward Arnold, Sevenoaks.

UNEPCOM, 1990 *Recommendations on application in the Sahelian zone of FAO/UNEP provisional methodology for desertification assessment and mapping.* Institute of Deserts, Turkmen SSR Academy of Sciences, Turkmen.

UNEP DC/PAC, 1984 *Activities of the United Nations Environment Programme in the combat against desertification.* UNEP, Nairobi.

UNEP DC/PAC, 1987 *Rolling back the desert.* UNEP, Nairobi.

UNEP–UNCOD, 1978 *United Nations Conference on Desertification 29 August–9 September 1977: Round up, plan of action and resolutions.* UN, New York.

UNOSTD, 1987 *Report of the panel of experts on 'The application of science and technology to the study, prevention, monitoring and combating of drought and desertification'.* UN, New York

Valenza, J., 1981 Surveillance continue de pâturages naturels Sénégalais: resultats de 1974 à 1978. *Révue d'Elèvage et de Médecine Vétérinaire des Pays Tropicaux* **34**: 83–100.

Verstraete, M.M., 1986 The United Nations Organisation and the issue of desertification. In F. El Baz and M.H.A. Hassan (eds) *Physics of desertification*. Martins Nijhoff, Dordrecht: 42–51.

Vita-Finzi, C., 1969 *The Mediterranean valleys*. Cambridge University Press, Cambridge.

Vokou, D., Diamantopoulos, J., Mardiris, Th. A. and Margaris, N.S., 1986 Desertification in northwestern Greece; the case of Kella. In R. Fantechi and N.S. Margaris (eds) *Desertification in Europe*. Reidel, Dordrecht: 155–160.

Walker, B.H., 1985 Structure and function of savannas: an overview. In J.C. Tothill and J.J. Mott (eds) *Management of the world's savannas*. Australian Academy of Science, Canberra.

Walker, B.H., 1987 (ed) *Determinants of tropical savannas*. IUBS Monograph Series 3. IUBS, Paris.

Walker, J.M. and Rowntree, P.R., 1977 The effect of soil moisture on circulation and rainfall in a tropical model. *Quarterly Journal of the Royal Meteorological Society* **103**: 29–46.

Walls, J., 1980 *Land, man and sand. Desertification and its solution*. Macmillan, New York.

Walls, J., 1984 Back to the war. *Supplement, Desertification Control Bulletin* **10**: 5–11.

Walsh, R.P.D., Hulme, M. and Campbell, M., 1988 Rainfall decline and its impact on hydrology and water supply in the semi-arid zone of Sudan. *Geographical Journal* **154**: 181–197.

Warren, A. and Agnew, C., 1987 *An assessment of desertification and land degradation in arid and semi-arid areas*. Drylands paper 2. International Institute for Environment and Development, London.

Warren, A. and Khogali, M., 1992 *Assessment of Desertification and Drought in the Sudano–Sahelian Region 1985–1991*. United Nations Sudano-Sahelian Office, New York.

Warren, A. and Maizels, J.K., 1977 Ecological change and desertification. In UN, 1977b: 169–260.

Warren, A., Sud, Y.C. and Rozanov, B.G., 1993 The future of deserts. *Palaeogeography, Palaeoclimatology, Palaeoecology* [in press].

Watson, A. 1990 The control of blowing sand and mobile desert dunes. In A.S. Goudie (ed) *Techniques for desert reclamation*. Wiley, Chichester: 35–85.

Weber, F., 1982 *Review of CILSS forestry sector program analysis papers*. USDA/OICD/TAD and AID/USDA/USFS, US Department of Agriculture, Washington DC.

Weisner, C.J., 1970 *Climate, irrigation and agriculture: a guide to the practice of irrigation*. Angus Robertson, London.

Weiss, T.G. and Jordan, R.S., 1976 Bureaucratic politics and the World Food Conference: the international policy process. *World Politics* **28**: 422–439.

Wigley, T.M.L. and Atkinson, T.C., 1977 Dry years in south-east England since 1698. *Nature* **265**: 431–434.

Wijkman, A. and Timberlake, L., 1985 Is the African drought an act of God or of man? *Ecologist* **15**: 9–18.

Wilcox, L.V., 1955 *Classification and use of irrigation waters*. US Department of Agriculture, Circular 969.

Wilhite, D. and Glantz, M., 1985 Understanding the drought phenomenon: the role of definitions. *Water International* **10**: 111–120

Williams, O.B., Suijdendorp, H. and Wilcox, D.G., 1977 *Associated case study. Australia, Gascoyne Basin*. UNCOD, document A/CONF. 74/15. UNEP, Nairobi.

Wolman, M.G. and Gerson, R., 1978 Relative scales of time and effectiveness of climate in watershed geomorphology. *Earth Surface Processes* **3**: 189–220.

Woodruff, N.P. and Siddoway, F.H., 1965 A wind erosion equation. *Soil Science Society of America, Proceedings* **29**: 602–608.

Woods, L.E., 1984 *Land degradation in Australia*. Australian Government Publishing Service, Canberra.

World Bank, 1985 *Desertification in the Sahelian and Sudanean zones of West Africa*. World Bank, Washington DC.

World Bank, 1992 *World development report 1992. Development and the environment*. Oxford University Press, New York.

Worster, D., 1979 *Dust bowl*. Oxford University Press, New York.

WRI (World Resource Institute), 1989 *World resources 1988-1989*. WRI, New York.

Yassin, T.E. and Alshanfari, S.A., 1991 Rangelands in Oman: management, problems and prospects. In R. Halwagy, F.K. Taha and S.A. Omar (eds) *Advances in range management in arid lands*. Kegan Paul, London: 119–130.

Zhao Songqiao, 1986 *Physical geography of China*. Scientific Press, Beijing, China; Wiley, New York.

Zhou Zhenda and Liu Shu, 1983 *Combating desertification in arid and semi-arid zones in China*. Institute of Desert Research, Academica sinica, Lanzhou, China.

Zhu Zhenda, Wand Xizhang, Wu Wiei, Kang Guoding, Zhu Che, Yao Fafeng and Wang Tao, 1992 China: desertification mapping and desert reclamation. In UNEP *World atlas of desertification*. Edward Arnold, Sevenoaks.

Index